For Vic & Jill
Werthof to
in answer to
my many
"questions" ☺

The Mysteries of Godliness

THE MYSTERIES OF GODLINESS

A History of
Mormon Temple Worship

by

David John Buerger

Smith Research Associates
San Francisco

Cover design by Ron Stucki

∞ *The Mysteries of Godliness* was printed on acid-free paper
and meets the permanence of paper requirements of the
American National Standard for Information Sciences.
This book was composed, printed, and
bound in the United States.

Published by Smith Research Associates in the United States of America.
Distributed by Signature Books Publishing, LLC, Salt Lake City, Utah.
First edition 1994 (cloth).
Second edition 2002 (paper).

—

2016   2015   2014   2013   2012   8   7   6   5   4

LIBRARY OF CONGRESS CATALOGING-IN-PUBLICATION DATA
Buerger, David John
The mysteries of Godliness : a history of Mormon temple worship /
by David John Buerger.
    p.   cm.
Includes bibliographical references and index.
ISBN 13: 978-1-56085-176-9
ISBN 10: 1-56085-176-7
1. Temple endowments (Mormon Church)–History.   I. Title.
BX8643.T4B84   1994
264' .09332099–dc20   94-37828
                                    CIP

CONTENTS

PREFACE

Your endowment is, to receive all those ordinances in the House of the Lord, which are necessary for you, after you have departed this life, to enable you to walk back to the presence of the Father, passing the angels who stand as sentinels, being enabled to give them the key words, the signs and tokens, pertaining to the Holy Priesthood, and gain your eternal exaltation in spite of earth and hell.

—Brigham Young, *Journal of Discourses* 2:31

For faithful members of the Church of Jesus Christ of Latter-day Saints, the modern temple endowment ceremony is a sacred and powerful ordinance. One official Mormon source calls it a temporal stepping stone which all people must traverse to achieve exaltation in heaven.[1] Since those who enter the temple agree to treat the ceremony with respect, I will confine my discussion to published accounts, journal and diary entries, autobiographies, and other public sources. I will not treat in any significant detail the speculative theological significance, spiritual meanings, or symbolic dimensions of the endowment, important though they are in the lives of Latter-day Saints.

---

1. *Gospel Essentials*, rev. ed. (Salt Lake City: Church of Jesus Christ of Latter-day Saints, 1979), 247.

Some readers may feel that any discussion of these ceremonies is inappropriate given their sacred nature. Certain aspects of the ritual are guarded by vows of secrecy. Although I do not wish to offend readers who may not share my understanding about what is appropriate, I have decided that, given exaggerated claims about the temple and its origin by some enthusiastic apologists, a degree of specificity in detail is unavoidable. Hopefully readers will see that I have tried to achieve a balance of scholarly objectivity, reverence for the sacred, regard for the sensibilities of others, and adequate documentation and development of the points to be discussed.

In 1912, one year after the LDS First Presidency asked James E. Talmage to write a book about temples, the church published *The House of the Lord*. In his chapter on ordinances, Talmage summarized the endowment as follows:

> *The Temple Endowment*, as administered in modern temples, comprises instruction relating to the significance and sequence of past dispensations, and the importance of the present as the greatest and grandest era in human history. This course of instruction includes a recital of the most prominent events of the creative period, the condition of our first parents in the Garden of Eden, their disobedience and consequent expulsion from that blissful abode, their condition in the lone and dreary world when doomed to live by labor and sweat, the plan of redemption by which the great transgression may be atoned, the period of the great apostasy, the restoration of the Gospel with all its ancient powers and privileges, the absolute and indispensable condition of personal purity and devotion to the right in present life, and a strict compliance with Gospel requirements.

Following this overview, Talmage stated more specifically:

> The ordinances of the endowment embody certain obligations on the part of the individual, such as covenant and promise to observe the law of strict virtue and chastity, to be charitable, benevolent, tolerant and pure; to devote both talent and material means to the spread of truth and the uplifting of the race; to maintain devotion to the cause of truth; and to seek in every way to contribute to the great preparation that the earth may be made ready to receive her King,—the Lord Jesus Christ. With the taking of each covenant and the assuming of each obligation a

promised blessing is pronounced, contingent upon the faithful observance of the conditions.[2]

In the discussion that follows I hope to expand this brief summary and enhance understanding of the temple for both Latter-day
Saints and others by providing a history of the endowment, its origins
and development, and possible directions for the future.

---

2. James E. Talmage, *The House of the Lord* (Salt Lake City: Church of Jesus Christ
of Latter-day Saints, 1912), 99-100.

4

CHAPTER 1

Prelude to the Endowment

The Lord Almighty . . . will continue to preserve me . . .
until I have fully accomplished my mission in this life,
and so firmly established the dispensation of the full-
ness of the priesthood in the last days, that all the pow-
ers of earth and hell can never prevail against it.

—Joseph Smith, Jr., 1842[1]

For Joseph Smith and successors in the presidency of the Church of
Jesus Christ of Latter-day Saints, the temple was at the heart of the
Mormon restoration. Both in Kirtland, Ohio, and later in Nauvoo,
Illinois, Smith labored to complete holy edifices where the Saints
might be "endowed with power from on high."[2] Ceremonial washings, anointings, and sealings were first administered in the Kirtland
temple (or House of the Lord) in 1836, and other temple instructions
and rites were added in Nauvoo in 1842 and 1843. Both have continued to the present in the LDS church. Not unexpectedly, given the

1. Joseph Smith, Jr., *History of the Church of Jesus Christ of Latter-day Saints*,
7 vols., ed. B. H. Roberts, 2d ed., rev. (Salt Lake City: Deseret Book Co., 1973), 5:139-40
(hereafter HC).
2. Ibid., 2:197; remarks made on 15 February 1835 by Oliver Cowdery.

developmental character of other early concepts, preliminary stages can be identified in the implementation of these rituals.

The evolving ceremonies can probably best be understood within the context of the similarly developing LDS concept of salvation.[3] Prior to mid-1831 Mormon theology was not predestinarian. The Book of Mormon, for example, does not employ "calling and election," "elect," "destined," "predestined," or "predestinate" when speaking of afterlife, judgment, or salvation. The sole use of the phrase "calling and election" in a June 1831 revelation published in Doctrine and Covenants 53:1, 7 (hereafter D&C) avoided eschatological implications.

Some time between June and November 1831, however, LDS salvation theology changed, tied to the 3 June 1831 conferral of High Priesthood on church elders.[4] According to later testimony by Book of Mormon witness David Whitmer, the introduction of the High Priesthood (an event he considered to be an aberration from scriptural sources) "originated in the mind of Sydney Rigdon": "Rigdon finally persuaded Brother Joseph [Smith] to believe that the high priests which had such great power in ancient times, should be in the Church of Christ to-day. He had Brother Joseph inquire of the Lord about it, and they received an answer according to their erring desires."[5]

Despite the controversy which surrounded this event, High Priesthood came to be regarded as the power to "seal" or perform earthly ordinances which were ratified in heaven. "[T]he order of the High priesthood," explained Smith on 25 October 1831, "is that they have power given them to seal up the Saints unto eternal life. And said it was the privilege of every Elder present to be ordained to the High priesthood."[6]

---

3. I am indebted to D. Michael Quinn and Anthony A. Hutchinson for assistance with the following discussion of salvation concepts, as well as the composition of the fullness of the priesthood ordinance and the conditional/unconditional nature of the ritual discussed below.

4. HC, 1:175-76.

5. David Whitmer, *An Address to All Believers in Christ* (Richmond, MO: the author, 1887), 64, 35; see also 32, 49, 62, 63, and 65.

6. "Far West Record," 25 Oct. 1931, archives, historical department, Church of Jesus Christ of Latter-day Saints, Salt Lake City, Utah (hereafter LDS archives); see also

This notion, when taken with key Book of Mormon passages, represented a departure from biblical precedent. In the New Testament, for example, the terms "to seal" and "to place a seal on" referred to the ancient practice of placing a wax or mud seal to close and protect a document from misappropriation. The confirmation effect of a sealing is seen in several Pauline passages in which God seals Christians by giving them the Holy Spirit or the Holy Spirit of Promise as a ratification of future blessings and promises to come. The Apocalypse of John depicts the servants of God receiving the seal or imprint of God on their forehead. In all pertinent New Testament references, however, it is God who applies the seals. There is no clear reference to a human intermediary performing the "sealing" function. (See, for example, Rom. 4:11; 2 Cor. 1:22; Eph. 1:13 and 4:30; and Rev. 13:16-18.)

Key players in the sixteenth-century Reformation used many of these sealing passages as evidence for their belief in predestination. Liberal reaction to Calvinist doctrine arose early in the seventeenth century when Arminians rejected this view, asserting that God's sovereignty and human free will were compatible, that such sealings depended on choices of the individual believer. The Arminian doctrines of free will and individual works continued to be propagated on the American frontier through such nineteenth-century groups as Alexander Campbell's followers and other primitivist Seekers. In 1829 when Joseph Smith was working on the Book of Mormon manuscript, these issues were important throughout the

---

Donald Q. Cannon and Lyndon W. Cook, eds., *Far West Record: Minutes of The Church of Jesus Christ of Latter-day Saints, 1830-1844* (Salt Lake City: Deseret Book Co., 1983), 20-21. Most of the research for this book was done during the late 1970s and early 1980s when temple-related materials housed in LDS archives were more accessible than they are today. Because it is now virtually impossible for researchers to consult the originals of these materials, I have included lengthy quotations from diaries and manuscript sources in this book and have deposited a copy of all research materials in the David J. Buerger Papers, Ms. 622, Manuscripts Division, Special Collections, Marriott Library, University of Utah, Salt Lake City, Utah. The collection has no access restrictions.

so-called "burned-over district" of western New York where he re-sided.[7]

With the exception of obvious non-figural usages of the term (as in sealing up a book or plates or hiding an object), the Book of Mormon employs this term similarly to the New Testament but in a more fully developed sense. Mosiah 5:15 (1st ed., 67) closely followed New Testament usage but emphasized works in opposition to Calvinistic themes: "I would that you should be steadfast and immovable, always abounding in good works, that Christ, the Lord God Omnipotent, may seal you his, that you may be brought to Heaven. . . ." Joseph Smith clearly defused predestinarian overtones by having the devil seal the wicked to damnation (Alma 34:35; 1st ed., 321): "[I]f ye have procrastinated the day of your repentance, even until death, behold, ye have become subjected to the spirit of the Devil, and he doth seal you his; . . . and this is the final state of the wicked."

The most significant development in Book of Mormon sealing theology was God's sealing power granted to Nephi, the son of Helaman (Hel. 10:7; 1st ed., 435). This story parallels biblical passages in several ways,[8] but the most important in our present context can be seen by comparing the passage in the Book of Mormon with Matthew 16:17-19: "Blessed art thou, Simon Bar-jona. . . . And I say also unto thee, That thou art Peter, and . . . whatsoever thou shalt bind on earth shall be bound in heaven: and whatsoever thou shalt loose on earth shall be loosed in heaven." Helaman 10:4-7 reads: "Blessed art thou, Nephi, . . . Behold, thou art Nephi, and I am God. . . . whatsoever ye shall *seal* on earth shall be *sealed* in heaven; and whatsoever ye shall

---

7. See discussion of the term "seal" in Rex Eugene Cooper, *Promises Made to the Fathers: Mormon Covenant Organization* (Salt Lake City: University of Utah Press, 1990), 64. Cooper emphasizes the comparison between Mormon and Puritan use of the term: "To Puritans it meant the visible symbol of a covenant; to Mormons it meant the authoritative ratification of covenantal promises, in a sense similar to that of Matthew 16:19, in which Christ gives Peter the keys of the kingdom. . . . After the [LDS] church was organized in 1830, the term appears to have first been employed about assurances of eternal salvation."

8. The story clearly is patterned on the account of Elijah the Tishbite sealing the heavens by drought in 1 Kings 17; also compare the Nephi-Elijah connection in Helaman 5:30 and 1 Kings 19:11-12. Additional parallels to Matthew 16:17-19 are Mark 8:29, Luke 9:20, and loose parallels in John 6:67-71 and 20:22-23. See also Gen. 14:26-32 in Joseph Smith's translation of the Bible (hereafter JST).

loose on earth, shall be loosed in heaven" (emphasis added). The term "seal" here, probably substituted for "bind" in order to remove any Catholic "papist" leaning of the text,[9] does not carry the soteriological and eschatological overtones usually associated with the figurative usage in the New Testament. Instead the sealing power is depicted as permitting miraculous physical events (such as the famine caused by drought in Helaman 11:4) in order to bring people to repentance. This same shift can be seen in 2 Nephi 33:15 ("For what I seal on earth, shall be brought against you at the judgment bar"). The New Testament had emphasized that God does the sealing; the Book of Mormon allows a *human* agent (i.e., Nephi) to seal at God's command. By allowing a human to be associated with this power, a way was prepared for further theological innovation by Joseph Smith.

In this context, the introduction of High Priesthood was one such innovation. In November 1831 these various concepts came together in a priesthood ritual allowing one to "seal [people] up unto eternal life" (D&C 68:2, 12; see also 1:8-9). Thus Mormon priesthood bearers themselves could perform a ritual paralleling what strict Calvinists, for example, reserved solely to God. This can be seen as one precursor for the endowment ceremony which would eventually be performed in the Kirtland temple.

Zebedee Coltrin's 1831 diary provides evidence that Mormon elders wasted no time in implementing this sealing ordinance: "Tuesday came to Sha[k]ersville held a meeting in the Evening with the Br and after laboring with them some length of time Br David seeled them up unto Eternal life."[10] Jared Carter recalled during his mission to Benson, Vermont, in 1831-32, being

> directed to pray most earnestly that God would grant unto us sealing grace. After this I felt directed by the spirit to declare unto the brethren that that day was a sealing time with them, as I had prayed in faith, that they might be blessed. My communication to them caused some of the brethren to tremble, for this was something that they had never before experienced; but I exhorted them to call more earnestly on the

---

9. For other passages which describe Roman Catholicism from the perspective of anti-papist frontiersmen, see 1 Ne. 13:4-9, 24-29; 14:10-17; and 2 Ne. 28:18-28.

10. Zebedee Coltrin Diary, 15 Nov. 1831, LDS archives. See also Journal of Joseph Knight, Sr., summer 1831, LDS archives.

Lord. We then began to pray, but the spirit, as I viewed it in my mind, was not yet poured out; therefore, I again arose and devoted a few minutes to call upon the Lord with one accord. Accordingly, all of us lifted our voices to God, and while we were praying, the Spirit rested down upon us. We then administered the Sacrament and it appeared to me that the Church of Christ in that locality was sealed up to the Lord, and it was likewise made plain to me that every one of us present should meet again in Zion. I then felt as though I could leave them without fear, for I had a testimony that God would keep them.[11]

Orson Pratt also remembered when in 1833 "some other brethren from other towns, met together and called upon the Lord; and the Lord heard their prayers and moved upon his servant Lyman Johnson by the power of the Holy Ghost to seal them up unto eternal life. And after this the brethren arose one by one and said that they knew that their names were sealed in the Lamb's Book of Life, and they all did bear this glorious testimony save two or three."[12]

Clearly this ordinance was not a one-on-one ceremony. A priesthood bearer was empowered to simultaneously seal a whole group of people to eternal life. Moreover, this ritual was a spoken one. No physical contact between officiator and recipient was mentioned.[13]

A second precursor to the Kirtland endowment came in an 1832 revelation (D&C 88) commanding that a "School of the Prophets" be established to instruct church leaders. On 23 January 1833 a number of men met in Kirtland in the upper room of Newel K. Whitney's store to organize the school. Those attending included Joseph Smith, Sidney Rigdon, Frederick G. Williams, Joseph Smith, Sr., Hyrum Smith, Samuel H. Smith, William Smith, Ezra Thayer, Newel K. Whitney, Martin Harris, Zebedee Coltrin, John Murdock, Lyman Johnson, Orson Hyde, Solomon Humphrey, Sylvester Smith, Orson Pratt, and Levi Hancock.[14] The 1832 revelation described ritual washing in detail:

---

11. See Journal History, 27 Sept. 1832, LDS archives.

12. Journal of Orson Pratt, 26 Aug., 8 Sept. 1833, LDS archives.

13. In some way this ordinance paralleled that revealed in D&C 60:15 and 84:92 wherein priesthood bearers sealed up the wicked to damnation with a washing-of-the-feet and a shaking-off-of-dust ceremony. This ordinance of damnation could also be performed with reference to a group of people.

14. List in Lyndon W. Cook, *The Revelations of the Prophet Joseph Smith: A*

74. And I give unto you, who are the first laborers in this last kingdom, a commandment that you assemble yourselves together, and organize yourselves, and prepare yourselves, and sanctify yourselves; yea, purify your hearts, and cleanse your hands and your feet before me, that I may make you clean;

75. That I may testify unto your Father, and your God, and my God, that you are clean from the blood of this wicked generation; that I may fulfil this promise, this great and last promise, which I have made unto you, when I will. . . .

85. Verily, I say unto you, let those who are not the first elders continue in the vineyard until the mouth of the Lord shall call them, for their time is not yet come; their garments are not clean from the blood of this generation. . . .

138. And ye shall not receive any among you into this school save he is clean from the blood of this generation;

139. And he shall be received by the ordinance of the washing of feet, for unto this end was the ordinance of the washing of feet instituted.

140. And again, the ordinance of washing feet is to be administered by the president, or presiding elder of the church.

141. It is to be commenced with prayer; and after partaking of bread and wine, he is to gird himself according to the pattern given in the thirteenth chapter of John's testimony concerning me. Amen.[15]

At the first meeting of the school this ordinance was administered as directed. The revelation did not state a relationship between washing of feet and the ritual of sealing which had been in practice for over a year, but when Smith actually implemented the washing ordinance in January, the minutes show him linking it to being "sealed up unto eternal life":

Opened with Prayer by the President [Joseph Smith] and after much speaking praying and singing, all done in Tongues proceded to washing hands faces feet in the name of the Lord . . . each one washing his own after which the president girded himself with a towel and again washed

---

Historical and Biographical Commentary of the Doctrine and Covenants (Provo, UT: Seventy's Mission Bookstore, 1981), 186-87; see also Salt Lake School of Prophets Minute Book 1883, 4, LDS archives.

15. "Kirtland Revelation Book," 41, LDS archives; see also D&C 88:139-41; esp. vv. 74-75; HC, 1:306-307, 311-12. For Smith's probable inspiration, see JST John 13.

the feet of all the Elders wiping them with the towel. . . . The President said after he had washed the feet of the Elders, as I have done so do ye wash ye therefore one anothers feet pronouncing at the same time through the power of the Holy Ghost that the Elders were all clean from the blood of this generation but that those among them who should sin wilfully after they were thus cleansed and sealed up unto eternal life should be given over unto the buffettings of Satan until the day of redemption. Having continued all day in fasting & prayer before the Lord at the close they partook of the Lords supper.[16]

The official account of this first meeting reads:

On the 23rd of January [1833], we again assembled in conference; when, after much speaking, singing, praying, and praising God, all in tongues, we proceeded to the washing of feet (according to the practice recorded in the 13th chapter of John's Gospel), as commanded of the Lord. Each Elder washed his own feet first, after which I girded myself with a towel and washed the feet of all of them, wiping them with the towel with which I was girded. Among the number, my father presented himself, but before I washed his feet, I asked of him a father's blessing, which he granted by laying his hands upon my head, in the name of Jesus Christ, and declaring that I should continue in the Priest's office until Christ comes. At the close of the scene, Brother Frederick G. Williams, being moved upon by the Holy Ghost, washed my feet in token of his fixed determination to be with me in suffering, or in journeying, in life or in death, and to be continually on my right hand; in which I accepted him in the name of the Lord.

I then said to the Elders, As I have done so do ye; wash ye, therefore, one another's feet; and by the power of the Holy Ghost I pronounced them all clean from the blood of this generation; but if any of them should sin wilfully after they were thus cleansed, and sealed up unto eternal life, they should be given over unto the buffetings of Satan until the day of redemption. Having continued all day in fasting, and prayer, and ordinances, we closed by partaking of the Lord's supper. I blessed the bread and wine in the name of the Lord, when we all ate and drank, and were filled; then we sang a hymn, and the meeting adjourned.[17]

---

16. Cook, *Revelations of the Prophet Joseph Smith*, 186, quoting "Kirtland Council Minute Book," 7-8, LDS archives.

17. HC, 1:323-34.

Zebedee Coltrin, one of the school's original members, later recalled these meetings:

> The salutation, as written in the Doctrine and Covenants was carried out at that time, and at every meeting, and the washing of feet was attended to, the Sacrament was also administered at times when Joseph appointed, after the ancient order; that is, warm bread to break easy was provided, and broken into pieces as large as my fist, and each person had a glass of wine and sat and ate the bread and drank the wine; and Joseph said that was the way that Jesus and his disciples partook of the bread and wine; and this was the order of the church anciently, and until the church went into darkness. Every time we were called together to attend to any business, we came together in the morning about sunrise, fasting, and partook of the Sacrament each time; and before going to school we washed ourselves and put on clean linen.[18]

It was announced that the School of the Prophets was to be held in a new edifice built to house the school and "to endow those whom I have chosen with power from on high" (D&C 95:8). Over the next

---

18. These recollections were given on the occasion of the reorganization of the Salt Lake School of the Prophets in 1883 under church president John Taylor (p. 38). The pentecostal outpourings associated with washings in the Kirtland temple were connected in Coltrin's recollections to the School of the Prophets as well.

"At one of these meetings after the organization of the school, [the school being organized] on 23rd of January, 1833, when we were all together, Joseph having given instructions, and while engaged in silent prayer, kneeling, with our hands uplifted each one praying in silence, no one whispered above his breath, a personage walked through the room from East to west, and Joseph asked if we saw him. I saw him and supposed the others did, and Joseph answered that is Jesus, the Son of God, our elder brother. Afterward Joseph told us to resume our former position in prayer, which we did. Another person came through; He was surrounded as with a flame of fire. I experienced a sensation that it might destroy the tabernacle as it was of consuming fire of great brightness. The Prophet Joseph said this was the Father of our Lord Jesus Christ. I saw Him. . . .

"I did not discover His clothing for He was surrounded as with a flame of fire, which was so brilliant that I could not discover anything else but His person. I saw His hands, His legs, His feet, His eyes, nose, mouth, head and body in the shape and form of a perfect man. He sat in a chair as a man would sit in a chair, but this appearance was so grand and overwhelming that it seemed I should melt down in His presence, and the sensation was so powerful that it thrilled through my whole system and I felt it in the marrow of my bones. The Prophet Joseph said: Brethren, now you are prepared to be the apostles of Jesus Christ, for you have seen both the Father and the Son, and know that They exist and that They are two separate Personages" (pp. 54-55; see also 100-104).

two years Smith encouraged completion of this House of the Lord with such glimpses of its potential as in the 5 October 1835 entry of the *History of the Church*:

> I returned home, being much fatigued from riding in the rain. Spent the remainder of the day in reading and meditation, and in the evening attended a Council of the Twelve Apostles; had a glorious time, and gave them much instruction concerning their duties for time to come; . . . also this fall to attend the solemn assembly of the first Elders, for the organization of the School of the Prophets; and attend to the ordinance of the washing of feet; and to prepare their hearts in all humility for an endowment with power from on high; to which they all agreed with one accord, and seemed to be greatly rejoiced.[19]

The following exhortation from 15 February 1835 similarly looks forward to and underscores the importance of this elusive endowment:

> Remember, you are not to go to other nations till you receive your endowments. Tarry at Kirtland until you are endowed with power from on high. You need a fountain of wisdom, knowledge and intelligence such as you never had. Relative to the endowment, I make a remark or two, that there may be no mistake. The world cannot receive the things of God. He can endow you without worldly pomp or great parade. He can give you that wisdom, that intelligence, and that power, which characterized the ancient saints, and now characterizes the inhabitants of the upper world.[20]

Even before the House of the Lord was dedicated on 27 March 1836 (see D&C 109), Smith introduced ordinances which Mormons today have come to think of as the first version of the endowment ritual. Clearly Smith and contemporaries considered these ceremonies to prepare the way for the real endowment of power—visions, prophesying, speaking in tongues, and feeling the Holy Ghost—which would follow dedication of the new temple.[21]

------

19. HC, 2:287.

20. Ibid., 197.

21. Ibid., 380-83, 386-88, 392, 427-28, 430-33. I am indebted to Lester E. Bush and Andrew F. Ehat for this insight.

CHAPTER 2

The Kirtland Ceremony

The Kirtland temple ritual was a simple, staged ceremony consisting of washing and anointing the body, blessing and sealing the individual, and washing the feet. These ordinances clearly were patterned after washings and anointings described in the Old and especially New Testaments (see Lev. 8; Mark 6:13; Luke 4:18, 7:38, 44; John 13:1-16; 1 Tim. 5:10; James 5:14).

According to Joseph Smith's diary, the first part of this ritual was introduced to members of the First Presidency and other church leaders on 21 January 1836.[1]

After washing and perfuming each other in the attic of the printing office, Smith and associates congregated in the unfinished temple where the First Presidency consecrated oil and progressively laid hands on each other's heads, blessing and anointing each other to

---

1. According to Book of Mormon witness Oliver Cowdery, five days prior to the 21st some preliminary washings took place: "met in the evening with bro. Joseph Smith, Jr. at his house, in company with bro. John Corrill, and after pure water was prepared, called upon the Lord and proceeded to wash each other's bodies, and bathe the same with whiskey, perfumed with cinnamon. This we did that we might be clean before the Lord for the Sabbath, confessing our sins and covenanting to be faithful to God. While performing this washing unto the Lord with solemnity, our minds were filled with many reflections upon the propriety of the same, and how the priests anciently used to wash always before ministering before the Lord. As we had nearly finished this purification, bro. Martin Harris came in and was also washed" (Oliver Cowdery Sketch Book, 16 Jan. 1836, pp. 4-5, archives, historical department, Church of Jesus Christ of Latter-day Saints, Salt Lake City, Utah [hereafter LDS archives]).

their offices. There followed visions and the expected endowment or
outpouring of God's spirit:

> At about 3. oclock P.M. I dismissed the school and the [First] presi-
> dency, retired to the loft of the printing office, where we attended to
> the ordinance of washing our bodies in pure water, we also perfumed
> our bodies and our heads, in the name of the Lord at early candlelight,
> I met with the presidency, at the west school room in the Chapel
> [Kirtland temple] to attend to the ordinance of annointing our heads
> with holy oil–also the [high] councils of ~~Zion~~ Kirtland and Zion, met
> in the two adjoining rooms, who waited in prayer while we attended
> to the ordinance,–I took the oil in my <left>~~right~~ hand, father Smith
> being seated before me and the rest of the presidency encircled him
> round about.–we then streched our right hands to heaven and blessed
> the oil and concecrated it in the name of Jesus Christ–we then laid our
> hands on our aged fath[er] Smith, and invoked, the blessings of
> heaven,–I then annointed his head with the concecrated oil, and sealed
> many blessings upon him, ~~head~~, the presidency then in turn, laid their
> hands upon his head, beginning at the eldest, untill they had all laid
> their hands on him, and pronounced such blessings, upon his head as
> the Lord put into their hearts–all blessing him to be our patriarch, ~~and~~
> <to> annoint our heads, and attend to all duties that pertain to that
> office.–I then took the seat, and father annoint[ed] my head, and sealed
> upon me the blessings, of Moses, to lead Israel in the latter days, even
> as moses led him in days of old,–also the blessings of Abraham Isaac
> and Jacob.–all of the presidency laid their hands upon me and pro-
> nounced upon my head many prophesies, and blessings, many of
> which I shall not notice at this time, but as Paul said, so say I, let us
> come to vissions and revelations,–The heavens were opened upon us
> and I beheld the celestial kingdom of God, and the glory thereof,
> whether in the body or out I cannot tell,–I saw the transcendant beauty
> of the gate ~~that enters~~, through which the heirs of that Kingdom will
> enter, which was like unto circling flames of fire, also the blasing
> [blazing] throne of God, whereon was seated the Father and the Son,–I
> saw the beautiful streets of that Kingdom, which had the appearance
> of being paved with gold–I saw father Adam, and Abraham and Michael
> and my father and mother, my brother Alvin that has long since slept,
> and marvled how it was that he had obtained ~~this~~ an inheritance <in>
> that Kingdom, seeing that he had departed this life, before the Lord
> <had> set his hand to gather Israel <the second time> and had not been
> baptised for the remission of sins–Thus ~~said~~ came the voice <of the
> Lord un>to me saying all who have died with[out] a knowledge of this

gospel, who would have received it, if they had been permited to tarry, shall be heirs of the celestial kingdom of God—also all that shall die henseforth, with<out> a knowledge of it, who would have received it, with all their hearts, shall be heirs of that kingdom, for I the Lord <will> judge all men according to their works according to the desires of their hearts—and ~~again I also beheld the Terrestial Kingdom~~ I also beheld that all children who die before they arive to the years of accountability, are saved in the celestial kingdom of heaven—I saw the 12, apostles of the Lamb, who are now upon the earth who hold the keys of this last ministry, in foreign lands, standing together in a circle much fatiegued, with their clothes tattered and feet swolen, with their eyes cast down-ward, and Jesus <standing> in their midst, and they did not behold him, the Saviour looked upon them and wept—I also beheld Elder [William E.] McLellen in the south, standing upon a hill surrounded with a vast multitude, preaching to them, and a lame man standing before him, supported by his crutches, he threw them down at his word, and leaped as an hart, by the mighty power of God

Also Eld[er] Brigham Young standing in a strange land, in the far southwest, in a desert place, upon a rock in the midst of about a dozen men of colour, who, appeared hostile He was preaching to them in their own toung, and the angel of God standing above his head with a drawn sword in his hand protec[t]ing him, but he did not see it,—and I finally saw the 12 in the celestial kingdom of God,—I also beheld the redemption of Zion, and many things which the toung of man, cannot discribe in full.—Many of my brethren who received this ordinance with me, saw glorious visions also,—angels ministered unto them, as well as my self, and the power of the highest rested upon, us the house was filled with the glory of God, and we shouted Hosanah to ~~the~~ God and the Lamb

I am mistaken, concerning my receiving the holy anointing first after father Smith, we received <it> in turn according to our age, (that is the presidency,)

"My Scribe also recieved his anointing <with us> and saw in a vision the armies of heaven protecting the Saints in their return to Zion—& many things that I saw

The Bishop of Kirtland with his counsellors and the Bishop of Zion with his counsellors, were present with us, and received their, annointing under the hands of father Smith and confirmed by the presidency and the glories of heaven was unfolded to them also—

We then invited the counsellors of Kirtland and Zion ~~and Kirtland~~ into our room, and President Hyrum Smith annointed the head of the president of the counsellors in Kirtland and President D. Whitmer the head of the president, of the counsellors of Zion—

The president of each quorum then annointed the heads of his colleagues, each in his turn beginning, at the eldest

The vision of heaven was opened to these also, some of them saw the face of the Saviour, and others were ministered unto by holy angels, and the spirit of prop[h]esy and revelation was poured out in mighty power, and loud hosanahs and glory to God in the highest, saluted the heavens for we all communed with the h[e]avenly host's,—and I saw in my vision all of the presidency in the Celestial Kingdom of God, and, many others who were present

Our meeting was opened by singing and prayer offered up by the head of each quorum, and closed by singing and invoking the benediction of heaven with uplifted hands, and retired between one and 2. oclock in the morning.[2]

According to Smith's diary, the next day's meeting of the School

2. Dean C. Jesse, ed., *The Papers of Joseph Smith* (Salt Lake City: Deseret Book Co., 1993), 2:155-59. The *History of the Church* recorded this as follows (angled brackets indicate intralinear additions which appear on the original holograph): "[T]he Presidency retired to the attic story of the printing office, where we attended the ordinance of washing our bodies in pure water. We also perfumed our bodies and our heads, in the name of the Lord.

"At early candle-light I met with the Presidency at the west school room, in the Temple, to attend to the ordinance of anointing our heads with holy oil. . . . I took the oil in my left hand, Father Smith being seated before me, and the remainder of the Presidency encircled him round about. We then stretched our right hands towards heaven, and blessed the oil, and consecrated it in the name of Jesus Christ.

"We then laid our hands upon our aged Father Smith, and invoked the blessings of heaven. I then anointed his head with the consecrated oil, and sealed many blessings upon him. The Presidency then in turn laid their hands upon his head, beginning at the oldest, until they had all laid their hands upon him, and pronounced such blessings upon his head, as the Lord put into their hearts, all blessing him to be our Patriarch, to anoint our heads. . . . The presidency then took the seat in their turn, according to their age, beginning at the oldest, and received their anointing and blessing under the hands of Father Smith.

"My scribe also received his anointing with us, and saw, in a vision, the armies of heaven protecting the Saints in their return to Zion, and many things which I saw.

"The Bishop of Kirtland with his Counselors, and the Bishop of Zion with his Counselors, were present with us, and received their anointings under the hands of Father Smith, and this was confirmed by the Presidency, and the glories of heaven were unfolded to them also" (Joseph Smith, Jr., *History of the Church of Jesus Christ of Latter-day Saints*, 7 vols., ed. B. H. Roberts, 2d ed. rev. [Salt Lake City: Deseret Book Co., 1973], 2:379-382 [hereafter HC]).

of the Prophets was spent "rehearsing to each other the glorious scenes that transpired on the preceding evening while attending to the ordinance of [the] holy anointing."[3] More anointings were performed in the temple that evening. Those receiving the ordinance included members of the Council of the Twelve, the presidency of the Seventies, and members of the high councils of Kirtland and Missouri. The events of this evening again concluded with the hosannah shout:

> At evening we met at the same place, with the council of the 12 and the presidency of the 70 who were to receive this ordinance; the high councils of Kirtland and Zion were present also: we called to order and organized; the Presidency then proceeded to consecrate the oil; we then laid our hands upon Elder Thomas B. Marsh who is the president of the 12 and ordained him to the authority of anointing his brethren, I then poured the concecrated oil upon his head in the name of Jesus Christ and sealed such blessings upon him as the Lord put into my heart; the rest of the presidency then laid their hands upon him and blessed him each in their turn beginning at the eldest; he then anointed <and blessed> his brethren from the oldest to the youngest, I also laid my hands upon them and prounounced many great and glorious [blessings] upon their heads; the heavens were opened and angels ministered unto us.
>
> The 12 then proceeded to anoint and bless the presidency of the 70 and seal upon their heads power and authority to anoint their brethren; the heavens were opened upon Elder Sylvester Smith and he leaping up [and] exclaimed, The horsemen of Israel and the chariots thereof. . . . President [Sidney] Rigdon, arose to conclude the servises of the evening by invoking the ben[e]diction of heaven of heaven upon the Lords anointed <which he did> in an eloquent manner the congregation shouted a loud hosannah [and] the gift of toungs, fell upon us in mighty pow[e]r, angels mingled themselves their voices with ours, while their presence was in our midst, and unseasing prasis swelled our bosoms for the space of half an hour,—I then observed to the brethren that it was time to retire, we accordingly <closed> our inter-

3. Scott H. Faulring, ed., *An American Prophet's Record: The Diaries and Journals of Joseph Smith* (Salt Lake City: Signature Books in association with Smith Research Associates, 1989), 120.

view and returned home at about 2. oclock in the morning & the spirit & visions of God attended me through the night.[4]

Book of Mormon witness and Joseph Smith confidant Oliver Cowdery described these events. Of the first night, 21 January, he wrote:

At about three o'clock P.M. I assembled in our office garret, having all things prepared for the occasion, with presidents Joseph Smith, jr. F. G. Williams, Sidney Rigdon Hyrum Smith, David Whitmer, John Whitmer and elder John Corrill, and washed our bodies with pure water before the Lord, preparatory to the annointing with holy oil. After we were washed, our bodies were perfumed with a sweet smelling oderous wash. At evening the presidents of the Church, with the two bishops and their counsellors, and elder Warren Parrish, met in the presidents' room, the high councils of Kirtland and Zion [Independence, Missouri] in their rooms. Those named in the first room were annointed with the same kind of oil and in the man[ner] that were Moses and Aaron, and those who stood before the Lord in ancient days, and those in the other rooms with annointing oil prepared for them. The glorious scene is too great to be described in this book, therefore, I say, that the heavens were opened to many, and great and marvelous things were shown.[5]

Of the second night Cowdery wrote,

At evening met in the president's room where were the presidents, the twelve, the presidents of the 70, the high councils of Kirtland and Zion, and the bishops and their counsellors. The presidents proceeded and annointed Thomas B. Marsh, the president of the twelve, and he annointed the other eleven. The Twelve then proceeded, president Marsh taking the lead, and annointed the presidents of the Seventy. Elder Don Carlos was ordained and annointed president of the high priesthood of the Melchisedek priesthood, by the presidents of the Church. Near the close of the meeting, 2 o'clock in the morning, almost all present broke out in tongues and songs of Zion.[6]

---

4. Jessee, 159-60.

5. Oliver Cowdery Sketch Book, 21 Jan. 1836, in Jesse, 159n1.

6. Jessee, 160n3.

Church bishop Edward Partridge remembered the ceremonial anointing:

> [January] 21st. Having previously washed once or twice, the [First] presidency with Bishop Whitney and his counsel, myself & my counsellors met for the purpose of being annointed with Holy oil. Meeting was opened by Prest. Joseph Smith, Jun., in behalf of the Presidency, Bishop Whitney in behalf of himself and counsellors, and myself in behalf of myself & counsellors. Then the presidency proceeded to sanctify the oil. Br. Joseph Smith, Jun., first anointed his father, pronouncing blessings upon him; then all the presidents beginning at the oldest rubbed their hand over his head & face, which had been annointed. Then Br. J. prayed to the Lord to accept of the anointing and all the Presidency with right hand uplifted to Heaven said Amen. Father Smith then proceeded to take the lead and pour on the oil; then Br. J. followed and then in rotation as before described, prophesying, &c., on one anothers heads. After the presidents, Bishop Whitney & his counsel were annointed after the same manner, then myself and counsel, then Br. Parrish as scribe for the presidency. After this Hyrum Smith annointed Father John Smith who annointed the rest of the High Council of Kirtland. Br. David Whitmer annointed Br. Simeon Carter, who anointed the High Council from Zion. Hymns were sung & a number saw visions & others were blessed with the outpouring of the Holy Ghost, and we shouted Hosanna to the Most High. The meeting was dismissed. Br. J. S. Jun, conferring the benedictions of Heaven upon us.
>
> The 22d. The forenoon was taken up in telling the visions of the preceding evening. We met in the evening for the purpose of anointing the traveling High Council, and the 7 Presidents of the 70. The Presidents of the Church anointed Br. Carlos Smith as President of the High Priests in Kirtland. Prest. J. S. Jun., requested Prest. Sidney Rigdon to ask the Lord to accept the performances of the evening, and instructed us, when he was done, to shout Hosannah, Blessed be the name of the Most High God. These things were performed; the shout & speaking in unknown tongues lasted 10 or 15 minutes. During the evening, more especially at the time of shouting, a number saw visions as they disclosed unto us.[7]

---

7. Edward Partridge Journal, 21-22 Jan. 1836, typescript, pp. 2-3, LDS archives.

As anointings continued through the final days of January, so did the miraculous. Of the 28 January meeting, Smith reported:

As I organized this quorem [presidency of seventies] in this room, Pres. Sylvester Smith saw a piller of fire rest down & abide upon the heads of the quorem as we stood in the midst of the Twelve.

When the Twelve & the seven were through with their sealing prayers I called upon Pres. S. Rigdon to seal them with uplifted hands & when he had done this & cried hossannah that all [the] congregation should join him & shout hosannah to God & the Lamb & glory to God in the highest—It was done so & Eld[er]. Roger Orton saw a ~~flaming~~ <mighty> Angel riding upon a horse of fire with a flaming sword in his hand followed by five others—encircle the house & protect the saints even the Lords anointed from the power of Satan & a host of evil spirits which were striving to disturb the saints—

Pres. Wm Smith one of the Twelve saw the h[e]avens op[e]ned & the Lords host protecting the Lords anointed. Pres. Z Coltrin one of the seven saw the saviour extended before him as upon the cross & [a] little after crowned with a glory upon his head above the brightness of the sun after these things were over & a glorious vision which I saw had passed. . . . after these quorems were dismissed I retired to my home filled with the spirit & my soul cried hossannah to God & the Lamb through <the> silent watches of the night & while my eyes were closed in sleep the visions of the Lord were sweet unto me & his glory was round about me praise the Lord.[8]

After several days of anointing other priesthood bearers, Smith on 6 February 1836 assembled these brethren together to "receive the seal of all their blessings."[9] This sealing was performed as a group ceremony by First Counselor Sidney Rigdon:

[C]alled the anointed together to receive the seal of all their blessings. The High Priests & Elders in the council room as usual—The Seventy with the Twelve in the second room & the Bishop in the 3—I laboured with each of these quorems for some time to bring [them] to the order which God had shown to me which is as follows—first part to be spent in solemn prayer before god without any talking or confusion & the conclusion with a sealing prayer by Pres. Sidney Rigdon when all the

8. Jessee, 163-64.
9. Ibid.

quorems are to shout with one accord a solemn hosannah to God & the Lamb with an Amen–amen & amen–& then all take seats & lift up their hearts in silent prayer to God & if any obtain a prophecy or vision to rise & speak that all may be edified & rejoice together I had considerable trouble to get all the quorems united in this order–I went from room to room repeatedly & charged each separately–assuring them that it was according to the mind of God yet notwithstanding all my labour– while I was in the east room with the Bishops quorems I f[e]lt by the spirit that something was wrong in the quorem of Elders in the west room–& I immediately requested Pres. O. Cowdery & H. Smith to go in & see what was the matter–The quorem of Elders had not observed the order which I had given them & were reminded of it by Pres. [Don] Carloss Smith & mildly requested to observe order & continue in prayer & requested–some of them replied that they had a teacher of their own & did not wish to be troubled by others[.] this caused the spirit of the Lord to withdraw This interrupted the meeting & this quorem lost th[e]ir blessing in a great mcasure–the other quorems were more careful & the quorem of the seventy enjoyed a great flow of the holy spirit many arose & spok[e] testifying that they were filled with the holy spirit which was like fire in their bones so that they could not hold their peace but were constrained to cry hosannah to God & the Lamb & glory in the highest. Pres. Wm Smith one of the twelve saw a vision of the Twelve & seven in council together in old England & prophecied that a great work would be done by them in the old co[u]ntries & God was already beginning to work in the hearts of the p[e]ople–Pres. Z. Coltrin one of the seven saw a vision of the Lords Host–& others were filled with the spirit & spake in tongues & prophecied–This was a time of rejoicing long to be remembered! praise the Lord.[10]

The elders' minutes reported problems that evening:

Met to proceed with the anointing of the Elders of the Most High. Counselor Morton organized those who were anointed in order for supplications. President Beman finished the anointing. The first presidency came and sealed our anointing by prayer and shout of Hosanna. The first counselor organized those who had been anointed in order for supplication. They gave us some instructions and left us. President Beman spoke to the assembly. Sever[al] spoke and there seemed to be a cloud of darkness in the room. Pres. O[liver]. Cowdery & H[yrum].

---

10. Ibid., 169-71; also HC, 2:391-92.

Smith came and gave some instructions and the cloud was broken and some shouted, Hosanna and others spake with tongues. The first president (J. Smith jr) returned and reprimanded us for our evil deeds which was the cause of our darkness. He prophesied saying this night the key is turned to the nations, and the angel John is about commencing his mission to prophesy before kings, and rulers, nations tongues and people. The assembly was dismissed with prayer.[11]

Oliver Cowdery wrote: "[M]et with the presidency and quorums in the Lord's house, when their anointing blessings were sealed by uplifted hands and praises to God. Many saw visions, many prophesied, and many spake in tongues. Closed a little before 12 o'clock."[12]

As intense as these experiences were, they were considered preparatory to a solemn assembly and further endowment upon completion of the temple. "They assure you, with the utmost confidence," wrote an Ohio journalist, "that they shall soon be able to raise the dead, to heal the sick, the deaf, the dumb, and the blind, &c. Indeed, more than one assured me, that they had, themselves, by the laying on of their hands, restored the sick to health."[13]

The temple was dedicated a month and a half later on Sunday, 27 March. The ceremony was attended by hundreds of men, women, and children. Smith read a written prayer (D&C 109) at the dedication. Then, according to Smith's diary, he "bore testimony of the administering of angels.—Presdt Williams also arose and testified that while Presdt Rigdon was making his first prayer an angel entered the

---

11. Jessee, 170n1, quoting "A Record of the First Quorum of Elders Belonging to the Church of Christ: in Kirtland Geauga Co. Ohio," 4-5, Library/Archives, Reorganized Church of Jesus Christ of Latter Day Saints, Independence, Missouri (hereafter RLDS archives).

12. Cowdery Sketch Book, 6 Feb. 1836, 12.

13. *Ohio Atlas*, 16 Mar. 1836, reprinted in *Painesville Telegraph*, 20 May 1836. The anticipation was mixed with uncertainty about exactly when the Solemn assembly would take place. See W. W. Phelps to his wife Sally, 5 Jan. 1836: "The whole work continually progresses, though somewhat slowly. I cannot tell when the Endowment will take place" ("Journal History," 5 Jan. 1836, LDS archives). Also Clarissa Bicknell Orton wrote to her parents: "I [e]xpect the house of the Lord will be finished about the first of febuary and that the solem assembly will be caled about the eight or te[n]th of the month." On 7 February she revised her estimate: "I thought when I wrote the first part of this letter that the house would be finished by the first of february but it will pro[b]ably be three weeks yet" (in L. B. Johnson, ed., *The Pines Letters* [n.p., 1954], 22-23).

window and <took his> seated ~~himself~~ between father Smith, and himself, and remained their during his prayer Presdt David Whitmer also saw angels in the house." As had become customary, the day's events were "sealed . . . by a shouting hosanah to God and the Lamb 3 times sealing it each time with Amen, Amen, and Amen." Those present also partook of bread and wine.

Stephen Post, who was in attendance, remembered:

> March 27 and 1836 This day was appointed to be a day when the house of the Lord built by the Church of the Latter day Saints was to be dedicated unto the Lord of the whole earth: there was also a contribution; each individual as they came into the house of the Lord donated as they could in order to defray the expense of the building as the committee had incurred much expense above what had before been contributed. the doors were opened at 8 and to be closed at 9 A.M. however they were closed before 9 on account of the house being full many retired to, and filled the school room, under the printing office which holds 400 or 450 and many went home. . . . President Joseph Smith Jun. Offered up a dedication prayer unto the Lord President Sidney Rigdon offered a short prayer and then led the way, followed by the whole congregation acknowledging the Lord to be King, this is the sample of the shout with uplifted hands unto the most high, by the Lord anointed Hosanna! Hosanna! Hosanna to God and the Lamb Amen! amen. and Amen. this was done three times. making 9 hosannas and 9 amens they next partook of the sacrament and then were dismissed after some testimony during the partaking by the congregation of the bread and wine in remembrance of our Lord and Savior Jesus Christ, Joseph Smith Jun. testified of the Angel of the Lord's appearing unto him to call him to the work of the Lord, and also of being ordained under the hands of the Angel of the covenant. . . . President F. G. Williams arose and testified that in the A.M. an angel of God came into the window (at the back of the pulpit) while P.t. Rigdon was at prayer and took his seat between him and Father Joseph Smith Sr. and remained there during the prayer.[14]

In the evening a priesthood meeting was held in which Smith "instructed the quorums respecting the ordinance of washing of feet"

---

14. Stephen Post Journal, 27 Mar. 1836, LDS archives.

which was to be introduced to a solemn assembly of the general priesthood "on wednesday following."[15] Oliver Cowdery wrote: "In the evening I met with the officers of the church in the Lord's house. The Spirit poured out—I saw the glory of God, like a great cloud, come down and rest upon the house, and fill the same like a mighty rushing wind. I also saw cloven tongues, like as of fire rest upon many. (for there were 316 present,) while they spake with other tongues and prophesied."[16] Bishop Partridge also wrote of the day's extraordinary events: "Many spoke in tongues; some saw visions, &c. Doct. F[rederick]. G. Williams saw an angel or rather the Savior, during the forenoon service."[17]

Post provided more details of the morning and evening of 27 March:

> The ordained members of the church were requested to meet in the Lords house this evening to receive instruction previous to their going forth to proclaim the gospel the congregation were now dismissed This eve assembled in the house of the Lord Joseph Smith jun. read the 6 chap. 11 Chron. and showed us the order of dedicating a house to God anciently: this evening was designed as a continuation of our pentecost, Angels of God came into the room, cloven tongues rested upon some of the Servants of the Lord like unto fire and they spake with tongues and prophesied. Last Saturday I received my patriarchal blessing under the hands of Joseph Smith Sen. Patriarch and Evangellist I write this monday march. 28 the roads are bare but there is plenty of snow in the woods, and considerable yet in the fields people are preparing for sugar making as they have not yet tapped any where yet as I have heard. the air is smoky today it was ascertained and told to us last eve that there was 1000 persons in the house of the Lord yesterday and they contributed as they went in $960. I will mention here that two of the Apostles Brigham Young and David Patten sang each a song of Zion in tongues and each spake in tongues and Elder Patten interpreted brother Youngs tongue which he spake During Last week there was 11 baptized in Kirtland. there was about 316 ordained members met in the house of the Lord Sunday eve and we received instruction from Joseph Smith Jr relative to our preaching and to our

---

15. Jessee (26-27 Mar. 1836), 191-203; see also HC, 2:410-28.
16. Cowdery Sketch Book, 21-22.
17. Partridge Journal, 27 Mar. 1836.

endowment this eve the spirit of the Lord rested on the congregation many spake in tongues many prophesied, Angels were in our midst, and ministered unto some, Cloven tongues like unto fire rested upon those who spake in tongues and prophesied when they ceased to speak the tongues ascended.[18]

Tuesday evening, the day before the anticipated solemn priesthood assembly, Smith and others "met in the most holy place in the Lords house" to pray for revelation and prepare for the next day's event.[19] They received the impression that they should call other leading brethren to the temple to "fast through the day and also the night and that during this, if we would humble ourselves, we should receive further communication from Him."[20] After the brethren were assembled, Smith said "that those who had entered the holy place must not leave the house untill morning but send for such things as were necessary, and also, that during our stay we must cleans[e] our feet and partake of the sacrament that we might be made holy before Him, and thereby be qualified to officiate in our calling upon the morrow in washing the feet of the Elders."[21] According to Smith's diary, those present first "proceeded and cleansed our faces and our feet, and then proceded to wash each others feet." After all were washed, "we partook of the bread and wine. The Holy S[p]irit rested down upon us and we continued in the Lords house all night prophesying and giving glory to God."[22]

The next day, 30 March, a group of about 300 of the church's male elite, those numbered among "the first of mine elders," met in the temple to have their feet washed and partake of the sacrament. At the beginning of the meeting, Smith, who had already spent the previous night in the temple, told those present:

> that this is a year of Jubilee to us and a time of rejoicing, and that it was expedient for us to prepare bread and wine sufficient to make our hearts glad, as we should not probably leave this house until morning; to this end we should call on the brethren to make a contribution, the

18. Post Journal, 27 Mar. 1836.
19. Jessee, 203.
20. Ibid., 204.
21. Ibid.
22. Jessee, 204-205; also HC, 2:429-30, and Faulring, 152-53.

stewards passed round and took up a liberal contribution and messen-
gers were dispatched for bread and wine, tubs [of] water and towels
were prepared and I called the house to order, and the presidency
proceeded to wash the feet of the 12 pronouncing many prophecy's
and blessings upon them in the name of the Lord Jesus, the brethren
began to prophesy upon each others heads, and cursings upon the
enimies of Christ who inhabit Jackson county Missouri continued
prophesying and blessing and sealing them with Hosanna and Amen
until nearly 7 oclock P.M. the bread <& wine> was then brought in, and
I observed that we had fasted all the day, and lest we faint; as the Saviour
did so shall we do on this occasion, we shall bless the bread and give
it to the 12 and they to the multitude, after which we shall bless the
wine and do likewise; while waiting for the wine I made the following
remarks, that the time that we were required to tarry in Kirtland to be
endued [endowed] would be fulfilled in a few days, and then the Elders
would go forth and each must stand for himself, that it was not
necessary for them to be sent out two by two as in former times. . . .

   [A]nd let the redem[p]tion of Zion be our object, and strive to
affect it by sending up all the strength of the Lords house whereever
we find them, and I want to enter into the following covenant, that if
any more of our brethren are slain or driven from their lands in Missouri
by the mob that we will give ourselves no rest until we are avenged of
our enimies to the uttermost, this covenant was sealed unanimously by
a hosanna and Amen. —I then observed to the quorums that I had now
completed the organization of the church and we had passed through
all the necessary ceremonies, that I had given them all the instruction
they needed and that they now were at liberty after obtaining their
lisences to go forth and build up the kingdom of God.[23]

At this point Smith told the assembly that he and the First
Presidency would retire because they had spent the previous night in
the temple and the next day, Thursday, the temple would be dedicated
again for those who had been unable to squeeze into the building the
previous Sunday. However, the others were not to leave:

   it was expedient for the brethren to tarry all night and worship before
   the Lord in his house I left the meeting in the charge of the 12 and

----

23. Jessee, 205-207. It is interesting that cursing one's enemies, a controversial
part of the later Nauvoo endowment, was intertwined with the ceremonies instituted
in Kirtland.

retired at about 9 o clock in the evening; the brethren continued exhorting, prophesying and speaking in tongues until 5 o clock in the morning—the Saviour made his appearance to some, while angels minestered unto others, and it was a penticost and enduement indeed, long to be remembered for the sound shall go forth from this place into all the world, and the occurrences of this day shall be hande[d] down upon the pages of sacred history to all generations, as the day of Pentecost, so shall this day be numbered and celebrated as a year of Jubileee and time of rejoicing to the saints of the most high God.[24]

Partridge similarly underscored the pentecostal events:

Tuesday the 29th. The 9 presidents, the two Bishops and their counsel met in the afternoon in the House of the Lord. We cleansed our hands and faces and feet, after which we had our feet washed in the name of the Lord; this took till dusk. We then partook of bread and wine, a feast. We prophesied and spoke in tongues and shouted Hosannas. The meeting lasted till daylight.

Wednesday [30 March 1836] all the officers of the Church met at 9 o'clock in the Lord's House, the Priests, Teachers & Deacons in one corner, the vails [curtains] having been let down, and the other officers occupied the rest of the lower room. The washing of feet was performed by noon, then they began to prophecy and speak in tongues adding shouts of Hosannas to God and the Lamb with Amen and Amen. This continued till dark, when they partook of a feast of bread and wine. The meeting was kept up till morning, the shouts were omitted during the night.

Thursday 31st. We met from 8 to 9 to accommodate those who could not get in at the Sunday dedication. The house was about filled and similar ceremonies performed that were performed on Sunday. This meeting rather surpassed the Sunday meeting, both in length & goodness.[25]

Arriving at Wednesday's solemn assembly, doubting that he would be asked to participate in the ritual washings, Post was overwhelmed:

Wen. 30. This day between the hours of 8 and 9 the ordained

24. Ibid.
25. Partridge Journal, 29-31 Mar. 1836.

members met in the house of the Lord to attend to the last ordinance
of the endowment viz: the ordinance of the washing of feet this
ordinance is administered to none but those who are clean from the
blood of the generation in which they live. I did not expect much to
receive the ordinance as I had not labored much in the vineyard, but I
had endeavoured to do as well as I could. However when we came
together the word of the Lord was that we all should receive the
ordinance. O the goodness and condescension of God. The washing
was commensed by the presidents who first washed the 12 and the 7
presidents of the seventies the 12 and 7 then commenced washing until
the whole were washed. The order of the house was that we tarry until
tomorrow morning in the house of the Lord and not go out only in cases
of necessity, after the washing the Brethren commenced prophesying
for the spirit of prophecy was poured out upon the congregation: the
house was divided into 4 parts by the curtains and they prophesied,
spake and sang in tongues in each room. we fasted until even when we
partook of bread and wine in commemoration of the marriage supper
of the Lamb. now having attended through the endowment I could
form an idea of the endowment anciently for Gods ordinances change
not.[26]

Such accounts provide an important context for the frenzied
millennial hymn that was sung by the choir at the dedication of the
House of the Lord:

> The Spirit of God like a fire is burning;
> The latter day glory begins to come forth;
> The visions and blessings of old are returning;
> The angels are coming to visit the earth.
>
> CHORUS: We'll sing & we'll shout with the armies of heaven;
> Hosanna, hosanna to God and the Lamb!
> Let glory to them in the highest be given,
> Henceforth and forever: amen and amen!
>
> The Lord is extending the saints' understanding—
> Restoring their judges and all as at first;

------

26. Post Journal, 30 Mar. 1836.

The knowledge and power of God are expanding;
The vail o'er the earth is beginning to burst.

CHORUS: We'll sing & we'll shout &c.

We call in our solemn assemblies, in spirit,
To spread forth the kingdom of heaven abroad,
That we through our faith may begin to inherit
The visions, and blessings, and glories of God.

CHORUS: We'll sing and we'll shout &c.

We'll wash, and be wash'd, and with oil be anointed,
Withal not omitting the washing of feet;
For he that receiveth his penny appointed
Must surely be clean at the harvest of wheat.

CHORUS: We'll sing and we'll shout &c.

Old Israel that fled from the world for his freedom,
Must come with the cloud and the pillar, again;
A Moses, and Aaron, and Joshua lead him,
And feed him on manna from heaven again.

CHORUS: We'll sing and we'll shout &c.

How blessed the day when the lamb and the lion
Shall lie down together without any ire;
And Ephraim be crowned with his blessings in Zion,
As Jesus descends with his chariots of fire!

CHORUS: We'll sing & we'll shout with *His* armies of heaven;
                  Hosanna, hosanna to God and the Lamb!
                  Let glory to them in the highest be given,
                  Henceforth and forever: amen and amen![27]

---

27. *Latter Day Saints' Messenger and Advocate* 2 (Mar. 1836): 280-81.

Although other participants reported pentecostal experiences,[28] not all remembered the incident in glowing terms. Years later two prominent apostates would denounce the events. William McLellin, at the time a member of the Quorum of the Twelve, subsequently wrote that "it was no endowment from God. Not only myself was not endowed, but no other man of the five hundred who was present—except it was with wine!"[29] David Whitmer later described the event as a "grand fizzle" and denied any angelic visitations.[30] In 1841 William Harris, by then a disaffected participant, wrote:

In 1836, an endowment meeting, or solemn assembly, was called, to be held in the Temple at Kirtland. It was given out that those who were in attendance at the meeting should receive an endowment, or blessing, similar to that experienced by the disciples of Christ on the day of Pentecost. When the day arrived, great numbers convened from the different Churches in the country. They spent the day in fasting and prayer, and in washing and perfuming their bodies; they also washed their feet, and anointed their heads with what they called holy oil, and pronounced blessings. In the evening, they met for the endowment. The fast was then broken by eating light wheat bread, and drinking as much wine as they saw proper. Smith knew well how to infuse the spirit which they expected to receive; so he encouraged the brethren to drink freely, telling them that the wine was consecrated, and would not make them drunk. As may be supposed, they drank to the purpose. After this, they began to prophesy, pronouncing blessings upon their friends, and curses upon their enemies. If I should be so unhappy as to go to the regions of the damned, I never expect to hear language more awful, or more becoming the infernal pit, than was uttered that night.

28. For example, Milo Andrus "saw the Spirit in the form of cloven tongues as a fire descend in thousands, and rest upon the heads of the Elders, and they spoke with tongues and prophesyed" ("Autobiography of Milo Andrus, 1814-1875," LDS archives); David Patten reported, "The heavens Was opened unto [us]. Angels & Jesus Christ was seen of [us] sitting at the right hand of the father" (in Scott G. Kenney, ed., *Wilford Woodruff's Journal*, 9 vols. [Midvale, UT: Signature Books, 1983], 1:67); and Erastus Snow remembered that "angels came & worsh[i]ped with us & some saw them yea even twelve legions of them the charriots of Israel & the horseman thereof" ("E[rastus]. Snows Sketch book No.1," 9 Nov. 1818-5 Dec. 1837, typescript, Huntington Library, San Marino, California).

29. William McLellin to M. H. Forscutt, Oct. 1870, RLDS archives.

30. *Chicago Inter-Ocean*, 17 Oct. 1886.

The curses were pronounced principally upon the clergy of the present day, and upon the Jackson county mob in Missouri. After spending the night in alternate blessings and cursing, the meeting adjourned.[31]

This account is echoed as well by John Corrill, a church historian: "The sacrament was then administered, in which they partook of the bread and wine freely, and a report went abroad that some of them got drunk: as to that every man must answer for himself. A similar report, the reader will recollect, went out concerning the disciples, at Jerusalem, on the day of pentecost."[32]

Apparently the solemn assembly and endowment were intended to be a one-time event only, not to be repeated. The relevant revelations imply, and at least one contemporary account confirms, this. In January 1836 Roger Orton wrote from Kirtland to his father: "Brother Joseph Smith ses [says] whoever is Her[e] at the endowment will always regois [rejoice] and whoever is not will away be Sorry[.] this thi[ng] will not take place a gain whil time last."[33] Yet it soon became evident that not everyone requiring the endowment for their work in the church could be there on 30 March. Therefore it was repeated at least three times in 1836. Fewer people participated in these events, but the same steps were repeated as in the March endowment: washings, anointing with oil, sealing the anointings, washing of feet, and pentecostal outpourings. Jeremiah Willey reported a solemn assembly on 6 April:

> I spent the night in the temple in prayer and fasting; the spirit of the Lord rested upon us, April 6 the presidency of the Church, the Twelve Apostles, and other quorums met in solemn assembly and sealed upon us our washings, anointings and blessings · with a loud shout of Hosannah to God and the Lamb, the Spirit of the Lord rested

31. William Harris, *Mormonism Portrayed; Its Errors and Absurdities Exposed, and the Spirit and Designs of its Authors Made Manifest* (Warsaw, IL: Sharp & Gamble, 1841), in John C. Bennett, *The History of the Saints; or, an Exposé of Joe Smith and Mormonism* (Boston: Leland & Whiting, 1842), 136.

32. John Corrill, *Brief History of the Church of Christ of Latter Day Saints (commonly called Mormons;) Including an Account of their Doctrine and Discipline: With the Reasons of the Author for Leaving the Church* (St. Louis: the Author, 1839), chap. 12.

33. Roger Orton to "Deer Father," Jan. 1836, in *Pines Letters*, 22.

upon us after spending three hours in the upper room, the quorums rejoined to the lower court. The Veils were lowered and the ordinance of washing of feet was administered. After this ordinance the veils of the temple were pulled up and the prophet addressed the Elders for three hours. Clothed with the power and spirit of God he unbosomed his feelings in the House of his friends and gave much instruction. He urged upon us the absolute necessity of giving strict heed to his teachings and counsel and the revelations of the Lord to the Church and us in all things, that Zion and her stakes may be redeemed and established no more to be thrown down. He said that the kings of the earth would yet come to behold the glory of Zion and that great and glorious blessings would be bestowed upon the Saints in the Last Days. Hyrum Smith bore testimony and was followed by Oliver Cowdery, who exhorted the Elders to keep within the bounds of their knowledge and let the mystery of the kingdom alone, for the Gentiles had not a knowledge even of the first principles of the Gospel. He said it is far better to preach what the people would call the small of the kingdom than to enter into the visions of Isaiah, Ezekiel and John. The Twelve broke bread, which was distributed to the multitude who eat and were filled. Thanks were returned and the meeting closed. The house was again filled at Candle Light. Pres. Joseph Smith requested the Elders to speak their feelings freely and sing, exhort and pray as the spirit would give utterance. The meeting continued during the whole night. Many of the gifts were poured out upon the people; at Break of Day we were dismissed. I also spent the night of the 7 in the Temple with several of the Elders in prayer and praise. Before the Lord the Holy Ghost rested upon us and the spirit of prophecy was given and many things were shown by the Holy Spirit.[34]

Charles C. Rich wrote of a 16 April meeting: "We then continued to fast and pray until the setting of the sun when we Broke Bread and Drank wine[.] we prophesied all night pronouncing blessings and cursings until the morning light there was Great manifestations of the power of God . . . and I was filled with the spirit of prophesy and I was endued with power from on high."[35] Additional elders participated on 30 April: "the [High] council met again in the Lord's house and

---

34. Journal of Jeremiah Willey, 1836, 10-12, LDS archives; HC, 2:475-77 for 6 April.

35. Charles Coulson Rich Diary, 16 Apr. 1836, LDS archives.

proceeded to anoint the following Elders. . . . These Elders with a Priest were anointed in the Lord's house with fasting and washing of feet according to the order given for the endowment of God, in the last days by the Pr[e]s. and assistant."[36]

A solemn assembly was held in the spring of 1837 on the anniversary of the first endowments and the anniversary of the founding of the church. Apostle Wilford Woodruff had been absent on a mission when the House of the Lord was dedicated the previous spring and now looked forward to participating:

> This being more particular the day of the Solumn assembly or a day that is looked upon annually with feeling of greater interest in Celebration of the 6th of April 1830 as upon that day the Church of Latter day Saints was first organized in this last dispensation & fulness of times. Henceforth the Solumn assembly of the Elders of Israel & all official members that can, will meet in the LORDS house annually to attend to the most Solumn ordinances of the house of GOD & of receieving the visions & great things of heavens. Therefore I shall be more particular in recording the transactions of this day than others for it is sumthing similar to the Pentecost that St Paul speak[s] of at Jerrusalem.[37]

During the two or three days before 6 April a number of priesthood holders were ritually washed and perfumed. Woodruff received his washing in the temple, but others were washed in private dwellings. Woodruff describes his own experience:

> April 3rd The day had now arived for preperations for the solumn assembly the Annointing & the endowment of the Elders of Israel or at least for those that were not endowed in Kirtland[,] the strong hold of the daught[ers] of Zion[,] in the spring of 1836 & as I was absent at that time my day is now come & my time at hand for those blessings & I shall record the events of each day of the endowment for the benefit of the generation to come.
>
> I upon this third day of April met in the house of the Lord with a number of the seventies to receive counsel respecting our washing & anointing. I was appointed with Elder G. Meeks to visit President F. G.

---

36. Lyndon W. Cook and Milton V. Backman, eds., *Kirtland Elders' Quorum Record, 1836-1841* (Provo, UT: Grandin Book Co., 1985), 18.

37. Kenney, 1:131.

Williams & have the perfumes & oil prepared against the day following. I consider'd it a privilege to wait upon the Elders of Israel in this thing that we might become the annointed of the Lord according to the words of the Poet & the Revelations of JESUS CHRIST.

> We'll wash and be washed and with oil be anointed
> > Withal not omit the washing of feet
> For he that receiveth his PENNY appointed
> > Must surely be clean at the hearvest of wheat.

After attending to the duties above spoken I repaired to a room in Company with Elder Meeks & Priest J Turpin to attend to our first washing. After washing our bodies from head to foot in soap & watter we then washed ourselves in clear watter next in perfumed spirits. The spirit of God was with us & we had a spiritual time. We spent the evening with several Elders in Prayer before God & the Power of God rested upon us.[38]

The next day Woodruff joined other brethren in the upper room of the temple. The men met according to their priesthood offices in appointed areas, and each man was individually consecrated, anointed, and blessed "as the testimony of Jesus shall direct which is the spirit of prophecy":

The quorums of the Deacons, Teachers, & Priest occupied one apartment the Elders another & the Seventies the third. Each quorums met for the anointing. . . .

President Coultrin opened the meeting by prayer & after conversing plainly to those who were to be anointed they proceded to business. The presidency consecrated the oil before God that it might be holy. The person to be anointed then took a seat & the presidency then laid hands upon his head & Consecrated him unto God & then anointed him in the name of the Lord & pronounced such blessings upon his head as the testimony of Jesus shall direct which is the spirit of prophecy. We had a glorious season indeed in this solumn ordinance of the house of the Lord.[39]

As had become apparent the previous year, Woodruff spent the

---

38. Ibid., 128-29.
39. Ibid., 129.

night in the temple fasting and praying. The anointing was sealed and further blessings pronounced the next day just before the solemn assembly. The *History of the Church* suggests that the Seventies were sealed as a group instead of individually to save time. Woodruff continues:

> While all of the anointed present lifted there hands towards heaven this first presidency of the Church Confirmed & sealed upon our heads all the blessings of our ordination, anointing, & Patriarchal [authority] with a seal in the presence of God & the Lamb & holy angels that they should all be fulfilled upon our heads that not one jot or tittle should fail & the seal was confirmed upon our heads with a shout of all the anointed with uplifted hand to heaven HOSANNA, Hosanna, Hosanna, to GOD & the LAMB, Amen, Amen, & Amen. Hosanna Hosanna, Hosanna, to GOD & the LAMB, Amen, Amen, & Amen. Hosanna, Hosanna, Hosanna, to GOD & the LAMB, Amen, Amen, & Amen. This was repeated as it is written & if ever a shout entered the Cabinet of heaven that did & was repeated by angels on high & caused the power of God to rest upon us.[40]

When the men descended to the general assembly room, they found that the veils had been lowered to segregate the congregation. There the anointed received the ordinance of washing the feet. "Elder Heber Kimble one of the twelve apostles attended to the washing of my feet & prophesied upon my head & pronounced me clean from the Blood of this generation. This as it was with JESUS when he washed his deciples feet. Great were the blessings that rested upon us in this ordinance," wrote Woodruff.[41] After this most of the veils were rolled up and the meeting began. The final ordinance of the day was again the sacrament: "After the Presidency Closed their remarks the twelve were Called upon to break bread for the multitude (as Jesus did in the days of the Apostles) that they might all be filled. They did so & we were all filled & was made glad while feasting with Patriarchs, Prophets, Apostles, Evangelest, Pasters, Teachers, & Deacons."[42]

---

40. Ibid., 132-33.

41. Ibid.

42. Ibid., 128-36. The *History of the Church* gives this abbreviated version of the proceedings (HC, 2:475-76): "A brief notice only was given, that a solemn assembly would be called, of the official members of the Church, on the 6th of April, for the

The departure of most Mormons from Kirtland between December 1837 and July 1838 resulted in the cessation of further endowments in the House of the Lord, except for John Taylor who had converted in July 1836 and was called to the Quorum of the Twelve in July 1838 after the Saints had left Kirtland. On their way to England with other members of the Twelve in the fall of 1839, some of the Twelve stopped in Kirtland. Taylor and fellow apostles Brigham Young, Heber C. Kimball, and George A. Smith met on 17 November in the House of the Lord, where Taylor and Theodore Turley, a Seventy, received the endowment. This consisted of a washing and anointing, washing of feet, and as before a spiritual outpouring: "President Young preached in the House of the Lord in the forenoon, and John Taylor in the afternoon. In the evening, President Brigham Young anointed Elder John Taylor in the House of the Lord, and Elder Daniel S. Miles anointed Theodore Turley, all of which was sealed with the shout of Hosanna."[43]

---

purpose of washing, anointing, washing of feet, receiving instructions, and the further organization of the ministry. Meetings were held by the different quorums on Monday, 3rd, Tuesday, 4th, and Wednesday, 5th, to anoint such of their respective members as had not been washed and anointed, that all might be prepared for the meeting on the 6th.

"At an early hour on Thursday, the 6th of April, the official members assembled in the House of the Lord, when the time for the first two or three hours was spent by the different quorums in washing of feet, singing, praying, and preparing to receive instructions from the Presidency. The Presidents, together with the Seventies and their presidents, repaired to the west room in the attic story, where, for want of time the preceding evening, it became necessary to seal the anointing of those who had recently been anointed and not sealed."

In Smith's attempt to restore ancient ritual, one diary suggests that he encouraged the practice of animal sacrifice in the Kirtland temple (*Excerpts from the Life Story of Wandle Mace* [n.p., n.d.], 4), but no other available evidence documents its practice in either Kirtland or Nauvoo.

43. "Manuscript History of Brigham Young," 17 Nov. 1839, LDS archives.

CHAPTER 3

Joseph Smith's Ritual

In Nauvoo, Illinois, Joseph Smith continued to expand Mormon salvation concepts, concepts which came to be intertwined with rituals later performed in temples. He defined the principle of "mak[ing your] calling and election sure" in a 27 June 1839 sermon. This was to be accomplished, after a lifetime of service and devotion, by being "sealed up" to exaltation while yet living.[1] This concept was based on 2 Peter 1:10-11: "Wherefore . . . brethren, give diligence to make your calling and election sure: for if ye do these things, ye shall never fail: For so an entrance shall be ministered unto you abundantly into the everlasting kingdom of our Lord and Saviour Jesus Christ" (see also v. 19 and Eph. 1:13-14).

This sermon was additionally important because Smith not only tied calling and election to sealing theology but also to the "second comforter" mentioned in John 14:26. According to Smith the second

---

1. Joseph Smith, Jr., *History of the Church of Jesus Christ of Latter-day Saints*, 7 vols., ed. B. H. Roberts, 2d ed. rev. (Salt Lake City: Deseret Book Co., 1973), 3:379-81 (hereafter HC). The original source is Willard Richards's Pocket Companion, "The Doctrine of Election," published in Andrew F. Ehat and Lyndon W. Cook, eds., *The Words of Joseph Smith: The Contemporary Accounts of the Nauvoo Discourses of the Prophet Joseph* (Provo, UT: Brigham Young University Religious Studies Center, 1980), 4-6. A brief discussion of this doctrine can be found in Roy W. Doxey, "Accepted of the Lord: The Doctrine of Making Your Calling and Election Sure," *Ensign* 6 (July 1976): 50-53; a more in-depth discussion is Hyrum L. Andrus, *Principles of Perfection* (Salt Lake City: Bookcraft, 1970), 331-400.

comforter was a personal manifestation of Jesus Christ. These ideas were also tied to the concept of personal revelation and the fact that the twelve apostles and all Mormons could and should follow Smith's steps and "become perfect in Jesus Christ." There was no reference to the temple in this sermon, nor were there functioning temples at this time.

In January 1841, well over two years after Mormons abandoned Kirtland, Joseph Smith announced another revelation. In it the Lord asked, "How shall your washings be acceptable unto me, except ye perform them in a house which you have built to my name?" (D&C 124:37). The Saints were instructed to build another temple "that I may reveal mine ordinances therein unto my people; For I deign to reveal unto my church things which have been kept hid from before the foundation of the world, things that pertain to the dispensation of the fulness of times" (vv. 40-41). Anointed Saints were advised that their Kirtland ordinances were forerunners to ordinances which would be revealed in a Nauvoo temple.

As in Kirtland, Smith elected to administer new rituals, an expanded "endowment," to selected leaders before the temple was finished. In 1842 the new endowment was performed only for men, but in 1843 wives were included. The pre-temple endowed were sometimes referred to as the "Holy Order," the "Quorum," the "Holy Order of the Holy Priesthood," or the "Quorum of the Anointed."[2] Preliminary initiations proved to be providential since Smith was killed before the temple's dedication.

On Wednesday, 4 May 1842, after two days of preparation in the upper story of his Nauvoo store, the prophet gathered together nine men. In a significant departure from the simple washings and anointings received in Kirtland, these men were introduced to new theological instructions and ritual. According to the account recorded in the "Book of the Law of the Lord," Smith spent the day "In council in the Presidents & General offices with Judge [James] Adams. Hyram Smith Newell K. Whitney. William Marks, Wm Law. George Miller. Brigham Young. Heber C. Kimball & Willard Richards. [*blank*] &

---

2. For a brief discussion of this group, see D. Michael Quinn, "Latter-day Saint Prayer Circles," *Brigham Young University Studies* 19 (Fall 1978): 84-96.

giving certain instructions concerning the priesthood. [*blank*] &c on the Aronic Priesthood to the first [*blank*] continuing through the day."[3] This was subsequently expanded to read in the *History of the Church* that Smith

> instruct[ed] them in the principles and order of the Priesthood, attending to washings, anointings, endowments and the communication of keys pertaining to the Aaronic Priesthood, and so on to the highest order of the Melchisedek Priesthood, setting forth the order pertaining to the Ancient of Days, and all those plans and principles by which any one is enabled to secure the fullness of those blessings which have been prepared for the Church of the First Born, and come up and abide in the presence of the Eloheim in the eternal worlds. In this council was instituted the ancient order of things for the first time in these last days. . . . therefore let the Saints . . . [know] assuredly that all these things referred to in this council are always governed by the principle of revelation.[4]

Joseph and Hyrum Smith received their endowments the next day.

One of the earliest accounts came from apostate John C. Bennett, who described the Holy Order in his 1842 exposé *The History of the Saints*. Although much of his description is obviously contrived, several specific comments on the ceremony parallel other descriptions published later in the nineteenth century. His account of the oaths, for example, includes promises of dedication to the Kingdom of God on earth, obedience, chastity, secrecy, a type of vengeance oath, and

---

3. Dean C. Jessee, ed., *The Papers of Joseph Smith* (Salt Lake City: Deseret Book Co., 1993), 2:380. The blanks indicate erased words in the original.

4. HC, 5:2. There are some problems with the published account. Of interest historically is the omission of two names, William Law and William Marks. Law left the church shortly before Smith's murder in June 1844; Marks became disaffected and, after briefly affiliating with Sidney Rigdon, James J. Strang, and other dissidents, ultimately joined the Reorganized Church of Jesus Christ of Latter Day Saints in 1859. Heber C. Kimball referred to the two as "worse than dead" (George D. Smith, ed., *An Intimate Chronicle: The Journals of William Clayton* [Salt Lake City: Signature Books in association with Smith Research Associates, 1991], 222). A complete list of names is found in the Heber C. Kimball Journal, 1840-45, section entitled "Strange Events, June 1842" (Stanley B. Kimball, ed., *On the Potter's Wheel: The Diaries of Heber C. Kimball* [Salt Lake City: Signature Books in association with Smith Research Associates, 1987], 55-56). See also D. Michael Quinn, "The Mormon Succession Crisis of 1844," *Brigham Young University Studies* 16 (Winter 1976): 214.

a penalty. Perhaps the most significant part of Bennett's description is the language borrowed from Psalms 133:1-3 to describe the anointing: "When the oath has been administered, the candidate is clothed with the robe of the order, and the precious ointment, or consecrated oil, poured upon his head, till it runs down upon his beard and the skirts of his garment."[5] Bennett's book also contains the earliest reference, in a letter from George W. Robinson, about the garments which participants wore: "After they are initiated into the lodge, they have oil poured on them, and then a mark or hole cut in the breast of their shirts, which shirts must not be worn any more, but laid up to keep the Destroying Angel from them and their families, and they should never die."[6]

Years later others more directly involved recalled the events of early May 1842. In 1884 Lucius N. Scovil remembered helping Smith prepare the room:

> I can testify that on the 3rd day of May, 1842, Joseph Smith the Prophet called upon five or six, viz: Shadrack [sic] Roundy, Noah Rogers, Dimick B. Huntington, Daniel Cairns [sic] and myself (I am not certain but that Hosea Stout was there also) to meet with him (the Prophet) in his business office (the upper part of his brick store). He told us that the object he had was for us to go to work and fit up that room preparatory to giving endowments to a few Elders that he might give unto them all the keys of power pertaining to the Aronic [sic] and Melchisedec [sic] Priesthoods.
>
> We therefore went to work making the necessary preparations, and everything was arranged representing the interior of a temple as much as the circumstances would permit, he being with us dictating everything. He gave us many items that were very interesting to us, which sank with deep weight upon my mind, especially after the temple was finished at Nauvoo, and I had received the ordinances in which I was among the first, as I had been called upon to work in the Temple as one of the hands during the winter. Some weeks previous to the dedication he told us that we should have the privilege of receiving the whole of the ordinances in due time. The history of Joseph Smith speaks for itself. But I can and do testify that I know of a

---

    5. John C. Bennett, *The History of the Saints; or, an Exposé of Joseph Smith and Mormonism* (Boston: Leland & Whiting, 1842), 277, see also 217-35, 272-78.
    6. Ibid., 247-48.

surety that room was fitted up by his order which we finished in the forenoon of the said 4th of May, 1842. And he gave us to understand that he intended to have everything done by him that was in his power while he remained with us. He said his work was nearly done and he should roll the burden of the kingdom upon the shoulders of the Twelve. I am the only one living that I know of, who helped to fit up that room, except Hosea Stout, [who] was there.[7]

Brigham Young reminisced:

When we got our washings and anointings under the hands of the Prophet Joseph at Nauvoo, we had only one room to work in with the exception of a little side room or office where we were washed and anointed, and had our garments placed upon us and received our New Name. After he had performed these ceremonies, he gave the Key words[,] signs, tokens and penalties. Then after this we went into the large room over the store in Nauvoo. Joseph divided upon the room the best that he could, hung up the veil, marked it, gave us our instructions as we passed along from department to another, giving us signs, tokens, penalties with the key words pertaining to those signs. After we had got through, Brother Joseph turned to me [Pres B. Young] and said, "Brother Brigham this is not arranged right but we have done the best we could under the circumstances in which we are placed . . ."[8]

Under a journal entry entitled "Strange Events, June 1842," Heber C. Kimball recorded his part in the ritual: "I was aniciated [initiated] into the ancient order was washed and annointed and Sealled and ordained a Preast, and so forth in company with nine others."[9] He also

---

7. "The Higher Ordinances," *Deseret News Semi-Weekly*, 15 Feb. 1884, 2. George Miller also recalled: "Many of the Apostles and Elders having returned from England Joseph washed and anointed as King and Priests to God, and over the House of Israel, the following named persons, as he said he was commanded of God, viz: James Adams (of Springfield), William Law, William Marks, Willard Richards, Brigham Young, Heber C. Kimball, Newel K. Whitney, Hyrum Smith, and myself; and conferred on us Patriarchal Priesthood. This took place on the 5th or 6th of May, 1842" (see George Miller to James J. Strang, 26 June 1855, in H. W. Mills, "De Tal Palo Tal Astilla," *Annual Publications—Historical Society of Southern California* 10 [Los Angeles: McBridge Printing Co., 1917], 7:364).

8. L. John Nuttall Journal, 7 Feb. 1877, Special Collections, Harold B. Lee Library, Brigham Young University, Provo, Utah.

9. Kimball, *On the Potter's Wheel*, 55.

wrote a letter to Parley P. Pratt describing the event a little over a month later:

> Brother Joseph feels as well as I Ever see him. one reason is he has got a Small company that he feels safe in thare hands. and that is not all he can open his bosom to and feel him Self safe I wish you was here so as to feel and hear fore your Self. we have recieved some pressious things through the Prophet on the preasthood that could caus your Soul to rejoice I can not give them to you on paper fore they are not to be riten. So you must come and get them fore your Self. —We have organised a Lodge here of Masons since we obtained a Charter. that was in March since that thare has near two hundred been made masons Br Joseph and Sidny was the first that was Recieved in to the Lodg. all of the twelve have become members Except Orson P. he Hangs back. he will wake up soon, thare is a similarity of preast Hood in masonary. Bro Joseph Ses Masonary was taken from preasthood but has become degen[e]rated. but menny things are perfect. we have a prosession on the 24th of June. which is cold [called] by Masons St Johns day in this country. I think I think it will result in good. the Lord is with us and we are prosperd.[10]

Kimball here posits matter-of-factly a connection with Freemasonry, which Smith joined about the same time he introduced the new endowment. Certainly the Nauvoo endowment ritual was a significant expansion from the washings and anointings of Kirtland. The *History of the Church* account implies a divine origin for the endowment, which it describes as embracing "the principles and order of the Priesthood, . . . and the communication of keys pertaining to the Aaronic Priesthood, and so on to the highest order of the Melchisedek Priesthood, . . . [and] the ancient order of things for the first time in these last days."[11] Believing that priesthood had been restored by angels, members may have assumed that ancient knowledge, like ancient authority, had been lost from the earth and was being restored to the prophet through revelation.[12] But nowhere did Smith leave a direct statement of how the endowment ceremony came to be.

10. Heber C. Kimball to Parley P. Pratt, 17 June 1842, LDS archives.

11. HC, 5:2.

12. See E. Cecil McGavin, *Mormonism and Masonry* (Salt Lake City: Bookcraft, 1956), 41; John A. Widtsoe, *Evidences and Reconciliations* (Salt Lake City: Bookcraft,

The *History of the Church* quotes Smith saying, "All these things referred to in this [endowment] council are always governed by the principle of revelation."[13] This "quotation" is actually a reconstruction[14] by Willard Richards composed between 14-18 April 1845, based on the very brief, incomplete entry from the "Book of the Law of the Lord" quote above. On so important and central an ordinance, it is unfortunate there is no revelatory document nor any known contemporary reference to a revelation by either Smith or his associates. With respect to this issue, most of the Doctrine and Covenants came about as a result of particular needs of the church or individuals. Important doctrines developed when outside forces and movements focused Smith's attention on a problem in a particular way. Thus it seems appropriate to inquire about influences from Smith's life that may have led to development of the temple ceremony.

A good place to begin such an investigation is the framework of the ceremony which, as Elder James Talmage has indicated in *The House of the Lord* (1912), retells the plan of salvation—the Creation, Fall, and Atonement. As a culmination of Smith's theology that human beings are the offspring of God and potential gods, the temple provided a synthesis of Mormon beliefs in the origin and purpose of men and women as well as a sacred ritual that reunited them with God and each other. This instructional material is drawn directly from scripture introduced by Smith in his revision of the Bible, pertinent sections of which are now published in the books of Moses and Abraham.

Latter-day Saints familiar with religions in the ancient mid-east and classical worlds have pointed out motifs that seem to find echoes

---

1960), 111-13.

13. HC, 5:2.

14. The story of this passage's reconstruction illustrates how much of the *History of the Church* was composed. According to Jessee, Smith wrote very little of his diary and history. At the time of his death in 1844, his history was completed only through 1838. Eleven men composed the history by using over twenty different manuscript sources. Key participant George A. Smith recalled that this task "was an immense labor, requiring the deep[e]st thought and the closest application, as there were mostly only two or three words (about half written) to a sentence" (Smith to Wilford Woodruff, 21 Apr. 1856, LDS archives, in Jessee, "The Writing of Joseph Smith's History," *Brigham Young University Studies* 11 [Summer 1971]: 472).

in the LDS temple. For example, apocalyptic and pseudepigraphic literature (written between the closing of the Old Testament and the opening of the New Testament and attributed to important prophets of the past such as Moses, Noah, and Enoch) commonly dealt with the existence of multiple gods, the creation of order out of chaos, the premortal existence of conscious beings, the creation of the earth, the creation of Adam and Eve, light versus darkness (as a symbol of the necessity of exercising free will to choose between opposites), Satan and his angels being cast out of heaven, the fall of Adam and Eve, the influence of angels in the world, the Savior's mission and atonement, his mission to spirit prison, the resurrection, the millennial kingdom, the crucial role of prophets and patriarchs, and secret covenants and "mysteries" by which earnest seekers could reach the highest heaven.

In addition, mystery cults in the ancient world, particularly Nag Hammadi, Qumran, and Greece, ring with such familiar motifs as preparatory purification through ritual bathing, special instruction in secret knowledge given only to initiates, use of sacred symbolic objects related to secret knowledge, narration or dramatic enactment of a sacred story, and fellowship in a secret brotherhood with a promise of immortality hereafter. A number of Latter-day Saints have pointed out the similarities between these ancient rites and Mormon rituals, usually suggesting that ancient ceremonies are vestiges, reshaped and distorted by time and cultural change, of an original ceremony first explained to Adam and Eve.[15]

Although this list of resemblances is provocative, ancient rites in which these common themes are embedded were based on cos- mological beliefs which had no anticipation of Christian eschatology,

---

15. See S. Kent Brown and C. Wilfred Griggs, "The Messiah and the Manuscripts: What Do Recently Discovered Documents Tell Us about Jesus?" *Ensign* 14 (Sept. 1974): 68-73; "The 40-Day Ministry," *Ensign* 15 (Aug. 1975): 6-11; Robert J. Matthews, "Were the Blessings of the Temple Available to the Saints in Jesus' Time, or Did They Become Available after His Death?" *Ensign* 14 (Sep. 1974): 50-51; Hugh Nibley, "The Expanding Gospel," *Brigham Young University Studies* 7 (Fall 1965): 3-27; "A New Look at the Pearl of Great Price," *Improvement Era*, Jan. 1968-May 1970; "Treasures in the Heavens: Some Early Christian Insights into the Organizing of Worlds," *Dialogue: A Journal of Mormon Thought* 8 (Fall-Winter 1973): 76-98; *The Message of the Joseph Smith Papyri: An Egyptian Endowment* (Salt Lake City: Deseret Book Co., 1975); "A Strange Thing in the Land," *Ensign*, Oct. 1975-Aug. 1977; and "The Facsimiles of the Book of Abraham: A Response to E. H. Ashment," *Sunstone* 4 (Dec. 1979): 49-51.

much less a resurrection of the dead as now believed by Latter-day Saints. As such these are at odds with the theological structure of the Mormon temple.[16] Even though we are accustomed to think of pagan "corruptions" of original truths, it has not proved fruitful to try to reconstruct an ancient Christian temple ceremony from pagan parallels.

It does not appear that Smith had any working knowledge of mystery cultures and apocalyptic/mystery cults from which to have drawn temple ideas. In short, ancient sources cannot be considered a direct influence on Smith except as they were revealed to him from a time predating corruption or except as they appear in the ancient scriptures that he brought forth. The influence of the creation accounts in the books of Moses and Abraham on the temple narrative is clear; but the only other scriptural reference directly linking ancient writings with the Mormon temple ceremony is found in Explanatory Note 8 to Facsimile 2 in the book of Abraham.

This facsimile shows a hypocephalus, an object placed by ancient Egyptians under the head of the deceased, the meaning of which is closely linked with chapter 162 of the Egyptian "Book of the Dead," where instructions for its construction and use are given. Smith's explanation for this portion of Facsimile 2 is: "Contains writings that cannot be revealed unto the world; but is to be had in the Holy Temple of God." This illustration was engraved by Reuben Hedlock under Smith's direction for the book of Abraham's publication in the February through March 1842 issues of the church's *Times and Seasons*. (This period just preceded Smith's initiation into Freemasonry and the subsequent introduction of the Nauvoo endowment ceremony.) A literal translation of this section of the hypocephalus is: "O God of the Sleeping Ones from the time of the Creation. O Mighty God, Lord of Heaven and Earth, the Netherworld and his Great Waters, grant that the souls of the Osiris Sheshonk, may live."[17] It is difficult to see how

16. I am indebted to Edward H. Ashment for this insight. See also Keith E. Norman, "Zeal in Quest of Knowledge," *Sunstone* 11 (Mar. 1987): 33-35, a review of Hugh Nibley's *Old Testament and Related Studies* (Salt Lake City: Deseret Book Co., 1986).

17. Michael Dennis Rhodes, "A Translation and Commentary of the Joseph Smith Hypocephalus," *Brigham Young University Studies* 17 (Spring 1977): 265.

this literal translation relates to the temple ceremony introduced by Smith in Nauvoo.

It is more reasonable (and I believe productive) to explore the source suggested by contemporary accounts such as the one quoted above in the letter from Heber C. Kimball: Freemasonry. The complex interplay of Masonic tradition on Mormon temple rites probably had its roots during the mid-1820s, given that Smith's father (apparently) and older brother Hyrum (definitely) had joined the fraternity in 1817 and between 1825 and 1827, respectively.[18] At this time Masonry's appeal, especially to young men in the northeastern United States, was at an all time high.[19] One reason for this popularity was Masonry's role as a surrogate religion for many initiates. Teaching morality (separate from an institutional church) was its most important ideal, a tack which set

---

18. Joseph Smith, Sr., was a member of Ontario Lodge No. 23, Canadaigua, New York, having been initiated an Entered Apprentice Mason on 26 December 1817, passed to the degree of Fellow Craft on 2 March 1818, and raised to the sublime degree of Master Mason on 7 May 1818 (Mervin B. Hogan, "Freemasonry and Mormon Culture," *Miscellanea* 12 [1991], Pt. 10:75-94; Art deHoyos brought this to my attention).

The definitive examination of Mormonism and Freemasonry has yet to be written. The best to date is Michael W. Homer, "'Similarity of Priesthood in Masonry': The Relationship between Freemasonry and Mormonism," *Dialogue: A Journal of Mormon Thought* 27 (Fall 1994). For a general introduction, see Reed C. Durham, Jr., "'Is There No Help for the Widow's Son?'" This was delivered as the presidential address to the Mormon History Association, 20 April 1974. See the version published in *Mormon Miscellaneous* 1 (Oct. 1975): 11-16. See also Kenneth W. Godfrey, "Joseph Smith and the Masons," *Journal of the Illinois State Historical Society* 64 (Spring 1971): 79-90; S. H. Goodwin, *Mormonism and Masonry: A Utah Point of View* (Salt Lake City: Grand Lodge, F. & A. M. of Utah, 1925); and *Additional Studies in Mormonism and Masonry* (Salt Lake City: Grand Lodge, F. & A. M. of Utah, 1927). Also Mervin B. Hogan, *The Origin and Growth of Utah Masonry and Its Conflict with Mormonism* (Salt Lake City: Campus Graphics, 1978); *Mormonism and Freemasonry: The Illinois Episode* (Salt Lake City: Campus Graphics, 1980); Anthony W. Ivins, *The Relationship of "Mormonism" and Freemasonry* (Salt Lake City: Deseret News Press, 1934); Gavin, *Mormonism and Masonry*; Allen D. Roberts, "Where Are the All-Seeing Eyes? The Origin, Use and Decline of Early Mormon Symbolism," *Sunstone* 4 (May-June 1979): 22-37; John E. Thompson, *The Masons, the Mormons and the Morgan Incident* (Iowa Research Lodge No. 2 A. & A.M., 1981); and Robin L. Carr, *Freemasonry and Nauvoo, 1839-1846* (Bloomington, IL: Masonic Book Club, 1989).

19. Dorothy Ann Lipson, *Freemasonry in Federalist Connecticut* (Princeton, NJ: Princeton University Press, 1977), 4, 143-440. After 1832 Masons concentrated on social and fraternal activities and, by reaching beyond the limitations of religious, political, and economic creeds, had grown to more than 3.25 million in the United States alone by the early 1980s.

well with those disenchanted with traditional churches. Furthermore, in the context of the influence of the Enlightenment during this period, Masons purported links between science and their mysteries which made their secret ceremonies attractive.[20] The lodge provided benefits of fraternal conviviality, charity, and security when traveling. Freemasonry also provided a form of recreation for members.[21]

The traditional origin of Freemasonry (which "enlightened" Masons view as mythological or legendary) is the construction of Solomon's temple by Master Mason Hiram Abiff. Actually Freemasonry was a development of the craft guilds during the construction of the great European cathedrals during the tenth to seventeenth centuries.[22] After the Middle Ages, lodges in Scotland and Great Britain began to accept honorary members and worked out rudimentary ceremonies to distinguish members of trade organizations. In 1717 four fraternal lodges, perhaps actual masons' lodges, united as the Grand Lodge of England, considered the beginning of organized Freemasonry or "speculative Masonry." The order spread quickly to other countries and included such prominent adherents as Mozart, Voltaire, George Washington, and Benjamin Franklin. Some historians believe that Masons staged the Boston Tea Party.

Latter-day Saints may feel that Masonry constitutes a biblical-times source of uncorrupted knowledge from which the temple ceremony could be drawn. However, historians of Freemasonry generally agree that the trigradal system of Entered Apprentice, Fellow Craft, and Master Mason, as practiced in Nauvoo, cannot be traced further back than the eighteenth century. According to Douglas Knoop and G. P. Jones, two knowledgeable twentieth-century historians, it is "highly probable" that the system of Masonry practiced at the organization of the Grand Lodge in London "did not consist of three distinct degrees." They warn, "It would probably not be safe to fix a date earlier than 1723 or 1725 for the origin" of the trigradal system. "Accepted Masonry underwent gradual changes throughout a period of years stretching from well before 1717 to well after that date.

---

20. Ibid., 117-21, 248-49.

21. Ibid., 9, 75; see also Wilson Carey McWilliams, *The Idea of Fraternity in America* (Berkeley: University of California Press, 1973).

22. I appreciate the advice of Art deHoyos on this point.

. . . The earliest speculative phase of Freemasonry may be regarded as beginning about 1730. . . . Though some symbolism had doubtless crept into Masonry by that date, it would not appear to have reached its full development for another forty or fifty years."[23]

The fundamental ceremonies of modern (American) York Rite and Scottish Rite Masonry occur on three distinct levels: (1) Entered Apprentice, (2) Fellow Craft, and (3) Master Mason. Each level contains instruction in morals and Masonic symbolism, coupled with secret signs, passwords, handshakes, and penalties for revealing secrets to non-Masons. Advanced degrees exist for both orders. Never-

---

23. Douglas Knoop and G. P. Jones, *The Genesis of Freemasonry: An Account of the Rise and Development of Freemasonry in its Operative, Accepted, and Early Speculative Phases* (Manchester, Eng.: Manchester University Press, 1949), 274, 275, 321, 322. Knoop and Jones have produced the most balanced scholarly historical studies of Freemasonry to date. Their publications by the Quatuor Coronati Lodge (the English Masonic research lodge) identify two schools of Masonic history dating from the 1870s: "verified" or institutional history, and "mythical" or philosophical speculations. Their most valuable works include collections of early Masonic catechisms (1943) and pamphlets (1978) as well as institutional histories through the early eighteenth century (1940, 1949). See also *A Short History of Freemasonry to 1730* (Manchester, Eng.: Manchester University Press, 1940); *The Early Masonic Catechisms* (Manchester, Eng.: Manchester University Press, 1943); and *Early Masonic Pamphlets* (London: Quatuor Coronati Correspondence Circle, Ltd., 1978).

John Hamill prefers the terms "authentic" and "non-authentic" rather than "verified" and "mythical." He explains, "The non-authentic school has four main approaches, which might be categorized as the *esoteric,* the *mystical,* the *symbolist,* and the *romantic.* All four approaches have two factors in common: a belief that Freemasonry has existed from 'time immemorial' and the apparent inability to distinguish between historical fact and legend" (*The Craft. A History of English Freemasonry* [Wellingborough: Crucible, 1986], 15-25; again Art deHoyos brought this source to my attention).

Other important careful histories include Robert Freke Gould, *A Concise History of Freemasonry* (New York City: Macoy Publishing and Masonic Supply Co., 1904); H. L. Haywood and James E. Craig, *A History of Freemasonry* (New York: John Day Co., 1927); Bernard E. Jones, *Freemasons' Guide and Compendium,* rev. ed. (London: Harrap, Ltd., 1950, 1956); Henry Wilson Coil, Sr., *Freemasonry Through Six Centuries,* 2 vols. (Richmond, VA: Macoy, 1967); Alex Horne, *King Solomon's Temple in the Masonic Tradition* (Wellingborough, Northamptonshire, Eng.: Aquarian Press, 1972); Norman MacKenzie, ed., *Secret Societies* (New York: Holt, Rinehart and Winston, 1967); Arthur Edward Waite, *A New Encyclopaedia of Freemasonry and of Cognate Instituted Mysteries: Their Rites, Literature and History,* 2 vols. (Philadelphia: David McKay Co., ca. 1923); David Stevenson, *The First Freemasons: Scotland's Early Lodges and Their Members* (Aberdeen, 1988); and David Stevenson, *The Origins of Freemasonry: Scotland's Century, 1590-1710* (Cambridge, Eng.: Cambridge University Press, 1988).

theless, the three initial degrees constitute the principal ceremonies experienced by active Masons.

Hyrum Smith's exact involvement on these levels is not known. Any early enthusiasm, however, may have been temporarily checked by widespread anti-Mason feelings which pervaded upstate New York during the late 1820s. This wave of public sentiment was precipitated by the announced publication of William Morgan's exposé of Masonic ceremonies and by his mysterious disappearance and presumed murder in September 1826. A public outcry against Masons who were thought to put themselves above the law followed. For a few years, American Masonic lodges were, for all practical purposes, inactive. Many lodges closed. Renouncements of affiliation were widespread. A number of newspapers dedicated to exposing Masonry were established in New York and other states. The anti-Masonic movement led to the creation of an independent political party where its energies were ultimately diffused. It was disbanded in 1832.[24]

Some scholars feel that anti-Masonry may be seen in the Book of Mormon and interpret some passages (for example, Alma 37:21-32; Hel. 6:21-22; Ether 8:18-26) as anti-Masonic. These passages condemn secret combinations, secret signs, and secret words in a manner which may be interpreted as reminiscent of anti-Masonic rhetoric prevalent during this period.[25]

A few references from contemporary newspapers confirm an early anti-Masonic perception of the Book of Mormon. On 15 March 1831, the *Geauga Gazette* of Painesville, Ohio, stated that "the Mormon Bible is Anti-masonick" and that "every one of its followers . . .

---

24. Charles McCarthy, "The Antimasonic Party: A Study of Political Antimasonry in the United States, 1827-1840," *Annual Report of the American Historical Association for the Year 1902* 1: 365-574; William Preston Vaughn, *The Anti-Masonic Party in the United States, 1826-1843* (Lexington: University Press of Kentucky, 1983).

25. Fawn M. Brodie, *No Man Knows My History: The Life of Joseph Smith,* 2d ed. (New York: Alfred Knopf, 1973), 65-66; Goodwin, *Mormonism and Masonry,* 9; *Additional Studies in Mormonism and Masonry,* 3-29; Thomas F. O'Dea, *The Mormons* (Chicago: University of Chicago Press, 1957), 23, 35; Blake Ostler, "The Book of Mormon as a Modern Expansion of an Ancient Source," *Dialogue: A Journal of Mormon Thought* 20 (Spring 1987): 73-76; Walter Franklin Prince, "Psychological Tests for the Authorship of the Book of Mormon," *American Journal of Psychology* 28 (July 1917): 373-95. The best study to date is Dan Vogel, "Mormonism's 'Anti-Masonick Bible,'" *The John Whitmer Historical Association Journal* 9 (1989): 17-30.

are anti-masons." This newspaper quoted Martin Harris as saying that
the Book of Mormon was an "Anti-masonick Bible." A similar story
appeared in *The Ohio Star* in Ravenna, Ohio, on 24 March 1831.
Another Painesville paper, *The Telegraph*, ran an article on 22 March
1831 challenging the 15 March story and claiming that the Book of
Mormon was printed by a "Masonic press" in Palmyra, New York. It
further asserted that there was "a very striking resemblance between
masonry and mormonism. Both systems pretend to have a very ancient
origin, and to possess some wonderful secrets which the world cannot
have without submitting to the prescribed ceremonies" (see also 24
Mar. 1831). Interestingly, Mormon converts in northeastern Ohio
were identified by the press as being as fanatical as the region's
anti-Masons.[26] Notably the first anti-Mormon book, *Mormonism Unvailed*, referred to ancient Book of Mormon Nephites as "Anti-masons."[27] Despite these Book of Mormon passages and press coverage,
no evidence exists to convincingly prove that early converts paid
serious attention to anti-Masonry.[28]

Perhaps more decisively, Freemasonry had little or no discernible
influence on the rites practiced in the Kirtland Temple, 1835-36. Reed
C. Durham, Jr., has noted, however, that some Masonic influence can
be seen in the temple's architectural patterns.[29] One quotation in the
History of the Church records Smith in 1835 using Masonic terms to
condemn the "abominations" of Protestants and praying that his "well
fitted" comments "may be like a nail in a sure place, driven by the
master of assemblies."[30] Smith's familiarity with and positive use of

------

26. *The Wayne Sentinel* (Palmyra, NY), 23 Aug. 1831; *The Churchman* (NY), 4
Feb. 1832.

27. E. D. Howe, *Mormonism Unvailed: or A Faithful Account of that Singular
Imposition and Delusion, from Its Rise to the Present Times, etc.* (Painesville, OH: E.
D. Howe, 1834), 81, 89.

28. Richard L. Bushman, *Joseph Smith and the Beginnings of Mormonism*
(Urbana: University of Illinois Press, 1984), 131; Grant Underwood, "The Earliest
Reference Guides to the Book of Mormon: Windows into the Past," *Journal of Mormon
History* 12 (1985): 69-89.

29. Durham, "The Widow's Son," 15-33. See also Laurel B. Andrew, *The Early
Temples of the Mormons: An Architecture of the Millennial Kingdom in the American
West* (Albany: SUNY Press, 1978).

30. HC, 2:347; Dean C. Jessee, ed., *The Personal Writings of Joseph Smith* (Salt
Lake City: Deseret Book Co., 1984), 120.

Masonic imagery is paradoxical in light of his anti-secret society rhetoric during the Missouri period.[31]

A full examination of the complex history of the church's transition to Nauvoo and its subsequent embrace of Masonry is beyond the scope of this discussion. Smith's involvement with Masonry is well documented, but the events leading him to consider joining the fraternity and endorsing its practice in Nauvoo are not. His ever-present fear of enemies may have led him to believe that affiliation would give some form of protection to church members. Perhaps he saw an additional level of protection from internal enemies resulting from the secrecy demanded of all initiates.[32] It is also possible that amid the translation and publication activities of the book of Abraham in spring 1842, Smith's preoccupation with ancient mysteries may have triggered an interest in tapping Masonic lore.

The influence of personal friends cannot be ignored. In 1838, for example, Smith stayed briefly in Far West, Missouri, with George and Lucinda Harris, eventually becoming close friends with Lucinda.[33] Lucinda had first been married to William Morgan in New York, when he was abducted for threatening to publish Masonic secrets. She became one of Smith's first plural wives.[34] Other prominent Freemasons who converted to Mormonism included Deputy Grand Master of Illinois James Adams, Heber C. Kimball,[35] Newel K.

---

31. HC, 3:178-82, 303.

32. Compare Heber C. Kimball's observation, 2 August 1857: "You have received your endowments. What is it for? To learn you to hold your tongues" (*Journal of Discourses*, 26 vols. [Liverpool: Latter-day Saints' Booksellers Depot, 1854-86], 5:133 [hereafter JD]), with Brigham Young's comment in 1860: "[T]he mane part of Masonry is to keep a secret" (in Scott G. Kenney, ed., *Wilford Woodruff's Journal*, 9 vols. [Midvale, UT: Signature Books, 1983], 5:418). A classic discussion on the sociology of secrecy and secret societies is by Georg Simmel in Kurt H. Wolff, trans. and ed., *The Sociology of Georg Simmel* (Glencoe, IL: Free Press, 1950), 330-76.

33. HC, 3:9; Linda King Newell and Valeen Tippetts Avery, *Mormon Enigma: Emma Hale Smith* (New York: Doubleday & Co., 1984), 70.

34. Brodie, *No Man Knows*, 459-60.

35. Stanley B. Kimball, *Heber C. Kimball: Mormon Patriarch and Pioneer* (Urbana: University of Illinois Press, 1981), 12. Kimball's daughter, Helen Mar Kimball Whitney, later reminisced: "I remember once when but a young girl, of getting a glimpse of the outside of the Morgan's book, exposing Masonry, but which my father always kept locked up."

Whitney, George Miller, John C. Bennett, John Smith, and Brigham Young.[36]

Of these associates, the most influential in accelerating Smith's interest in Freemasonry was John C. Bennett.[37] Bennett has typically been characterized as an opportunistic scoundrel whose brief (eighteen-month) sojourn with the Saints at Nauvoo was unfortunate and embarrassing. Actually, Bennett was a powerful confidante to Smith and a key figure in Nauvoo. His accomplishments included: "Assistant President" of the church, first mayor of Nauvoo, Major General in Nauvoo Legion, and secretary of the Nauvoo Masonic Lodge. He was instrumental in gaining the Illinois legislature's approval of the Nauvoo Charter, Nauvoo Legion, and the University of Nauvoo.[38] Although his own status as a Mason in good standing prior to Nauvoo has been called into question,[39] Bennett may well have advised Smith to adopt Freemasonry as a means to end persecution.[40] Ebenezer Robinson, editor of the *Times and Seasons* until February 1842, reminisced: "Heretofore the church had strenuously opposed secret societies such as Freemasons . . . but after Dr. Bennett came into the Church a great change of sentiment seemed to take place."[41]

Smith's official experience in Freemasonry began five months before the first Nauvoo endowment. He petitioned for membership in the Nauvoo Masonic Lodge on 30 December 1841. The favorable results of the lodge's investigation into his petition were reported on 3 February 1842.[42] Smith was initiated as an entered apprentice Mason

---

36. Godfrey, "Joseph Smith and the Masons," 81-82; Leonard J. Arrington, *Brigham Young: American Moses* (New York: Alfred A. Knopf, 1985), 99; James J. Tyler, "John Cook Bennett, Colorful Freemason of the Early Nineteenth Century," reprinted from the *Proceedings of the Grand Lodge of Ohio* (n.p., 1947), 8.

37. Robert Bruce Flanders, *Nauvoo: Kingdom on the Mississippi* (Urbana: University of Illinois Press, 1965), 247.

38. Richard S. Van Wagoner and Steven C. Walker, *A Book of Mormons* (Salt Lake City: Signature Books, 1982), 10-14.

39. Mervin B. Hogan, *John Cook Bennett and Pickaway Lodge No. 23* (n.p., 1983); and Mervin B. Hogan, *John Cook Bennett: Unprincipled Profligate Cowan* (Salt Lake City: Campus Graphics, 1987).

40. "Joseph Smith and the Presidency," *Saints' Herald* 68 (19 July 1921): 675.

41. *The Return* 2 (June 1890): 287.

42. Mervin B. Hogan, comp., *Founding Minutes of Nauvoo Lodge, U.D.* (Des

on 15 March 1842 and received the fellow craft and master degrees the next day. Since the customary waiting period before receiving a new degree is thirty days, Smith's elevation to the "sublime degree" (Master Mason) without prior participation was unusual.[43] During the organization of the Female Relief Society one day later in the Nauvoo Masonic Lodge room, Smith filled his founding address with Masonic allusions: "Let this Presidency serve as a *constitution*";[44] Smith "proposed that the Society go into a close *examination* of every *candidate*. . . . that the Society should grow up by *degrees*. . . . he was going to make of this Society a *kingdom of priests* as in *Enoch's day*."[45] Kent L. Walgren, a student of Mormon/Masonry connections, concluded from reading other early Female Relief Society minutes that Smith's aim in establishing the Society was to "institutionalize secrecy."[46] He cites an entry from the minutes where Emma Smith, probably during the organizational period, read an epistle signed by Joseph Smith, Brigham Young, and four others: "there may be some among you who are not sufficiently skill'd in Masonry to keep a secret. . . . Let this Epistle be had as a private matter in your Society, and we shall learn whether you are good Masons."[47]

Over the next several weeks, Smith participated in other lodge meetings, witnessing the Entered Apprentice degree five times, the

---

Moines, IA: Research Lodge No. 2, 1971), 8, 10.

43. Smith's accelerated advancement came at the hand of Abraham Jonas, Grandmaster of the Illinois Lodge. Given that Jonas was running for political office, it is possible that he thought his action would secure him the Mormon vote.

44. Relief Society, Minutes of the Nauvoo Female Relief Society, 17 Mar. 1842, italics added, LDS archives.

45. Ibid., 30 Mar. 1842, italics added. Freemasons are enjoined to study their Book of Constitutions which contains fundamental Masonic principles; every man considering becoming a Mason is called a "candidate" and must pass a character examination before being approved for initiation; new initiates progress in Masonry through a system of ceremonial degrees; and several officers in a lodge have different titles employing the word "Priest." See R. W. Jeremy L. Cross, *The True Masonic Chart, or Hieroglyphic Monitor; Containing All the Emblems Explained in the Degrees of Entered Apprentice, Fellow Craft, Master Mason, etc.* (New Haven, CT: Jeremy L. Cross, 1824), 7, 15-19, 63, 65, 157; William Morgan, *Freemasonry Exposed* (1827; reprint ed., Chicago: Ezra Book Publications, Inc., n.d.), 16-18.

46. Kent L. Walgren, "James Adams: Early Springfield Mormon and Freemason," *Journal of the Illinois State Historical Society* 75 (Summer 1982): 131.

47. Ibid., 132n49; recorded after minutes for 28 Sept. 1842.

Fellow Craft degree three times, and the Master Mason degree five times—all prior to his introduction of the extended endowment.[48] An important sermon on 1 May 1842 contained references carrying Masonic overtones:

> The *keys* are certain *signs* and *words* . . . which cannot be revealed . . . till the Temple is completed—The rich can only get them in the Temple. . . . There are *signs* in heaven, earth, and hell, the Elders must *know them all* to be endowed with power. . . . The devil *knows many signs* but does not know the *sign of the Son of Man*, or Jesus. No one can truly say he knows God until he has handled something, and this can only be in the Holiest of Holies.[49]

On 4 and 5 May, forty-nine days after his Masonic initiation, Smith introduced the new endowment ceremony to trusted friends in the upper story of his red brick store.[50]

The clearest evidence of Masonic influence on the Nauvoo temple ceremony is a comparison of texts. Three elements of the Nauvoo endowment and its contemporary Masonic ritual resemble each other so closely that they are sometimes identical. These are the tokens, signs, and penalties. The two accounts which may be most useful for the purposes of comparison are those of Catherine Lewis and William Morgan. Morgan's 1826 account was an exposé of his local York Rite's "Craft" degrees (the same rite introduced in Nauvoo, though the wording differed from state to state).[51] Catherine Lewis joined the LDS church in 1841 in Boston. After Smith's death in 1844, she moved to Nauvoo and was among those who received their endowment in the new temple. Lewis received the ordinance at the urging of Heber Kimball and one of his wives. Repulsed by Kimball's subsequent proposal of plural marriage, she left Nauvoo and published a book in 1848 which includes a description of the temple ceremony.[52]

---

48. Hogan, *Minutes of Nauvoo Lodge*, 12-18.

49. Ehat and Cook, *Words of Joseph Smith*, 119-20, emphasis added; D&C 129:4-9. Before passing each degree, every Masonic candidate is tested in his knowledge of special signs and words by the presiding lodge officer. See Cross, *The True Masonic Chart*, 97; Morgan, *Freemasonry Exposed*, 18-27, 49-61, 70-89.

50. HC, 4:550-53, 570, 589, 594, 608; 5:1-2, 446; 6:287.

51. Morgan, *Freemasonry Exposed*, see esp. 23-24, 53-54, 76-77, 84-85.

52. Catherine Lewis, *Narrative of Some of the Proceedings of the Mormons, etc.*

NAUVOO ENDOWMENT CEREMONY RITES COMPARED
TO CONTEMPORARY PUBLISHED FREEMASONIC RITES

Nauvoo Temple Ceremony Rites

Freemasonic Rites

I will now give you the signs and tokens of the priesthood . . . the first sign or token is to take hold of the right hand, placing the ball of the thumb between the two upper joints of the fore-fingers.

[The grip of the Entered Apprentice:] The right hands are joined together as in shaking hands and each sticks his thumb nail into the third joint or upper end of the forefinger. . . . [After receiving the Boaz, the initiate is given a lambskin or white apron which is donned.]

[The pass-grip of the Fellow Craft] is given by taking each other by the right hand, as though going to shake hands, and each putting his thumb between the fore and second fingers where they join the hand, and pressing the thumb between the joints.

The second sign is to place the thumb on the upper joint of the second finger; —these tokens signify you have two names; one of which is a new name.

The third sign is called the Patriarchal grip, and has three names; the first, Patriarchal grip; second, the Son; the third, you will receive at the veil. . . .

[The pass-grip of the Master Mason] is given by pressing the thumb between the joints of the second and third fingers where they join the hand.

[The sign and Due-Guard of the Master Mason] is given by raising both hands and arms to the el-

We then held up both hands

(Lynn, MA: the Author, 1848), 9-10; see also, *Warsaw Signal*, 15 Apr. 1846, 2; Increase McGee Van Dusen and Maria Van Dusen, *The Mormon Endowment; A Secret Drama, or Conspiracy, in the Nauvoo-Temple, in 1846* (Syracuse, NY: N. M. D. Lathrop, 1847), 6, 9.

above the head,

bows, perpendicularly, one on each side of the head, the elbows forming a square. The words accompanying this sign, in case of distress, are, "O Lord, My God! Is there no help for the widow's son?" . . . The Due Guard is made by holding both hands in front palms down.

[The sign and Due-Guard of the Entered Apprentice] is given by holding your two hands transversely across each other, the right hand upwards and one inch

and placed our right hand under the left ear, drew it across the throat,

from the left . . . [and] by drawing your right hand across your throat, . . .

[Sign and Due-Guard of the Fellow Craft:] The sign is given by drawing your right hand flat, with the palm of it next to your breast,

the left hand was placed to the right shoulder, then drawn across the breast, and the right hand suddenly thrust down the right side.

across your breast from the left to the right side with some quickness, and dropping it down by your side; the Due-Guard is given by raising the left arm until that part of it between the elbow and that part above it form a square.

The Penal Sign is given by putting the right hand to the left side of the bowels, the hand open, with the thumb next to the belly, and drawing it across the belly, and letting it fall; this is done tolerably quick.

We then raised our hands again, and were taught how to pray. This ceremony concluded, we proceeded singly to the veil, (which is a large sheet separating us from the upper part of the hall, having five holes in it—two for the eyes, one for the mouth, and two for the arms,) the person representing the Lord is on the other side of the vail, to take the signs and converse with us. Our Instructor tells us how to answer.

Then the Lord asks for the signs; we give them; our new name is whispered in his ear; he then whispers the third name of the Patriarchal Grip in our ear, viz: —"Marrow in the bones, Strength in the sinews, and virtue in the loins throughout all generations."

"He (candidate) is raised on what is called the five points of fellowship, which are foot to foot, knee to knee, breast to breast, hand to back and mouth to ear. This is done by putting the inside of your right foot to the inside of the right foot of the person to whom you are going to give the word, the inside of your knee to his, laying your right breast against his, your left hands on the back of each other, and your mouths to each other's right ear (in which position alone you are permitted to give the word), and whisper the word Mahhahbone. The Master's grip is given by taking hold of each other's hand as though you were going to shake hands, and sticking the nails of each of your fingers to the joint of the other's wrist where it unites with the hand. . . .He is also told that Mahhah-bone signifies marrow in the bone.

Other similarities with Masonic rites include the prayer circle which required Masonic initiates to assemble around an altar, place their left arm over the person next to them, join hands, repeat the words of the Most Excellent Master, and give all the signs from the initial ceremonial degrees.[53] Historian D. Michael Quinn has pointed out

53. David Bernard, *Light on Masonry: A Collection of All the Most Important Documents on the Subject of Speculative Free Masonry, etc.* (Utica, NY: William Williams, 1829), 116-17; Jabez Richardson, *Richardson's Monitor of Free-Masonry; Being a Practical Guide to the Ceremonies in All the Degrees Conferred in Masonic Lodges, Chapters, Encampments, etc.* (1860; reprint ed., Chicago: Ezra Cook, 1975),

that nineteenth-century American Protestant revivals also had prayer circles in which, "when the invitation was given, there was a general rush, the large 'prayer ring' was filled, and for at least two hours prayer ardent went up toe God."[54] Two other Masonic elements with Mormon echoes are initiates' receiving a new name and donning a white apron as part of the rite.[55] An explanatory lecture always follows the conferral of each Masonic degree ceremony, a practice not unlike the Mormon temple endowment's lecture at the veil.

This pattern of resemblances indicates that Smith drew on Masonic rites in shaping the temple endowment and specifically borrowed tokens, signs, and penalties, as well as possibly the Creation narrative and ritual anointings. Still, the temple ceremony cannot be explained as wholesale borrowing, neither can it be dismissed as completely unrelated. As Mervin Hogan, a Mormon Mason, explained in 1991, "[L]ittle room for doubt can exist in the mind of an informed, objective analyst that the Mormon Temple Endowment and the rituals of ancient Craft Masonry are seeming intimately and definitely involved."[56]

An interesting question is the response of Smith's contemporaries to the temple ceremony, since many were also familiar with Masonry. How did they understand the resemblances? Although modern Latter-day Saints are generally unfamiliar with Masonry, this was not the case in Nauvoo. According to the Manuscript History of Brigham Young, Heber C. Kimball later said, "We have the true Masonry. The Masonry of today is received from the apostasy which took place in the days of Solomon, and David. They have now and then a thing that is correct, but we have the real thing."[57]

61, 66.

54. Rev. James Erwin, *Reminiscences of Early Circuit Life* (Toledo, OH: Spear, Johnson & Co., 1884), 68, in Quinn, "Latter-day Saint Prayer Circles," 81-82.

55. The reception of the new name was a feature of William Morgan's 1826 New York exposé but did not form part of the Masonic ritual practiced in Nauvoo. Art deHoyos pointed this out to me.

56. Mervin B. Hogan, *Freemasonry and Mormon Ritual* (Salt Lake City: author, 1991), 22.

57. "Manuscript History of Brigham Young," 13 Nov. 1858, 1085, LDS archives; see also Stanley B. Kimball, "Heber C. Kimball and Family, The Nauvoo Years," *Brigham Young University Studies* 15 (Summer 1975): 458.

Another of Smith's close friends, Joseph Fielding, wrote in 1844: "Many have joined the Masonic Institution this seems to have been a Stepping Stone or Preparation for something else, the true Origin of Masonry."[58] According to one of Brigham Young's ex-wives, Young "delight[ed] to speak of it [the endowment] as 'Celestial Masonry.'"[59] Young's brother Phineas thought that a part of the ceremony referred directly to the "marks of a Master Mason."[60] John D. Lee, in narrating his duties as a worker in the Nauvoo temple after Joseph Smith's death, used explicitly Masonic words (italicized below) to describe his entrance into the temple:

> Tuesday Dec 16th 1845 about 4 oclock in the morning I entered the Poarch in the lower court where I met the Porter who admitted me through the door which led to the foot or nearly so of a great flight of Stairs which by ascending led me to the door of the outer court which I found *tyled* within by an officer. I having the *proper implements* of that *degree* gained admittance through the outer and inner courts which opened and led to the sacred departments. . . . Having entered I found myself alone with the *Tyler* [guard] that kept the inner courts set about and soon got fires up in the different rooms and setting things in order—for the day—at about 9 oclock in the morning the washing and anointing commenced . . .[61]

More than sixty years later Elder Franklin D. Richards explained to his colleagues in the Quorum of Twelve Apostles,

> A Masonic Lodge . . . was established in Nauvoo and Joseph Smith, Brigham Young, Willard Richards, John Taylor, Lorenzo Snow, Orson Hyde, F. D. Richards, and about 1000 others in all became Masons. Joseph, the Prophet, was aware that there were some things about Masonry which had come down from the beginning and he desired to know what they were, hence the lodge. The Masons admitted some keys of knowledge appertaining to Masonry were lost. Joseph enquired

58. Andrew F. Ehat, ed., "'They Might Have Known That He Was Not a Fallen Prophet': The Nauvoo Journal of Joseph Fielding," *Brigham Young University Studies* 19 (Winter 1979): 145.

59. Ann Eliza Webb Young, *Wife No. 19: Or, The Story of a Life in Bondage* (Hartford, CT: Dustin, Gilman and Co., 1876), 371.

60. In Kimball, *On the Potter's Wheel*, 166.

61. John D. Lee Diary, 16 Dec. 1845, LDS archives (emphasis added).

of the Lord concerning the matter and He revealed to the Prophet true Masonry, as we have it in our temples.[62]

The LDS First Presidency went so far in 1911 as to refer publicly to the "Masonic characters [of] the ceremonies of the temple."[63] Apostle Melvin J. Ballard[64] and historian E. Cecil McGavin[65] were among early twentieth-century Mormons who believed that Masonry's trigradal degree system of Entered Apprentice, Fellow Craft, and Master Mason dated back to Solomon's temple or to the time of Adam.

To summarize Mormon participation in Freemasonry during the Nauvoo period, it is useful to note that in 1840 only 147 men in Illinois and 2,072 in the United States were Masons.[66] By the time of the exodus to Utah in 1846-47, approximately 1,366 Mormon males in Nauvoo had been initiated into the Masonic order.[67] While it is uncertain exactly why Freemasonry was initially embraced, its activities undoubtedly provided fraternal benefits and its ceremonies clearly provided part of the specific wording for the Nauvoo temple endowment, although most nineteenth-century Masonic rituals have no resemblance to early temple ceremonies. It is significant that, following conferral of endowment rites on Nauvoo adults and their subsequent relocation to Utah, Masonry never regained the prominence among Mormons it received in Nauvoo.

Two additional ceremonies were introduced in 1843 about a year following the initial conferral of the new endowment: celestial marriage for time and eternity and the fullness of the priesthood or the second anointing. Celestial marriage was applied to and equated with

---

62. Stan Larson, ed., *A Ministry of Meetings: The Apostolic Diaries of Rudger Clawson* (Salt Lake City: Signature Books in association with Smith Research Associates, 1993), 42.

63. Statement of the First Presidency (Joseph F. Smith, Anthon H. Lund, and John Henry Smith), 15 Oct. 1911, in *Oakland Tribune*, 15 Oct. 1911, and in *Deseret News*, 4 Nov. 1911; see also James R. Clark, ed., *Messages of the First Presidency of the Church of Jesus Christ of Latter-day Saints* (Salt Lake City: Bookcraft, 1970), 4:250.

64. *Conference Report of the Church of Jesus Christ of Latter-day Saints* (Salt Lake City: Deseret News Press, Apr. 1913), 126; *Salt Lake Tribune*, 29 Dec. 1919, in S. H. Goodwin, *Mormonism and Masonry*, 49-50.

65. McGavin, *Mormonism and Masonry*, 192.

66. Godfrey, "Joseph Smith and the Masons," 83.

67. Durham, "Help for the Widow's Son," 15-33.

plural marriage until the late nineteenth century.[68] Although in March 1836 and again in May 1842 Smith declared the endowment complete and the fullness of the priesthood restored, by late August 1842 he prayed that "the Lord Almighty . . . will continue to preserve me . . . *until* I have fully accomplished my mission in this life, and so firmly established the dispensation of the fullness of the priesthood in the last days, that all the powers of earth and hell can never prevail against it."[69] Almost a year later on 6 August 1843, Brigham Young confirmed that the fullness of the priesthood had not yet been given: "[I]f any in the Church had the fullness of the Melchisedec Priesthood, [I do] not know it." Clearly, Smith had discussed this concept with Young, for Young added, "For any person to have the fulness of that pristhood *must be a king & a priest.* . . . A person may be *anointed king & priest* before they receive their kingdom &c."[70]

---

68. After the Wilford Woodruff Manifesto in 1890, association of celestial marriage with polygamy was discouraged. Mormons now perceive celestial marriage and plural marriage as separate concepts. Andrew F. Ehat, "Joseph Smith's Introduction of Temple Ordinances and the 1844 Mormon Succession Question," M.A. thesis, Brigham Young University, 1982, 59-62, maintained that Smith never taught plural marriage to the Quorum of the Anointed, but Quinn, *The Mormon Hierarchy: Origins of Power* (forthcoming), shows that this quorum was the nucleus for polygamy and that plural wives were anointed and sealed.

69. HC, 5:2, 139-40, 31 Aug. 1842 (italics added). Since this citation is not in the regular Nauvoo Relief Society minutes or in the Manuscript History of the Church, it probably represents an anachronistic reinterpretation of Joseph Smith's original comments.

70. HC, 5:527. This account is from Wilford Woodruff's Journal, 6 Aug. 1843, Kenney, 2:271-72. Compare Orson Pratt's sermon, 24 May 1845, *Times and Seasons* 5 (1 June 1845): 920.

Young's remarks on kings and priests originated in the endowment ritual. As Heber C. Kimball explained to a Nauvoo temple audience on 21 December 1845, "You have been anointed to be kings and priests, but you have not been ordained to it yet, and you have got to get it by being faithful" (Smith, *An Intimate Chronicle*, 227). This concept was mentioned again by George Q. Cannon in 1883: "in the washing that takes place in the first endowment, they are washed that they might *become* clean from the blood of this generation . . . in the same way they are ordained *to be* Kings and Priests—that ordinance does not make them . . . Kings and Priests. If they fully received of another endowment [i.e., the second anointing], a fulness of that power, and the promises are fulfilled in the bestowal of the power upon them" (Salt Lake School of the Prophets Minute Book, 2 Aug. 1883, 14, LDS archives). In 1941 Apostle David O. McKay explained that the "first anointing" is conferred in the initiatory ordinances of the endowment where "one . . . is anointed to become a king and a priest of the Most High;

Other facets of Mormon thinking had also matured by the time Brigham Young made that statement. Particularly important was a refinement of the Latter-day Saint view of "eternal life." Prior to receiving the "three degrees of glory" vision in February 1832 (now D&C 76), Mormons, including Smith, understood eternal life in the same sense as other Protestants—as an undifferentiated heaven as the only alternative to an undifferentiated hell. Even after February 1832 and possibly as late as 1843, Smith apparently still conceived "eternal life" as dwelling in the presence of Elohim (God) forever. It was not until May 1843 that Smith ostensibly taught that the celestial king-dom[71] contained gradations, with the highest gradation reserved solely for men and women who entered into the new and everlasting covenant of marriage (see D&C 131:1-4).[72] In July 1843 Smith dictated another revelation (now D&C 132) which defined those achieving "exaltation" in the highest degree of the celestial kingdom as "gods."[73]

---

a queen and priestess in the realms of God. . . . We are anointed that we may become such" ("The Temple Ceremony," address at the Salt Lake Temple Annex, 25 Sept. 1941, LDS archives, in Joseph C. Muren, comp., *The Temple and Its Significance*, rev. ed. [Ogden, UT: Temple Publications, 1974]).

In terms of the Nauvoo endowment prior to Smith's death, it may be that the "first anointing" was an actual, not promissory, ordination, for Heber Kimball's own diary recollection of the 4 May 1842 ceremony was that he was "ordained a Preast." Notably the Kirtland endowment actually pronounced recipients "clean from the blood of this generation"; yet Kimball's 21 December 1845 diary also records him telling the same temple audience cited above of more blessings to come "if you are faithful and keep your tongue in your mouth." Apparently the concept of purification was also undergoing development and the actual form of this ceremony changed as Smith developed a fuller understanding of the priesthood ordinances and their relationship to the Mormon concept of godhood.

71. Although this is the current interpretation of this teaching, some have argued that Smith was merely redescribing the trilogistic concept of three general degrees of glory as outlined in D&C 76. In other words the "highest degree" spoken of in D&C 131:2 would be synonymous with "celestial kingdom," while the "celestial glory" in D&C 131:1 would only be referring to the "resurrection of the just" described by D&C 76.

72. An early letter published by W. W. Phelps, *Messenger & Advocate* 9 (June 1835): 130, suggests that Smith may have taught a variation of this doctrine eight years prior to D&C 131: "We shall by and bye learn that . . . we may prepare ouselves for a kingdom of glory; become archangels, even the sons of God where the man is neither without the woman, nor the woman without the man in the Lord."

73. Although the doctrine and limited practice of plural marriage had been extant for several years prior to the 12 July 1843 dictation of D&C 132, the recording of this

The importance of this teaching is seen in another sermon given shortly thereafter on 27 August 1843. Significantly, these comments occurred in a discussion of three orders or levels of priesthood: the Levitical or Aaronic order, the patriarchal order of Abraham, and the fullness of the priesthood of Melchizedek which included "kingly powers" of "anointing & sealing—called elected and made sure."[74] Said Smith: "No man can attain to the Joint heirship with Jesus Christ with out being administered to by one having the same power & Authority of Melchisedec." This authority and power came not from "a Prophet nor apostle nor Patriarch only but of [a] King & Priest [of Jesus Christ]."[75]

During this same sermon Smith said: "Abrahams [sic] Patriarchal power" was the "greatest yet experienced in this church."[76] His choice of words is particularly revealing, for by this date ten men had received the initiatory washings and anointings, as well as the Aaronic and Melchizedek portions of the endowment of the "Patriarchal Priesthood" on 4 May 1842. Many of these had also received the ordinance of celestial marriage for time and eternity with their wives. Joseph and Emma Hale Smith, for example, were sealed in May 1843, as were James and Harriet Adams, Brigham and Mary Ann Angell Young, Hyrum and Mary Fielding Smith, and Willard and Jenetta Richards.[77] When Joseph Smith said late in August that the Patriarchal Priesthood was the "greatest yet experienced in this church," he was well aware that the fullness of the Melchizedek priesthood was yet to be conferred through a higher ordinance.

---

important revelation introduced several crucial ideas which are pivotal in understanding the theology surrounding the second anointing ritual. See Robert J. Woodford, "The Historical Development of the Doctrine and Covenants," Ph.D. diss., Brigham Young University, 1974, 3:1731-61; and Danel Bachman, "A Study of the Mormon Practice of Plural Marriage before the Death of Joseph Smith," M.A. thesis, Purdue University, 1975.

74. Joseph Smith Diary, 27 Aug. 1843, in Ehat and Cook, *Words of Joseph Smith*, 244.

75. In "Scriptural Items," in Ehat and Cook, *Words of Joseph Smith*, 245.

76. Compare Joseph Smith sermon of 27 June 1839, in Ehat and Cook, *Words of Joseph Smith*, 4-6.

77. Joseph Smith Diary, 28 May 1843, in Scott H. Faulring, ed., *An American Prophet's Record: The Diaries and Journals of Joseph Smith* (Salt Lake City: Signature Books in association with Smith Research Associates, 1987), 381.

In a sense the institution of this higher ordinance was the logical next step. The previous twelve years of pronouncements, sealings, and anointings "unto eternal life" guaranteed a status that, according to Smith's 1843 teachings, was subservient to that of the gods. From the perspective of these teachings, even the Nauvoo endowment administered to members of the Holy Order simply provided that the men who received it would live in the celestial kingdom as angels and servants. Until 1843 women had been excluded from these ordinances, possibly because of Smith's personal reluctance, certainly because of his first wife Emma's rejection of polygamy, as well as because of John Bennett's lurid exposé and/or the apostasy and subsequent reconciliation of Orson and Sarah Pratt over polygamy. Doctrine and Covenants 131 and 132 indicated that this exclusion deprived the men (who had received the previous ordinances) of the highest kingdom of glory—godhood. The higher ordinance was necessary to confirm the revealed promises of "kingly powers" (i.e., godhood) received in the endowment's initiatory ordinances. Godhood was the meaning of this higher ordinance, or second anointing, for the previously revealed promises in Doctrine and Covenants 132:19-26 implicitly referred not to those who had been sealed in celestial marriage but to those who had been sealed and ordained "kings and priests," "queens and priestesses" to God. Such individuals would necessarily have received a higher anointing: "Then shall they be gods, because they have all power, and the angels are subject unto them."

This special priesthood ordinance was first administered on 28 September 1843 to Joseph and Emma Smith. The *History of the Church* gives a discreet account of this event:

> At half-past eleven, a.m., a council convened over the store, consisting of myself, my brother Hyrum, Uncle John Smith, Newel K. Whitney, George Miller, Willard Richards, John Taylor, Amasa Lyman, John M. Bernhisel, and Lucien Woodworth; and at seven in the evening we met in the front upper room of the Mansion, with William Law and William Marks. By the common consent and unanimous voice of the council, I was chosen president of the special council.
>
> The president led in prayer that his days might be prolonged until his mission on the earth is accomplished, have dominion over his

enemies, all their households be blessed, and all the Church and the world.[78]

Joseph Smith's journal, the original source, gives a fuller account: "Beurach Ale [a code name for Joseph Smith] was by common consent, & unanimous voice chosen President of the quorum. & anointed & ord[ained] to the highest and holiest order of the priesthood (& companion)."[79] This "companion" was his wife, Emma, to whom he had been sealed for time and eternity four months earlier on 28 May. Wilford Woodruff's record of this event, found in his 1858 Historian's Private Journal, was equally explicit: "Then by common consent Joseph Smith the Prophet Received his second Anointing of the Highest & Holiest order."[80]

During the next five months this higher priesthood ordinance was conferred on at least twenty men and the wives of sixteen of these men. As the accompanying table[81] shows, fullness of priesthood blessings during Smith's lifetime was reserved primarily for church leaders. His concern about administering to these leaders before the temple was completed, besides emphasizing secrecy and loyalty among those who entered plural marriage, was so that "the Kingdom will be established, and I do not care what shall become of me." As George Q. Cannon asserted in 1869, "It was by the virtue of this authority, on the death of Joseph Smith, that President Young, as President of the quorum of the Twelve, presided over the Church."[82]

In an important discourse on priesthood on 10 March 1844 Smith was recorded as saying:

---

78. HC, 6:39.

79. Joseph Smith Diary, 28 Sept. 1843, in Faulring, *An American Prophet's Record*, 416. Beurach Ale was a scriptural "code" designation for Joseph Smith; see D&C 103:21 (1971 ed.), which spells it Baurak.

80. Wilford Woodruff, Historian's Private Journal, 1858, 24, LDS archives.

81. This table is based on independent research by Lisle G. Brown, especially with respect to the table's design, Andrew F. Ehat, whose "Ehat Endowment Data Summary," cited in his "Joseph Smith's Introduction of Temple Ordinances," 98-100, provides most of the dating, and my own research. The listing contains only names and dates for which documentation is fairly certain. Some of the names included are documented as having received one or more of these ordinances, but no precise date has been located.

82. George Q. Cannon, sermon, 5 Dec. 1869, JD 13:49.

Known Endowments, Marriage Sealings, and Second Anointings during Joseph Smith's Lifetime

Second Anointing	Endowment	Males	Marriage Sealing(s)	Females	Endowment	Second Anointing
dbi*	4 May 42	James Adams	28 May 43	Harriet Adams	8 Oct 43	
	12 May 44	Almon Babbitt				
dnr*	28 Sep 43	John Bernhisel				
12 Nov 43	12 Oct 43	Reynolds Cahoon	nd*	Thirza Cahoon	29 Oct 43	12 Nov 43
dnr	3 Feb 44	William Clayton	22 Jul 43	Ruth Clayton		dnr
15 Nov 43	12 Oct 43	Alpheus Cutler	nd	Lois L. Cutler	29 Oct 43	15 Nov 43
				Elizabeth Durphy	1 Oct 43	
			nd	Mercy R. Fielding	1 Nov 43	
	9 Dec 43	Joseph Fielding		Hannah Fielding	Dec 43 - Feb 44	
	11 May 44	John P. Greene				
25 Jan 44	2 Dec 43	Orson Hyde	dnr	Miranda N. Hyde	18 Feb 44	dnr
20 Jan 44	4 May 42	Heber C. Kimball	nd	Vilate Kimball	1 Nov 43	20 Jan 44
	4 May-31 Jul 42	Vinson Knight				
dnr	4 May 42	William Law	dnr	Jane Law	1 Oct 43	dnr
4 Feb 44	9 Dec 43	Cornelius Lott	20 Sep 43	Permilla Lott	23 Dec 43	4 Feb 44
	28 Sep 43	Amasa M. Lyman				
22 Oct 43	4 May 42	William Marks	nd	Rosanna Marks	1 Oct 43	22 Oct 43
	4 May 42	George Miller	nd	Mary Miller		by 3 Feb. 44
26 Feb 44	23 Dec 43	Isaac Morley	26 Feb 44	Lucy G. Morley	23 Dec 43	26 Feb 44
				Fanny Y. Murray	23 Dec 43	
2 Feb 44	9 Dec 43	William Phelps	2 Feb 44	Sally W. Phelps	23 Dec 43	2 Feb 44
26 Jan 44	23 Dec 43	Orson Pratt				
12 Jan 44	2 Dec 43	Parley P. Pratt	23 Jun 43	Mary Ann Pratt	nd	nd
nd	9 Dec 43	Levi Richards				
27 Jan 44	4 May 42	Willard Richards	29 May 43	Jenetta Richards	1 Nov 43	27 Jan 44
dnr	11 May 44	Sidney Rigdon				
31 Jan 44	2 Dec 43	George A. Smith	20 Jan 44	Bathsheba Smith	23 Dec 43	31 Jan 44
8 Oct 43	5 May 42	Hyrum Smith	8 Oct 43	Mary F. Smith	29 May 43	8 Oct 43
				Mercy Thompson	1 Nov. 43	dnr
26 Feb 44	28 Sep 43	John Smith	nd	Clarissa Smith	8 Oct 43	26 Feb 44
				Lucy Mack Smith	8 Oct 43	12 Nov 43
28 Sep 43	5 May 42	Joseph Smith, Jr.	28 May 43	Emma Hale Smith	28 Sep 43	28 Sep 43
	17 Dec 43	Samuel H. Smith				

Known Endowments, Marriage Sealings, and Second Anointings during Joseph Smith's Lifetime (continued)

Second Anointing	Endow-ment	Males	Marriage Sealing(s)	Females	Endow-ment	Second Anointing
	12 May 44	William Smith				
nd	2 Dec 43	Orson Spencer	nd	Catherine Spencer	23 Dec 43	nd
30 Jan 44	28 Sep 43	John Taylor	30 Jan 44	Leonora Taylor	1 Nov 43	30 Jan 44
27 Oct 43	4 May 42	Newel K. Whitney	21 Aug 42	Elizabeth Whitney	8 Oct 43	27 Oct 43
	14 May 44	Lyman Wight				
28 Jan 44	2 Dec 43	Wilford Woodruff	11 Nov 43	Phoebe Woodruff	23 Dec 43	28 Jan 44
dnr	28 Sep 43	Lucien Woodworth	nd	Phebe Woodworth	29 Oct 43	dnr
22 Nov 43	4 May 42	Brigham Young	29 May 43	Mary Ann Young	1 Nov 43	22 Nov 43
	3 Feb 44	Joseph Young		Jane A. Young	3 Feb 44	

*dbi = died before introduced; dnr = did not receive during Joseph Smith's lifetime; nd = no date available but probably received during Joseph Smith's lifetime; blank space = nothing known, or received after Joseph Smith's death.

[T]he spirit power & Calling of Elijah is that ye have power to hold the keys of the revelations ordinances, oricles powers & endowments of the fulness of the Melchezedek Priesthood & of the Kingdom of God on the Earth & to receive, obtain & perform all the ordinances belong-ing to the kingdom of God even unto the sealing of the hearts of the fathers unto the Children & the hearts of the Children unto the fathers even those who are in heaven.[83]

Formally conferring this sealing power of Elijah completed the basic form of the priesthood endowment. As Brigham Young would explain after Smith's death, "Every man that gets his endowment . . . [has been] ordained to the Melchisedeck Priesthood, which is the highest order of Priesthood. . . . those who have come in here and have received their washing & anointing will be ordained Kings & Priests, and will then have received the fulness of the Priesthood, all that can be given

---

83. Wilford Woodruff Journal, 10 Mar. 1844, in Kenney, 2:361-62.

on earth, for Brother Joseph said he had given us all that could be given to man on the earth."[84]

In practice today the second anointing is actually the first of two parts comprising the fullness of the priesthood ceremony.[85] Although there have been refinements in the ceremony since Nauvoo, a brief discussion of it may be helpful. First, a member of the Quorum of Twelve Apostles or First Presidency recommends a couple to the president of the church. The president then issues a letter to the husband and wife inviting them to attend the temple at a specific time and date and to bring their regular temple recommend with them. In the Salt Lake temple, second anointings are usually administered on Sunday afternoons. In newly constructed temples, they are often performed after the temple has been dedicated but before it opens to members generally.

The first part of the ceremony—being anointed and ordained a king and priest or queen and priestess—is administered in a Holy of Holies or special sealing room and is performed by or under the direction of the president of the church. There are usually but not always two witnesses. Only the husband and wife need to dress in temple robes. The husband leads in a prayer circle, offering signs and praying at an altar. He is then anointed with oil on his head, after which he is ordained a king and a priest unto God to rule and reign in the House of Israel forever. (The anointing oil is usually contained in a special receptacle shaped like a horn, which can be transported from temple to temple.) He is also blessed with the following (as the officiator determines): the power to bind and loose, curse and bless; the blessings of Abraham, Isaac, and Jacob; the Holy Spirit of Promise; to attain godhood; to be sealed to eternal life (if not done previously); to have the power to open the heavens; and other blessings.

Next the wife is anointed with oil on her head, after which she is ordained a queen and a priestess unto her husband, to rule and

---

84. Smith, *An Intimate Chronicle*, 234.
85. Prior to receiving the second anointing, a man receives the ordinance of the washing of the feet under the direction of the church president. This cleanses the man from the blood and sins of his generation and should not be confused with the last ordinance of the second anointing (discussed below) when the man's feet are washed by his wife.

reign with him in his kingdom forever. She is blessed with the following: to receive all the blessings of the everlasting priesthood; to be an heir to all the blessings sealed upon her husband; to be exalted with her husband; to have ministering angels attend her; to be sealed up to eternal life; to receive the blessings of godhood; to live as long as desired; to have the power of eternal lives (of posterity without end); and other blessings. The specifics of the anointing are recorded by hand in a large leather-bound register.

At the conclusion of this ordinance, the washing of the husband's feet by his wife is explained to the couple. It is a private ordinance, without witnesses. Its significance is related to the resurrection of the dead, as Heber Kimball noted.[86] The couple is told to attend to the ordinance at a date of their choosing in the privacy of their home. At the determined time the husband dedicates the home and the room in which they perform the ordinance, which then follows the pattern of Mary's anointing Jesus in Matthew 12. The ordinance symbolically prepares the husband for burial, and in this way the wife lays claim upon him in the resurrection.[87] Having authority, she also pronounces those blessings she feels appropriate upon her husband. Kimball's journal entry derives from a speculative belief taught by early Mormons that Jesus married Mary and Martha, the sisters of Lazarus.[88] Historical records indicate that the husband and wife perform the second part of the priesthood ordinance from a few days to as much as a few years after the second anointing.[89] Only the first part of the second anointing

---

86. Kimball, *On the Potter's Wheel*, 55.

87. Compare the patriarchal blessing Hyrum Smith gave John Taylor on 23 July 1843 that "shall be sealed upon your head in the day that you shall be anointed & your body prepared for its buriel" (Patriarchal Blessing Book, 3:144, LDS archives). For biblical accounts of Jesus Christ's anointing for his burial, see Matthew 26:6-12, Mark 14:3-9, John 12:1-8.

88. See Ogden Kraut, *Jesus Was Married* (n.p., 1969) for a compilation of early LDS citations on this belief.

89. See Phineas Richards Journal, 22 Jan., 1 Feb. 1846, LDS archives; Robert McQuarrie Journal, 13 Nov. 1890, 1 June 1894, LDS archives; and Sylvester Q. Cannon Journal, 30 Sept. and 28 Oct. 1904, LDS archives. Wasatch Stake president William H. Smart's account of his and his wife's second anointing illustrates the two-part ceremony:

"31 May 1901: Went to Temple this morning presenting recommend which Pres. Snow gave me about 3 months ago. We had not come before for our second anointing as the baby was young, and because we desired to become settled in our new home.

can be performed vicariously for the dead, and only by those who have already received the ordinance.[90]

Centrally embedded in the evolution of the anointing ritual in early Mormon history is the concept of hierarchy.[91] As the ritual evolved, lay members of the church advanced into the inner circle, receiving ordinances and symbols formerly held only by Smith and his immediate associates, while Smith and other leaders then moved on to higher kingdoms, more sure promises, and more secret rituals. Although change in the fundamental framework of the ritual was frozen by Smith's death in June 1844, theologic perceptions dealing with certain aspects of the endowment—and more particularly the second anointing—underwent further modification.

. . . Bp John R Winder annointed us and Elder Madsen instructed us. These are the greatest blessings that are bestowed upon man in the flesh. We were both melted in tears and I felt the patriarchal spirit of pure affection more than I have done before. The witnesses to the annointing were John R. Winder [who] annointed. Adolph Madsen assisted John Nicholson Recorder. . . .

"21 June 1901 [at home]: This evening from about 9-30 to 12 O.C. my wife and I attended to the second part of the ordinance of second anointings. We besides the ordinance itself sang 'We thank thee O God for a prophet,' conversed concerning our duties to each other and children, read from John XII: 1-8 verses, read the Rev. on the Eternity of the Marriage Covenant, Section 132. We dedicated [the] room for the purpose of this meeting. Closed by singing: 'Oh my father thou that dwellest.' Anna was mouth in preliminary prayer, I gave the dedicatory prayer and the benediction. The spirit of the Lord was with us and we felt nearer together than usual: were much encouraged in pressing onward in an endeavor to succeed in life. We fasted during the day and broke our fast together a little after 12 O.C.'" (William H. Smart Diary, 31 May, 21 June 1901, Special Collections, Marriott Library, University of Utah, Salt Lake City, Utah).

90. The description of second anointings as performed in temples today was verified by a knowledgeable individual who wishes to remain anonymous.

91. Although it oversimplifies this complex developmental process, Andrew Ehat has attempted to show how Smith's additions to the Kirtland endowment in Nauvoo did not disrupt the ultimate order of the ceremony. His listing of temple ordinances, based on the *History of the Church*, is intended to illustrate this point. Items first revealed in Nauvoo are italicized, while those found in both the Kirtland and Nauvoo ceremonies are not: (1) Washing of the body with water and perfumed alcohol *(set wording)*; (2) *Sealing the washing;* (3) Anointing *the body* with oil; (4) Sealing the anointing *(set wording)*; (5) *Aaronic portion of the endowment*; (6) *Melchizedek portion of the endowment*; (7) *Marriage for time and eternity*; (8) *Anointing with oil;* and (9) Washing of feet (cited in Ehat and Cook, *Words of Joseph Smith*, 140-41n6, and in his "Introduction of Temple Ordinances," 169).

CHAPTER 4

Brigham Young's Revisions

One of the potential successors to Joseph Smith in mid-1844 was Smith's counselor in the First Presidency, Sidney Rigdon. Although Rigdon had received his endowment on 11 May 1844, he had not received his second anointing, which became a matter of crucial importance to those who had. Orson Hyde, not always a reliable commentator, described the succession conundrum at Nauvoo in a letter one month later:

> We have had a charge given us by our prophet, and that charge we intend to honor and magnify. It was given in March last.... "To us were committed the Keys of the Kingdom, and every gift, key and power, that Joseph ever had," confirmed upon our heads by an anointing, which Bro. Rigdon never did receive.
>
> We know the charge which the prophet gave us, and the responsibility which the Spirit of the living God laid on us through him, and we know that Elder Rigdon does not know what it was. We have counted the cost of the stand we have taken, and have firmly and unitedly, with prayer and with fasting—with signs and with tokens, with garments and with girdle, decreed in the name of Jesus Christ, that we will honor our calling, and faithfully carry out the measures of the prophet so far as we have power, relying on the arm of God for strength in every time of need.[1]

---

1. Orson Hyde to Ebenezer Robinson, 19 Sept. 1844, in *The Return* 2 (Apr. 1890), 4:253.

None of the major contenders to Brigham Young and the Council of
the Twelve—Sidney Rigdon, William Smith, James Jesse Strang, Lyman
Wight, and later Joseph Smith III—had received the higher ordinance.[2]
After a special conference rejected Rigdon as "guardian" of the church
in August 1844, he tried to undermine the authority of the Quorum of
the Twelve by administering his own ceremony of washing and
anointing. This resulted in his excommunication by the Twelve on 8
September 1844.[3]

Little actual ordinance work was done for a year or more after
Smith's death. But from the time he assumed leadership in early
August, Brigham Young kept construction of the temple before the
Saints and used the promise of its completion to keep them together
in Nauvoo. On 18 August 1844, Young told the Saints:

> I discover a disposition in the sheep to scatter, now the shep-
> herd is taken away. I do not say that it will never be right for this
> people to go from here. . . . but I do say wait until . . . you are
> counseled to do so. . . . *stay here in Nauvoo*, and build the Temple
> and get your endowments; do not scatter; "united we stand, divided
> we fall". It has been whispered about that all who go into the wilder-
> ness with [Lyman] Wight and [George] Miller will get their endow-
> ments, but they cannot give an endowment in the wilderness. If we
> do not carry out the plan Joseph has laid down and the pattern he
> has given for us to work by, we cannot get any further endowment.
> . . . North and South America is Zion and as soon as the Temple is
> done and you get your endowments you can go and build up stakes,
> but do not be in haste, wait until the Lord says go.[4]

2. For the relationship of these contenders to the second anointing and the
succession issue, see Andrew F. Ehat, "Joseph Smith's Introduction of Temple
Ordinances and the 1844 Mormon Succession Question," M.A. thesis, Brigham Young
University, 1982, 189ff, esp. fig. 1.

3. See Lisle G. Brown, "The Holy Order in Nauvoo," 12-17, privately circulated.

4. Joseph Smith, Jr., *History of the Church of Jesus Christ of Latter-day Saints*, 7
vols., ed. B. H. Roberts, 2d ed. rev. (Salt Lake City: Deseret Book Co., 1973), 7:254-55,
258 (hereafter HC). Wilford Woodruff's handwritten report of Young's comments
expands: "If we do not carry out the plan Joseph has laid down & the pattern he has
given for us to work by, we cannot get any further endowment—I want this to sink deep
into your heart that you may remember it. If you stir up the flame of dissention will you
get an endowment? No! You get a party to run here and another there, and divide our
strength, and weaken our hands, and we will be left and our enemies will flock around
us & destroy us—in that case you will not get your endowments, but will sink & not

Young and the apostles made more and more explicit what they saw at stake in defection from the temple and its ordinances. James Emmett was a member of the Council of Fifty who grew impatient and led a company of about one hundred Mormons into Iowa. The apostles warned:

> [Emmett] has led you forth from our midst and separated you from the body and like a branch severed from a tree you must and will perish together with your posterity and your progenitors unless you are engrafted again thereon before you wither and die. . . .
>
> Do you desire the eternal seal of the priesthood placed upon your head by which your progenitors for ages past and your posterity for endless generations to come shall be secured to you in a covenant that is everlasting? . . .
>
> All of you are ready to answer yes, and respond with a hearty affirmative. But remember there is but one way by which you can realize or partake of these thngs; it is by hearkening to our counsel in all things.[5]

In response to such council and warning, the Saints donated money, time, art, furnishings, and other material to make the temple attic ready for use.[6] In late 1845 church leaders began to prepare to administer the endowment to the general membership, and the first ceremonies were performed in the temple on 10 December. The first recipients were members of the Quorum of the Anointed who wanted to go through the ritual again within the walls of the temple. But by 7

---

rise—go to hell and not to the bosom of Abraham. . . . [W]ould the Lord give an endowment to a people that would be frightened away from [their] duty?" (Brigham Young Addresses, 1843-55, archives, historical department, Church of Jesus Christ of Latter-day Saints, Salt Lake City, Utah [hereafter LDS archives]).

5. HC, 7:378.

6. For details concerning the construction of the Nauvoo temple, including the administration of endowments in 1842 as well as December 1845-February 1846, see Lisle G. Brown, "The Sacred Departments for Temple Work in Nauvoo: The Assembly Room and the Council Chamber," *Brigham Young University Studies* 19 (Spring 1979): 361-74; and Andrew F. Ehat, ed., "'They Might Have Known That He Was Not a Fallen Prophet': The Nauvoo Journal of Joseph Fielding," *Brigham Young University Studies* 19 (Winter 1979): 133-66.

February 1846 when Young officially closed the temple, 5,200 members were endowed.[7]

Locations Where Nauvoo Temple Ordinances Were Performed Prior to the Nauvoo Temple

Location	Date	Type of Temple Ordinance
Joseph Smith Store	4 May 1842	Endowment
	27 June 1842	Prayer Circle
	28 Sep. 1842	Endowment
	5 Nov. 1843	Endowment
	31 Dec. 1843	Prayer Circle
	20 Jan. 1844	Second Anointings
Joseph Smith Homestead	26 June 1842	Prayer Circle
	12 Nov. 1843	Second Anointings
	19 Nov. 1843	Prayer Circle
The Mansion House	27 Aug. 1843	Prayer Circle
	28 Sep. 1843	Second Anointings
	29 Oct. 1843	Endowment
Brigham Young Residence	22 Jan. 1844	Prayer Circle
	25 Jan. 1844	Second Anointing
	1 Aug. 1844	Prayer Circle
	15 Aug. 1844	Second Anointings
	24 Jan. 1845	Prayer Circle
Hyrum Smith House	14 Sep. 1844	Prayer Circle
Heber Kimball House	1 Oct. 1844	Prayer Circle
Parley Pratt Store	12 Jan. 1845	Second Anointings
Trustee's Office	26 Jan. 1845	Endowment

---

7. HC, 7:541-80; the last entry on page 580 gives two possible figures for the final day's ordinance count: the Seventy's Record, LDS archives, brings the cumulative total to 5,210; George A. Smith's estimate boosts this to 5,634 endowments. The lower figure is probably more representative, however, for by using a third source (Heber C. Kimball Journal, 7 Feb. 1846, LDS archives), the cumulative total is 5,154.

Location	Date	Type of Temple Ordinance
Willard Richards	21 Jan. 1845	Prayer Circle
House	4 Nov. 1845	Prayer Circle
Joseph Noble House	20 Mar. 1845	Prayer Circle
John Smith House	17 Apr. 1845	Second Anointings
John Taylor House	5 Oct. 1845	Prayer Circle

Years later Young recalled that Smith's endowment included ritualistic signs, tokens, and penalties. But he also suggested that the structure and order of the ritual expanded into a more elaborate and detailed ceremony as it moved from the constricted quarters over Smith's store to the larger stage of the temple:

> Bro Joseph turned to me [President Brigham Young] and said: "Brother Brigham this is not arranged right, but we have done the best we could under the circumstances in which we are placed, and I wish you to take this matter in hand and organize and systematize all these ceremonies with the signs, tokens, penalties and key words." I did so and each time I got something more; so that when we went through the Temple at Nauvoo, I understood and knew how to place them there. We had our ceremonies pretty correct.[8]

No written text of the 1842 or 1843 ritual exists. The first descriptions in any detail date from 1845, and it is on these that one must rely for comparisons.

On 30 November the Quorum of the Twelve met in the temple, dedicating its attic in preparation for performance of the rituals. According to the diary of William Clayton, a scribe in attendance:

> At about 12 o'clock we clothed and . . . then offered up the signs of the Holy Priesthood and repeated them to get them more perfect. I was requested to keep minutes. President offered up prayers and dedicated the Attic story, the male room and ourselves to God, and prayed that God would sustain and deliver from the hands of our enemies, his servants untill they have accomplished his will in this house. Elder

---

8. L. John Nuttall Journal, 7 Feb. 1877, Special Collections, Harold B. Lee Library, Brigham Young University, Provo, Utah; Nuttall was Young's secretary at the time.

Taylor then sang "A poor wayfaring man of grief &c." after which we again offered up the signs and Elder Kimball prayed that the Lord would hear and answer the prayers of his servant Brigham, break off the yoke of our enemies and inasmuch as they lay traps for the feet of his servants, that they may fall into them themselves and be destroyed.[9]

Heber Kimball detailed some of the final preparations inside the temple. On 4 December, a Thursday, he recorded: "About 2 in the after noon went to the Temple. . . . Soon after P. Pratt, O. Hide ingaged in putting up canvas and other things to prepare our room. W. W. Phelps brought in some seders [cedar] trees to adorn our garden [room in the temple]. About sun set Bishop N. K. come in with the [temple] Vail, the old one and new one. The holes ware cut by By B. Young and others assisted."[10] The next day he wrote that his wife and daughter "Came in fore the purpus of Heming the Veil." He added that W. W. Phelps also "come in with some seders trees."[11] He noted that on the coming Sunday morning: "the Holy Order will assemble fore prair and council. Our wives will come and pertack [partake] with us. The Sacrament will be administer[ed] and spend the day in those thing[s] that the Spirrit shall teach. This was the advise of President B. Young— this gave great joy to our wimmen. To morrow will finish our rooms." He described the finishing touches the next day: "The trees set in order in the garden. Sister Elzebeth Ann Whitney come in and sode [sewed] on the fringe, going over the Top of the canvas running threw the room crost from North to South. . . . Sister Clarisa and Emily Cutler mad[e] a Coten [cotton] Veil going before the Linnen Veil."[12]

The Sunday meeting on 7 December was the first meeting of the full Quorum of the Anointed in the Nauvoo temple. Kimball wrote: "The following Persons are members of the Holy Order of the Holy Preasthood having Recieved it in the Life time of Joseph and Hirum,

---

9. George D. Smith, ed., *An Intimate Chronicle: The Journals of William Clayton* (Salt Lake City: Signature Books in association with Smith Research Associates, 1991), 192-93.

10. Heber C. Kimball Journal, 4 Dec. 1845, in Stanley B. Kimball, ed., *On the Potter's Wheel: The Diaries of Heber C. Kimball* (Salt Lake City: Signature Books in association with Smith Research Associates, 1987), 158.

11. Ibid., 159.

12. Ibid., 162-63.

the Prophets. Elder B. Young went and gave the Brethren and Sisters present a view of the Seprate rooms, and the object of them, then pute up the Veil and choe [showed] the Order of it. The Brethren and Sisters clothed [in temples robes at] half past one [and] commenced our meeting at two Oclock."[13] William Clayton, who Kimball noted was one of seven present who had not yet received the second anointing, described the meeting:

> In the Temple all day. All the first quorum with one or two exceptions were present both male and female. About 1 o'clock we clothed. Dressed in ceremonial robes and aprons. The meeting was opened by prayer by Joseph Fielding. . . . President Young then addressed the company. . . . He stated "that a few of the quorum had met twice a week ever since Joseph and Hyrum were killed and during the last excitement, every day and in the hottest part of it twice a day to offer up the signs and pray to our heavenly father to deliver his people and this is the cord which has bound this people together. If this quorum and those who shall be admitted into it will be as diligent in prayer as a few has been I promise you in the name of Israels God that we shall accomplish the will of God and go out in due time from the gentiles with power and plenty and no power shall stay us." After the exhortation we offered up the signs and had prayers for the usual subject.[14]

More finishing touches were made to the attic rooms for the first endowments which were held on Wednesday, 10 December. The Monday before, Kimball wrote, "Elder Phelps Brought in some grape Vines, and hung cluster[s] of rasens hung to them as the chois fruit. . . . John D Lee and others have been fitting up stoves in the two west rooms. as they will be devoted to washing and Anointing and to heet water. we have two Large traves [troughs]. . . . Three men can wash in either of them at the same time."[15] The next day Kimball again described preparations and the anticipation of the next day's events: "The stoves in the wash rooms are fitted up and fire in them. We shall begin our opperations to morrow Morning if the Lord will. O Lord be with Thy servents and inspire thare hearts with lite and knowlledge,

13. Ibid., 164.
14. Smith, *An Intimate Chronicle*, 193-94.
15. Kimball, *On the Potter's Wheel*, 165-66.

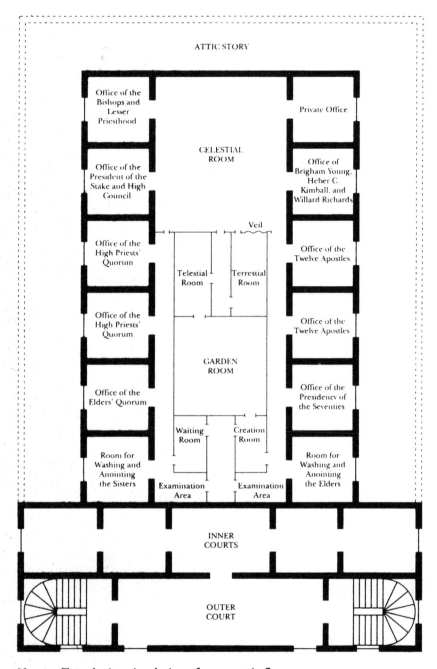

ATTIC STORY

Office of the Bishops and Lesser Priesthood

Private Office

CELESTIAL ROOM

Office of the President of the Stake and High Council

Office of Brigham Young, Heber C. Kimball, and Willard Richards

Veil

Office of the High Priests' Quorum

Office of the Twelve Apostles

Telestial Room

Terrestial Room

Office of the High Priests' Quorum

Office of the Twelve Apostles

GARDEN ROOM

Office of the Elders' Quorum

Office of the Presidency of the Seventies

Waiting Room

Creation Room

Room for Washing and Anointing the Sisters

Room for Washing and Anointing the Elders

Examination Area

Examination Area

INNER COURTS

OUTER COURT

Nauvoo Temple, interior design of top or attic floor.

so that they may not go [w]rong in the ordanance of the Holy Preasthood and Thy name shall have all the Glory."[16]

On 10 December Clayton began to keep a temple-related diary for Heber Kimball that tracks the day's events in some detail. First he describes the "16 bottles of Oil which had been perfumed by Bishop Whitney for the purpose of anointing."[17] Then he outlines the first preparatory ritual for the endowment:

> At 3 o clock Sister Mary Ann Young and Vilate Kimball, Elizabeth Ann Whitney, commenced washing and anointing each other being the first in this holy Temple of the Lord. This was done in the preparation room in the North West corner of the Attic story. About the same time President Young put up the vail in its place which things finish and complete the Celestial Room preparatory to the endowment. . . .
>
> At 25 minutes past 4 o clock President Young and Heber C. Kimball commenced washing Elder Willard Richards. . . . We continued washing and anointing those present till about 7 1/2 o clock.
>
> At 20 minutes to 8 o clock President Young announced that all things were now ready to commence and go through with the ordinances. He said that after we get properly organized and ready to go on without confusion, no person will be permitted to talk, nor walk about in the main rooms, neither would any person be expected to be in the Celestial room only those who were necessary to carry on the work. At the same hour he took the chair and appointed P. P. Pratt and John Taylor to assist him in taking those through who were now prepared. W. W. Phelps acted as serpent. . . . These went through all the ordinances untill they were passed through the vail at which time it was half past nine o clock. President Young then called all present into the Celestial room where we kneeled down and Amasa Lyman offered up prayers.
>
> Some of the brethren and sisters then retired home and the rest continued washing and anointing and taking through the whole ordinance until half past 3 o clock in the morning. . . .
>
> After all was lead through those present offered up the signs of the Holy Priesthood and offered up Prayers. Elder Orson Hyde gave praise to the Most High for his goodness. H. C. Kimball presides as

16. Ibid., 167.
17. Smith, *An Intimate Chronicle,* 202.

Eloheem, Orson Hyde as Jehovah and George A. Smith as Michael and N. K. Whitney as the serpent.[18]

The diary entry for the next day, Thursday, 11 December, describes both the temple arrangements and the ceremony in more detail:

> The main room is divided into apartments for the ceremonies of the endowment. . . . On each side of the Alley is a small room partitioned off where the saints receive the first part of the ceremony or where the man is created and a help mate given to him. From these rooms to the third partition in the Arch is planted the garden, which is nicely decorated and set off with shrubs and trees in pots and Boxes to represent the Garden of Eden. In this apartment is also an altar. Here the man and woman are placed and commandments given to them in addition to what is given in the creation. Here also after the man and woman has eaten the forbidden fruit is given to them a charge at the Alter and the first and second tokens of the Aaronic Priesthood. They are then thrust out into a room which is dark being the one on the North side between the four and fifth division of the arch which represents the telestial kingdom or the world. Opposite to this is another apartment of the same size representing the terrestrial kingdom and between these two is an alley about 4 feet wide. In the telestial kingdom, after the man has proved himself faithful he receives the first signs and tokens of the Melchizedek priesthood and an additional charge. Here also he vouches for the conduct of his companion. They are then left to prove themselves faithful, after which they are admitted into the terrestrial kingdom, where at the alter they receive an additional charge and the second token of the Melchizedek Priesthood and also the key word on the five points of fellowship.
>
> There are words given with every token and the new name is given in the preparation room when they receive their washing and annointing.
>
> After [they have] received all the tokens and words and signs they are led to the vail where they give each to Eloheem through the vail and are then admitted into the Celestial Room. . . .
>
> Brigham Young and wife, H. C. Kimball and G. A. Smith, also Sister Mary Smith, Mercy R. Thompson, W. W. Phelps and his wife tarried in the Temple all night. We only obtained about an hour and a

---

18. Ibid., 203-204.

half sleep. . . . From thence we returned back to the Temple and found several brethren had come in with the expectations of receiving their anointings. . . . A little before six we commenced taking them through the ceremonies, Heber C. Kimball acting as Eloheem, George A. Smith as Jehovah, Orson Hyde as Michael, W. W. Phelps as the serpent. We were also assisted by P. P. Pratt. . . .

President having gone out some time ago returned while we were in the garden. The signs and tokens were all given by H. C. Kimball. He also received them through the vail. It was about half past seven when we got through. Those last who were taken through were then instructed farther regarding the signs by Elder Orson Hyde.

The President then called all those who were present into the Celestial room. We formed a circle, offered up the signs, and then offered up prayers for the sick; for our families and that the Lord would frustrate the plans of our enemies.[19]

At the end of the third day, Friday, Clayton wrote: "During the whole of the three days already spent in the endowment, President Brigham Young presided and dictated the ordinances and also took an active part in nearly every instance except when entirely overcome by fatigue through his constant labors to forward the work."[20]

Norton Jacob and his wife were among those who received their endowments on Friday. This was the first day, according to Jacob, that endowments were performed for those who had not received them from Joseph Smith:

Wm. Weeks come to me and said he wanted me to go home and prepare myself and wife and come to the temple at 12 o'clock a.m. ready to receive our endowments. We most joyfully complied with the request and at about 8 o'clock p.m. we were washed and anointed in the House of the Lord. It was the most interesting scene of all my life and one that afforded the most peace and joy that we had ever experienced since we were married, which has been over fifteen years. [Six brethren] were the first that received their endowment in this House of the Lord, which took place on this day, the time before having been occupied in the washing and anointing those that had before received their endowments under the hands of Joseph Smith the Prophet, which he con-

19. Ibid., 205-208.
20. Ibid., 209.

ferred upon them one year ago last winter. After those six went in with
their wives, [several others] and myself with our wives were called in
and all passed through the endowment at the same time.[21]

These accounts of the first three days describe only four roles in
the endowment ceremony: Elohim, Jehovah, Michael, and the serpent.
A meeting held after the third day of endowments provides an example
of the process of revising the dramatic elements of the ceremony. On
13 December, Clayton writes:

> Last evening an arrangement was made establishing better order in
> conducting the endowment. Under this order it is the province of
> Eloheem, Jehovah and Michael to create the world, plant the Garden
> and create the man and give his help meet. Eloheem gives the charge
> to Adam in the Garden and thrusts them into the telestial kingdom or
> the world. Then Peter assisted by James and John conducts them
> through the Telestial and Terrestrial kingdom administering the
> charges and tokens in each and conducts them to the vail where they
> are received by the Eloheem and after talking with him by words and
> tokens are admitted by him into the Celestial kingdom . . .[22]

In drawing out the story, Eve, the companion for Adam/Michael, is
also introduced. After Elohim, Jehovah, and Michael create the world
and plant the Garden of Eden, Eve is created and enables the Fall. Peter,
assisted by James and John, helps Adam and Eve reach the veil and win
readmittance into the Father's presence.[23]

Initially there was a wide difference in the time required for an
endowment. "Companies" or groups of participants averaging about
a dozen members took an hour to an hour and a half. But some sessions
lasted up to four hours. One company of thirty-five had a ceremony of
five hours and ten minutes. Clayton's diary does not comment on the
reasons for the variations, but they are probably related to the size of
the company, the experience of those officiating, the interjection of

21. Norton Jacob Journal, 20, Special Collections, Lee Library.

22. Smith, *An Intimate Chronicle*, 210.

23. Christian ministers were added in the 1850s. See William Cook, *The Mormons*
(London: Joseph Masters, 1857), 37-42. By 1905 the ceremony had been edited to allow
only one minister. See "The Mormon Temple Endowment Ceremony," *The World
Today*, Feb. 1905, 165-70.

explanatory lectures, and the use of a single veil station. Some days over one hundred endowments were performed.

As we reconstruct these 1845-46 sessions, it appears that initiates normally participated in a washing and anointing ceremony, had a brief recess, then participated in the main endowment. Sessions began with the ringing of a bell. A "lecture at the veil" was sometimes given (usually by Brigham Young or Heber C. Kimball) at the end of the endowment. On at least two occasions, the lecture seems to have been postponed and delivered a few days later.[24]

The earliest accounts of the Nauvoo temple endowment indicate that initiatory washings followed a literal Old Testament model of actual bathing. Large tubs of water are specified in the separate men's and women's rooms. The anointing was performed by liberally pouring consecrated oil from a horn over the head and allowing it to run over the whole body. Originally everyone participating took the roles of Adam and Eve. Early endowment administrations were primarily restricted to a man and his wife or wives,[25] although few men were endowed without their spouse's participation. Initially all were admitted through the veil by the same officiator. Men began conducting their wives through the veil by 1857.[26]

By 21 December, a Sunday, over 500 had received their endowment. That day a meeting of the expanded Quorum of the Anointed convened in the temple, including "all those who could clothe themselves in the garments of Priesthood."[27] Norton Jacob wrote of the meeting, "I with my wife, first had the exquisite pleasure of meeting with the holy order of the Lord's anointed in his holy House, whose motto is 'Holiness to the Lord.'" According to Clayton, seventy-five were in attendance. At the meeting plans were announced to take at least 100 people through the temple daily.[28] By the next Sunday, "About 200 persons were present, clothed in priestly garments." Brigham Young warned, "We shall not be able to have another public

---

24. Smith, *An Intimate Chronicle*, 193-94, 199-215, 256-58.

25. Ehat, "Joseph Smith's Introduction of Temple Ordinances," 106-107.

26. John Hyde, Jr., *Mormonism: Its Leaders and Designs* (New York: W. P. Fetridge & Co., 1857), 99.

27. Smith, *An Intimate Chronicle,* 220.

28. Ibid., 238.

meeting here on account of the weight on the floor, it has already caused the walls to crack, prevents the doors from shutting, and will injure the roof."[29] Those in attendance heard sermons about the ordinances and the holy garments they were asked to make and wear. Amasa Lyman spoke of the endowment journey in a general way and pointed to further ordinances yet to come:

> He said Doubtless with the most of the present assembly it is the beginning of a new era, in their lives, they have come to a time they never saw before. They have come to the commencement of a knowl-edge of things, and it is necessary they should be riveted on their minds, one important thing to be understood in this, that those portions of the priesthood which you have received are all essential matters, it is not merely that you may see these things [that are promised], but it is matter of fact, a matter that has to do directly with your salvation. . . . It is putting you in possession of those keys by which you can ask for things you need and obtain them. This is the Key by which to obtain all the glory and felicity of eternal life. It is the key by which you approach God. No impression which you receive here should be lost. It was to rivet the recollection of the tokens and covenants in your memory like a nail in a sure place, never to be forgotten.
>
> The scenery through which you have passed is actually laying before you a picture or map by which you are to travel through life, and obtain an entrance into the celestial kingdom hereafter. . . .
>
> If you are found worthy and maintain your integrity, and do not run away and think you have got all your endowment you will be found worthy after a while, which will make you honorable with God. You have not yet been ordained to any thing, but will be by and by. You have received these things, because of your compliance with all the requisitions of the law, and if faithful you will receive more.
>
> You have now learned how to pray. You have been taught how to approach God and be recognized. This is the principle by which the Church has been kept together, and not the power of arms. A few individuals have asked for your preservation, and their prayers have been heard, and it is this which has preserved you from being scattered to the four winds.
>
> Those who have learned to approach God and receive these blessings, are they better than you? The difference is, they have been

---

29. Ibid., 240.

permitted to have these things revealed unto them. The principles which have been opened to you are the things which ought to occupy your attention all your lives. They are not second to any thing. You have the key by which if you are faithful, you will claim on you and on your posterity, all the blessings of the Priesthood.[30]

Kimball followed with his version of the endowment journey, focusing specifically on the way the participants "personify Adam." He ended by similarly looking forward to second anointings:

> The ideas advanced by brother Lyman are good and true. We have been taken as it were from the earth, and have travelled until we have entered the Celestial Kingdom and what is it for, it is to personify Adam. And you discover that our God is like one of us, for he created us in his own image. Every man that ever came upon this earth, or any other earth will take the course we have taken. Another thing, it is to bring us to an organization, and just as quick as we can get into that order and government, we have the Celestial Kingdom here. You have got to honor and reverence your brethren, for if you do not you never can honor God. The man was created, and God gave him dominion over the whole earth, but he saw that he never could multiply, and replenish the earth, without a woman. And he made one and gave her to him. He did not make the man for the woman; but the woman for the man, and it is just as unlawful for you to rise up and rebel against your husband, as it would be for man to rebel against God.
>
> When the man came to the vail, God gave the key word to the man, and the man gave it to the woman. But if a man don't use a woman well and take good care of her, God will take her away from him, and give her to another.
>
> Perfect order and consistency makes Heaven but we are now deranged, and the tail has become the head.
>
> We have now come to this place, and all your former covenants are of no account, and here is the place where we have to enter into a new covenant, and be sealed, and have it recorded. One reason why we bring our wives with us, is, that they make a covenant with us to keep these things sacred. You have been anointed to be kings and priests, but you have not been ordained to it yet, and you have got to get it by being faithful. You can't sin so cheap now as you could before

---

30. Ibid., 224-26.

you came to this order. It is not for you to reproach the Lord's anointed nor to speak evil of him. You have covenanted not to do it.[31]

During the next Sunday meeting, Young elaborated further the significance of the Adam and Eve story in the endowment ceremony:

The keys or signs of the Priesthood are for the purpose of impressing on the mind the order of the Creation. In the first place the name of the man is given, a new name, Adam, signifying the first man, or Eve, the first Woman. Adam's name was more ancient than he was. It was the name of man long before him, who enjoyed the Priesthood. The new name should be after some ancient man. Thus with your ancient name, your modern name and the name that was last given you, you enquire concerning things past present and future.

After his fall, another name was given to Adam, and being full of integrity, and not disposed to follow the woman nor listen to her was permitted to receive the tokens of the priesthood.

I wish you to cease talking about what you see and hear in this place. No man or woman has a right to mention a work of the appearance of this building in the least; nor to give the signs and tokens except when assembled together, according to the order of the Priesthod, which is in an upper room. There are not a dozen persons that can give the signs and tokens correct, and the reason is that person would run to that vail, one of the most sacred places on the face of the earth, that had not understood the right manner of giving the signs and tokens.

The order and ordinances passed through here prove the principles taught in the Bible. First men should love their God supremely. Woman will never get back, unless she follows the man back, if the man had followed the woman he would have followed her down until this time. Light, liberty and happiness will never shine upon men until they learn these principles. The man must love his God and the woman must love her husband. The love which David and Jonathan had for each other was the love of the priesthood. God is a personage of tabernacle, the Son is a personage of tabernacle, the Spirit or Holy Ghost is also a personage, but not a personage of tabernacle, but is a personage of Spirit. God dwells in eternal burnings puts his hand through the vail and writes on the wall. Any persons that goes through

---

31. Ibid., 226-27.

these ordinances, unless they cleanse their hearts and sanctify themselves, and sanctify the Lord, it will damn them.[32]

The following Tuesday, 30 December, the work of the endowment finished early, and an innovation occurred which seems by
Clayton's account to have been spontaneous:

> The labors of the day having been brought to a close at so early
> an hour viz; half past 8, it was thought proper to have a little season of
> recreation, accordingly, Brother Hans Hanson was invited to produce
> his violin. He did so, and played several lively airs, among the rest some
> very good lively dancing tunes. This was too much for the gravity of
> Brother Joseph Young, who indulged in a hornpipe, and was soon
> joined by several others, and before the dance was over several French
> fours were indulged in. The first was opened by President B. Young
> with Sister Whitney and Elder H. C. Kimball with Sister Lewis. The spirit
> of dancing increased until the whole floor was covered with dancers.
> After this had continued about an hour, several excellent songs were
> sung, in which several of the brethren and sisters joined. The Upper
> California was sung by Erastus Snow. After which Sister Whitney being
> invited by President Young, stood up and invoking the gift of tongues,
> sung one of the most beautiful songs in tongues, that ever was heard.
> The interpretation was given by her husband, Bishop Whitney, it
> related to our efforts to build this House, and to the privilege we now
> have of meeting together in it, of our departure shortly to the country
> of the Lamanites, and their rejoicing when they hear the gospel, and of
> the ingathering of Israel. Altogether, it was one of the most touching

---

32. Ibid., 238-40. John D. Lee also recorded this sermon in his diary: "Pres.
Brigham Young then arose draped in linen clean and white in the midst of about 300
that were arrayed in white robes—which is an emblem of the righteousness of the
saints—He spoke in reference to the order of the Priesthood—the signs and tokens
connected there with—he observed that there were 4 penal signs and 4 penal tokens
and each one of them aludes to certain names—the first aludes to your New or 1st Name
the 2nd to the 2nd and so on and should I or any of you want to inquire of the Lord—for
anything ancient that transpired on Plannets that rolled into existence long after this
world or theater of action I would use my New Name because it is more ancient than
myself and refers to ancient times—and should I want to enquire for things that are
modern I would use my own name and to inquire for things that are future I would use
the name which refers to things in future—using the signs that are connected with the
3 names—the spirit of Elijah's God was in our midst and surely we had a time of
rejoicing—while we partook of the Bread and Wine and that of our own make pure and
good—such a scene my eye never before beheld" (28 Dec. 1845, LDS archives).

and beautiful exhibitions of the power of the Spirit in the gift of tongues which was ever seen. (So it appeared to the writer of this.) After a little conversation of a general nature, the exercises of the evening were closed by prayer by President B. Young, and soon after most of the persons present left the Temple for their homes.[33]

Two days later a wedding occurred in the temple. Young people attended, and again there was dancing. Wrote Clayton,

> After dancing a few figures, President Young called the attention of the whole company, and then gave them a message, of this import, viz; that this temple was a Holy place, and that when we danced, we danced unto the Lord, and that no person would be allowed to come on to this floor, and afterwards mingle with the wicked. He said the wicked had no right to dance, that dancing and music belonged to the Saints.[34]

After the dancing ended at about two in the morning, the "sisters retired to the side rooms, and the brethren stretched themselves on the floor, or on the sofas and all were soon in the embraces of 'tired nature's sweet restorer, balmy sleep,' with the exception of the Bridegroom and Bride, and a few of their friends who, being unable to close their eyes in sleep, from the abundance of their joy, passed the short hours of the morning, in agreeable conversation, in the office."[35] This pattern of performing endowments during the day and dancing in the temple at night continued at least during the next week. At this point Clayton's diary for Kimball ends.

The final pages of Clayton's record describe the new altar which was being installed in the temple. On 7 January, Clayton's final temple entry reads,

> This afternoon and evening the new altar was used, for the first time, and four individuals and their wives were sealed. The altar is about 2 1/2 feet high, and 2 1/2 feet long, and about one foot wide, rising from a platform about 8 or 9 inches high and extending out on all sides about a foot, forming a convenient place to kneel upon. The top of the altar and the kneeling place are covered with cusions of scarlet damask

33. Smith, *An Intimate Chronicle*, 244.

34. Ibid., 247.

35. Ibid., 249.

cloth. The sides of the upright part, or body of the altar are covered with white linen.

The Twelve and the Bishops with their wives, were present at the dedication this afternoon . . .[36]

The next day the fullness of the priesthood, or second anointing, was administered for the first time in the temple. Once again the earliest to receive the second anointing had already received it from Joseph Smith. A "Book of Anointings" was begun on this day to supplement the temple record Clayton had been keeping for Heber C. Kimball. Kimball and his wife Vilate were the first to receive the ordinance. The record begins:

> President Brigham Young as president of the whole church anointed Brother Heber C. Kimball first this being according to the order in which the ordinances of the Lords House are at all times first communicated to the children of men that he who holds the Keys of the Kingdom of Heaven to minister to men on Earth as President Brigham Young now does should confer the ordinances upon some faithful man who should in turn minister to him according to the pattern of heavenly things
>
> This is the order observed by the Prophet Joseph he first baptized Oliver then Oliver baptized him.

> Entry No. 1., Jan. 8th 1846.
>
> 6. o. clock eve. Pres. Brigham Young Heber Chase Kimble Parley Parker Pratt, Orson Pratt John Taylor, Amasa Lyman, Newell Kimble Whitney Vilate Kimble, Elizabeth an Whitney, Sarah Marinda Pratt, & Leonara Taylor—assembled in Pres. B. Young's Room No 1. dressed themselves [in] Holy Robes. The Hymn now let us rejoice in the Day of Salvation, was sung & Elder Heber C. Kimble offered Prayre at the alter after offering up the Signs of the Presthood. Pres. Brigham Young, proceeded to anoint Br. Heber C. Kimble and Vilate his wife—and pronounced the following blessings namely Bro Heber Chase Kimble in the name of Jesus Christ we poor upon thy head this Holy oil a Priest & we anoint thee a King & unto the most High God in & over the Church of Jesus Christ of Latter Days Saints and also Iseral in this the Holy Temple of the Lord at Nauvoo the City of Jos[eph] State. of. Ills. & I seal upon you power to bind on Earth & it Shall be bound in Heaven &

---

36. Ibid., 257-58.

whomsoever thou Shalt loose on Earth shall be loosed in Heaven, & whomsoever thou shalt curse shalt be cursed, & whomsoever thou shalt Bless shall be blessed—I anoint thy head that it may be sound & thy brain shall be quick to think & to regulate thy whole body & thine ears to hear the cries of the Poor & needy of thy Brethren, who shall come to the[e] for council & thine eyes—that thou mayest see and understand the things of God—& that thou mayest behold Angels & thy mouth that thou mayest Speak fourth the great things of God. & I Seal upon you all the blessings of thy Progenetors Even Abraham Isaac & Jacob—& even as Far back as the Priesthood: & I say that thou Shall live to a good old age—Even to three Score & ten (years) & longer if thou desire it—& thou sha[l]t have Power to redeem thy progenitors & thou shall have power over thy Posterity & shall Save all of them & bring them into thy Kingdom we also Seal upon the[e] all the Power & blessing of the Holy reserection, Even to the Eternal Godhead & no blessing that thy heart can conceive will be withheld from you—& in the Name of the Father & of the Son & of the Holy Spirit Amen—
He then anointed sister Vilate Kimble a Queen & Priestess unto her Husband (H. C. Kimble) in the Church of Jesus Christ of Latter Days Saints & in Iseral. & pronounced all the blessings upon her head in common with her husband.
      /s/ John D Lee

Three days later the second entry continued:

Sunday Jan 11*th* 1846. 31 minutes to 7 P.M. Assembled in Pres. Brigham Youngs Room No. 1. in the atic Story of the Lords House. Pres. B. Young Heber C. Kimble, Orson Hyde, P P Pratt, Orson Pratt, Williard Richards John Taylor Amasa Lyman N. K. Whitney Geo. Miller Edmund—Ellsworth, Maray Young Vilate Kimble Leonora Taylor Elizabeth an Whitney & Elizabeth Ellsworth. Br J. Taylor started the Hymn This Earth was once a garden place all being clothed in Priestly garments [robes]—Pres. B. Young Prayed all having nealed [knelt] a round the Alter—previous to Prare [prayer] they all arose—Sang a Hymn & offered up the Signs of the Holy Priesthood—Then Br Heber C. Kimbal proceeded to anoint and consecrate Pres. Brigham Young a King & a Priest unto the most high god—over the Church of Jesus Christ of Latter Day Saints & over the whole House of Iseral—

      Brother Brigham Young, I pour this holy, consecrated oil, upon your head, and anoint thee a King and a Priest of the Most High God over the Church of Jesus Christ of Latter Day Saints, and unto all Israel: and I anoint thy head, that thy brain may be healthy and active and quick to think and to understand and to direct thy whole body and I anoint thy eyes that they may see and perceive, and that thou mayest not be deceived in what thou beholdest, and that thy sight may never fail thee: and I anoint thy ears that they may be quick to hear and communicate to thy understanding; and that thou mayest hear the secret deliberations of thy enemies, and thereby thou shalt be enabled to overreach their designs: and I anoint thy nose that thou may scent, and relish the fragarence of the good things of the earth: and I anoint thy mouth that thou mayest be enabled to speak the great things of God, and confound all the wisdom of man, and put to nought all who shall raise up to oppose thee, in all countries where thou goest for thou shalt build up the Kingdom of God among many people, and in the midst of mighty nations: so thy glory shall be established, and whosoever thou shalt bind on earth, shall be bound in heaven, and whomsoever thou shalt loose on earth, shall be loosed in heaven; for there shall be given unto thee crowns, and kingdoms, and dominions; and thou shalt receive all thy heart shall desire; and thy soul shall be satisfied with a multitude of blessings which thou shalt receive; for princes shall bow at thy feet and deliver unto thee their treasures; and thou shalt teach them the principles of salvation. And I seal thee up unto Eternal Life, that thou shalt come forth in the morn of the first resurrection, and receive all these blessings, in their fulness. And thou shalt attain unto [the] Eternal Godhead, and receive a fulness of joy, and glory, and power; and that thou mayest do all things whatsoever is wisdom that thou shouldest do, even if it be to create worlds and redeem them: so shall thy joy be full to the praise and glory of God: Amen.

Elder Heber Chase Kimble then anointed Mary An Young, a Queen & Priestes unto her husband (Brigham Young) in the Church of Jesus Christ of Latter Days Saints & in the house of Iseral—

Sister Mary Ann Young, I pour upon thy head this holy, consecrated oil, and seal upon thee all the blessings of the everlasting priesthood, in conjunction with thy husband: and I anoint thee to be a Queen and Priestess unto thy husband, over the Church of Jesus Christ of Latter Day Saints; and thou shalt be heir to all the blessings which are sealed upon him, inasmuch as thou dost obey his counsel; and thou shalt receive glory, honor, power and exaltation in his exaltation: and thou shalt be a strength in thy mind for thou shalt have visions, and manifestations of the Holy Spirit, and the time shall come that Angels shall visit thee, and minister unto thee, and teach thee: and in abscence of thy husband shall comfort thee, and make known his situation.

Thou shalt be a wise counsellor to many of thy sex, and they shall look unto thee for precept and or example.

Thou shalt be noted and honored for thy generosity, and the freedom and good feelings with which thou shalt relieve the wants of the distressed; and the disgression [discretion] with which thou shalt act in thy sphere in all things. And I seal thee up unto Eternal Life, thou shalt come forth in the morning of the first resurrection and inherit with him all the honors, glories, and power of Eternal Lives, and that thou shalt attain unto the eternal Godhead, so thy exaltation shall be perfect, and thy glory be full, in a fulness of power and exaltation.

And the glory, honor and power shall be ascribed unto the Father, Son, and Holy Ghost: Amen.[37]

Within the next few weeks, other leading brethren and their wives received their second anointing, and church leaders began performing adoption sealings tying men of lower priesthood rank to men of higher priesthood rank, as well as children to parents. When the temple was closed on 7 February 1846, over 2,000 couples had been sealed for time and eternity, and just under 600 men and women had received the fullness of the priesthood through their second anointing. In addition to Young, at least nineteen other men were authorized to perform second anointings.[38] On a typical day, six to

---

37. "Book of Anointings," ca. 1845-46, 2-6, LDS archives. The "Book of Anointings" lists all recipients of the second anointing in the Nauvoo temple, including texts of several of the personal blessings received with the anointings. Kimball and his wife Vilate originally received the second anointing on 20 January 1844, and the second part of the fulness of the priesthood ceremony on 1 April 1844. Based on the discussion earlier, it is possible that Kimball's ordination to the "Eternal Godhead" reflected an elite modification for this early Mormon leader's second anointing, which normally anointed a recipient to godhood; Brigham Young was blessed by Kimball to "attain unto [the] Eternal Godhead," as was Young's wife Mary Ann. It is noteworthy that one week prior to the commencement of second anointings in the Nauvoo temple, Clayton recorded a "temple wedding" between William G. Young and Adelia C. Clark wherein Brigham Young "pronounced them Husband & Wife, and sealed them together as such for time and for all eternity, and also sealed them up to eternal life, against all sins, except the sin of the Holy Ghost, which is the shedding of innocent blood, and pronounced various blessings upon them" (1 Jan. 1846, in Smith, *An Intimate Chronicle*, 247; the Book of Anointings contains no record of a second anointing for William G. Young and Adelia C. Clark).

38. Those listed in the "Book of Anointings" included Ezra T. Benson, Zebedee Coltrin, Winslow Farr, William Huntington, Orson Hyde, Aaron Johnson, Heber C. Kimball, Amasa M. Lyman, George Miller, Isaac Morley, William W. Phelps, Orson Pratt,

twelve couples received this ordinance. A few women were sealed to their current husband for time but as a queen to a deceased man (usually Joseph Smith) for eternity. Several polygamous second anointing sealings were also performed.

These brief weeks in Nauvoo and its temple reflect a unique emphasis on second anointings. Although the endowment was sporadically administered after the Saints trekked westward and until another edifice was dedicated for its consummation, no available records or diaries indicate that the higher ordinance of the fullness of priesthood was given for over two decades.

Despite injunctions for secrecy, accounts soon began to circulate about the temple rituals. During the 28 December 1845 meeting of the Quorum of the Anointed, Kimball had, according to Clayton, "alluded to the stories in circulation that several persons had been killed on their way through the ordinances, and that men and women were stripped naked here. Joseph said that for men and women to hold their tongues, was their salvaton."[39] An example of such a lurid contemporary account can be found in the *Warsaw Signal*, edited by rabid Mormon critic Thomas Sharp, for 18 February 1846:

> The Saints have endeavored to keep the ceremony of the endowment perfectly quiet; but some of them have let the cat out of the bag and disclosed all. We have the story from two different sources, and as both correspond, we give it credit, although persons abroad, not acquainted with Mormonism, will be loath to believe that so much depravity as is evinced in the invention of this ceremony can exist, and that men and women can be found who consider the obscene rites sacred.
>
> There must always be two candidates, a male and female presented for the endowment at once. These must pay one dollar each as a fee. If a male cannot find a female to take the endowment with him, the heads of the church provide one, and *vice versa*. The candidates are first taken into a room together, where they are stripped of all their clothing and are made to wash each other from head to foot. They are then separated and put into different rooms, where they are oiled—with

Parley P. Pratt, Charles C. Rich, William Smith, William Snow, Daniel Spencer, Orson Spencer, John Taylor, and Brigham Young.

39. Smith, *An Intimate Chronicle*, 240.

perfumed sweet oil, by one of the functionaries of the church. They then pass into another room still separate, where one of the Twelve pronounces a blessing upon them and gives them extensive powers and privileges—such as a plurality of wives to the male, and other similar blessings to the female. The ceremony being ended, the candidates are brought together, still in a state of nudity, into a room where they are allowed to remain together, alone, as long as they see proper. They are then invested with their robes and take their departure.

The really deluded among the Saints consider this ceremony as sacred and intended as a trial of their virtue. But it was invented by the Twelve, evidently for the purpose of offering them an opportunity for gratifying their brutal lusts.

A woman who had been through the temple herself but had since left the Mormons wrote to correct this distorted account. Her letter was published in the 15 April 1846 number of the *Warsaw Signal*. Although her personal response to the temple and an unrelated polygamous proposition were negative, her description in large part fits with the more sympathetic accounts provided by Clayton's record and adds some intriguing details. Writes "Emeline":

I discover by your paper, in what you have published in regard to the Mormon endowments, given of late in the temple, that you have been wrongly informed at least, so far as actual experience has taught me [what transpires] in the orgies of an afternoon, in that (as I have been taught to believe) most holy building. In revealing what I am about to do, I have no lashing of conscience; notwithstanding I took upon myself, during the laughable farce, several oaths and obligations of a serious character, not to reveal the secrets of the priesthood—had they been given me by any thing other than assumed authority, and vile, corrupt, licentious libertines, taking upon themselves the livery of Heaven, and essaying to represent the characters of our God and Savior—knowing those characters as I did previously to be the most debased wretches upon earth, the whole farce appeared to me to be nothing less than fearful blasphemy.

I went into this pretended holy operation, in company with 14 others, all sisters in the Mormon church, and with most of whom I was well acquainted. They were, in the main, women of good character, and appeared sincere in their respective devotions. We were first received past the Guard into a private room on the north side of the Temple—this was the room of preparation or purif[i]cation.—We were divested of all our apparel, and in a state of perfect nudity we were washed from head to foot,—a blanket was then thrown about our persons, and then commencing at the head we were anointed from head to foot with sweet oil scented (I think) with lavender. We were then clothed in a white robe. All this was done by sisters in the church—none others were present—it is false to say that men and women are admitted together in an indecent manner. We were then conducted into a room called the Garden of Eden; here we found several of our brethren robed in white also, and apparently in a soperfic state. We were presented before them and a voice from the Lord awoke them from sleep. After a considerable ceremony, which I do not recollect much of, we were left by the Lord and soon a very dandy-like fellow appeared with a black cap on, that had a long veil attached to it; he appeared very familiar—and by his very insinuating and friendly manner induced some of our sisters eat of the "forbidden fruit." Soon after the voice of the Lord appeared again in the garden; we all appeared frightened, and both men and women huddled together into the corner of the room, as if in the act of hiding. The fellow in the black cap presents himself before the Lord and engages in a controversy, boasting of what he had done. The Lord pronounced a curse upon him—he gets down upon his belly and crawls off. At this period of the holy ceremony, I could not suppress my visible passions; for this fellow acted his part well—undoubtedly his part being the part of a Devil—was the most natural. We were then presented with aprons, which we put on about this time, a sword was shook at us through the partition of the room, which was to guard the Tree of Life. After considerable ceremony, which I do not recollect, we were passed into another room, which was dark and was dreary. This was called the Terrestrial Kingdom; immediately the dandy in the black cap made his appearance; at first he appeared very sly—peeping about, and when he found the Lord was not present, he became very familiar and persuasive. Said he, "here we are, all together, and all good fellows well met. Come Methodists, come Presbyterians, come Baptists, come Quakers, come Mormons, and come Strangites, &c. &c. Come let us drink together." In this way he tempted us, and we partook with him. After a considerable parade and ceremony, we passed into another room, or Celestial Kingdom. Here I saw some of the Twelve, and particularly Brigham Young, with a white crown upon his head, and so I have since been told, representing God himself. We passed this room without much ceremony into another. I have forgotten what it represented, not much of interest transpired here, & we were conducted back and put in possession of our clothing—all save sister ——; she had a very fine alopacca dress stolen during our absence, and has never been able to recover it.

In the different apartments of this singular farce, we took upon ourselves oaths and obligations not to reveal the secrets of the priesthood. I do not consider them binding; as I have had ample and repeated opportunity to prove the administrators of these obligations are corrupt as the Devil in Hell. In one place I was presented with a new name, which I was not to reveal to any living creature, save the man to whom I should be sealed for eternity. By this name I am to be called in eternity, as after the resurrection. This name was ——; and from all that I can gather, all the females had the same name given them, but we were not allowed to reveal it to each other, under no less penalty than to have our throats cut from ear to ear, our hearts torn out, &c., &c. I have forgotten a part of the penalties. In one place something was spoken to me which I do not recollect—the meaning was "marrow in the bone;" the token was a firm hold of the hand, pressing the finger nail firmly into the wrist of the right hand. I have since been told by a brother, that there was a mystical meaning in this, that will hereafter be revealed to me.

Now, sir, this is the substance of the Mormon endowment—and the Mormon who says it is not true, is a liar, and the truth is not in him! I have been a member of this farce of Priestcraft for the last six years; the first four years I suspected nothing but what I was in the right of all holy things. The last two years I have been doubtful, seeing the abandoned conduct of the priests; but I toiled on, expecting something would be revealed in the endowments of the Temple that would strengthen my faith, and qualify me for heavenly purposes. For this I have toiled by night and by day; for this I have worked my fingers to the quick, to gain something from my scanty allowance, to assist in the completion of that building, the motto of which was to be "HOLINESS TO THE LORD" and illumined by the Shekina of heaven. Imagine then my disappointment in the blasphemous farce I saw acted before me, and by men who have at repeated trials, attempted to seduce me into the lowest degradation and ruin. But, thanks to my Heavenly Protector! I have been enabled to withstand the shock, and hope and trust I shall outlive the disgrace of once being associated with such a set of heartless scoundrels. I hope, sir, for the good of community, you will give my "revelation" a place in your columns, for in the presence of high heaven, I pronounce every word of it truth, and nothing but truth.

Other exposés followed, some more reliable than others, but by this time the majority of Saints had departed Nauvoo and environs for the exodus to the Rocky Mountains.

CHAPTER 5

Developments in
Nineteenth-century Utah

Following the exodus of Mormons from Nauvoo in 1846, the endowment entered a period of dormancy. Aside from a few prayer circles held on the open prairies during the trek west, Mormons did very little temple work immediately following their resettlement. One known exception occurred on Ensign Peak in the Salt Lake Valley on 21 July 1849. Addison Pratt had been on a mission when the endowment was initiated in Nauvoo. Thus, according to Brigham Young's account: "Addison Pratt received his endowments on Ensign Hill on the 21st, the place being consecrated for the purpose." Afterwards, Pratt was among those called at October 1849 general conference on a mission to the Society Islands in the South Pacific.[1]

The explanation for this hiatus is unknown. On 7 July 1852 it was recommended that endowment ordinances be performed in the "Old Council House," the first permanent public building erected in Salt

---

1. "Manuscript History of Brigham Young," 4:107, archives, historical department, Church of Jesus Christ of Latter-day Saints, Salt Lake City, Utah (hereafter LDS archives); see also B. H. Roberts, *A Comprehensive History of The Church of Jesus Christ of Latter-day Saints*, 6 vols. (Provo, UT: Brigham Young University Press, 1965), 3:386-87; hereafter CHC. Also Elden Jay Watson, ed., *Manuscript History of Brigham Young, 1846-1847* (Salt Lake City: Elden J. Watson, 1971), 556; William Clayton, *William Clayton's Journal*, ed. Clayton Family Association (Salt Lake City: Deseret News, 1921), 202-203; D. Michael Quinn, "Latter-day Saint Prayer Circles," *Brigham Young University Studies* 19 (Fall 1978): 79-105.

Lake City. The building was used by the territorial legislature and territorial public library. No action was taken on the proposal.

On 6 April 1853, at the laying of the cornerstone of the Salt Lake temple, Brigham Young looked back to Kirtland and Nauvoo and forward to a House of the Lord in Utah:

> And those first Elders who helped to build it [the Kirtland temple], received a portion of their first endowments, or we might say more clearly, some of the first, or introductory, or initiatory ordinances, preparatory to an endowment.
>
> The preparatory ordinances there administered, though accompanied by the ministration of angels, and the presence of the Lord Jesus, were but a faint similitude of the ordinances of the House of the Lord in their fulness; yet many, through the instigation of the devil, thought they had received all, and knew as much as God; they have apostatized, and gone to hell. But be assured, brethren, there are but few, *very few* of the Elders of Israel, now on earth, who know the *meaning* of the word *endowment.* To know, they must experience; and to experience, a Temple must be built.
>
> Let me give you the definition in brief. Your *endowment* is, to receive all those ordinances in the House of the Lord, which are necessary for you, after you have departed this life, to enable you to walk back to the presence of the Father, passing the angels who stand as sentinels, being enabled to give them the key words, the endowment, pertaining to the Holy Priesthood, and gain your eternal exaltation in spite of earth and hell.[2]

A new building called the Endowment House was dedicated for baptisms for the dead, marriage sealings, and endowments on 5 May 1855. Located in the northwest corner of Temple Square, a total of 54,170 endowments and 694 second anointings were conducted there until 16 October 1884. No such ordinances were administered for the dead.[3] When later church leaders decided to refocus attention and

---

2. *Journal of Discourses,* 26 vols. (Liverpool, Eng.: Latter-day Saints' Bookseller's Depot, 1854-86), 2:31 (emphasis in original); see also 2:315; 5:133; 6:63, 154-55; 8:339; 9:25-26, 91; 10:172; 11:27; 18:132; 19:250 (hereafter JD).

3. Laureen R. Jaussi and Gloria D. Chaston, comps., *Register of LDS Church Records* (Salt Lake City: Deseret Book Co., 1968), 366-67, cited in James Dwight Tingen, "The Endowment House: 1855-1889," Dec. 1974, privately circulated. Also Richard Cowan, *Temple Building—Ancient and Modern* (Provo, UT: Brigham Young University

funds upon completion of the temple, they ordered the Endowment House razed. Young too felt it was necessary to restrict sealing, endowment, and second anointing ceremonies to Utah temples, believing that to do otherwise "would destroy the object of the gathering."[4] The Nauvoo temple had since burned and Young announced in 1858 that the Kirtland temple had been "disowned by the Father and the Son."[5]

A year after the Endowment House opened, First Presidency counselor Heber C. Kimball gave the following advice to bishops about who could be admitted to receive their endowment:

> [The] men and women whom you recommend, must be individuals, who pay their tithing from year to year; who pray in their families, and do not speak against the authorities of the Church and Kingdom of God; nor steal; nor lie; nor interfere with their neighbors things; nor their neighbors wives or husbands; who attend strictly to meetings and prayer meetings, and those who pay due respect to their presiding officers, and Bishops and those who do not swear.
>
> We shall expect you to Pickup the old and infirm; the lame and blind and the righteous poor, but not the devils poor.
>
> We would like to see many of the young and sprightly young persons who are strict to obey their parents.
>
> We shall require the Bishops to send their names in a letter fully recommended and tell them to qualify themselves by washing their bodies in pure water and bringing Temple clothing and oil for their anointings. As they live in the country, we want them to bring their eggs, butter, meat, bread and flour, and the luxuries of [the farm] fit to grace the tables of the House of the Lord, to feed the men and women who administer unto them; and if there should be any left, that we may give it to the poor; and in so doing God will bless you and we will bless you. This by order of the First Presidency.[6]

A letter from the First Presidency written the same spring to bishops in Iron and Washington counties similarly advised that

---

Press, 1971), 29.

4. Scott Kenney, ed., *Wilford Woodruff's Journal*, 9 vols. (Midvale, UT: Signature Books, 1984), 6 (26 Dec. 1866): 307-308.

5. JD 2:32.

6. Heber C. Kimball to Bishop Evans, 19 May 1856, LDS archives.

the person who can get their endowments must be those who pray, who pay their tithing from year to year; who live the lives of saints from day to day; setting good exampels before their neighbors. Men and women, boys and girls over 16 years of age who are living the lives of saints, believe in the plurality [polygamy], do not speak evil of the authorities of the Church, and possess true integrity towards their friends, can come up after their spring crops are sown, and their case shall be attended to.

A postscript to the letter asked bishops to "send us word 10 days before you send your company that we may have the rooms vacant for them."[7]

In the mid-1860s Brigham Young added the following advice: "[W]hen Persons Came to get their Endowments [they] Should be Clean & pure. A man should not touch a woman for 10 days before getting their Endowments. And the Twelve while traveling should hold meetings with the male members as priesthood meetings & teach these [things] but they have to [be] handled in wisdom or Evil will grow out of it."[8] Young and others reiterated similar advice at a meeting in Salt Lake City two years later: "spoke on the impropriety of the youth of Zion marrying instead of getting sealed. He also spoke of cleanliness of person, before going to get their endowments; a woman should not go for a week after her menses were upon her, a man should not have intercourse with his wife for several days, but should be clean in body and exercised in spirit previous thereto; his clothing should be changed once or twice before going there."[9]

Although the endowment was thus resumed during the mid-1850s, another decade would pass before second anointings were continued. The reason is unknown. Unquestionably the subject continued to be discussed. On 26 November 1857, for example, Wilford Woodruff recorded in his diary that "in company with G. A. Smith I called upon President Brigham Young and asked Council about publishing the Endowments or an outline of it telling the time when the

---

7. Parowan Historical Record, 13, 16 Mar. 1856, LDS archives.

8. Kenney, 7 (26 Dec. 1866): 308.

9. Journal History, 31 Jan. 1868, LDS archives; also "Manuscript History of Brigham Young" for 1868, 131.

Twelve Received their 2d Anointing & also the organization of the Council of 50. He gave his Concent for us to publish an account of it so that the Saints might understand it."[10] Apparently this proposal never appeared in print. A few weeks later on 18 December as he worked to update the official history of the church, George A. Smith made a few relevant procedural comments noting "that Joseph taught that but one King & Priest could be anointed at one meeting in a private Room Dedicated by permission to Anoint in. But one person Could be anointed in a day but in the Temple several could be anointed in a day. But at each anointing the meeting was dismissed and then Came together." In Young's view, "When the Temple is finished & a place duly prepared we should not be confined to any particular Number in sealing and anointing."[11]

It is not clear whether Young initially intended to await completion of a temple before reinstating second anointings. Whatever the factors in his timetable, a decision clearly had been made by early January 1867 (ten years before the St. George temple was dedicated) to resume the highest ordinance. On 26 December 1866 Young met in council with the First Presidency and Quorum of the Twelve to clarify several procedural issues prior to recommencing the ordinance a week later. Woodruff's diary reports the meeting:

> Presidet Young said that the order of the 2d anointing was for the persons to be anointed to be cloathed in their Priestly robes the man upon the right hand and wife or wifes upon the left hand. The Administrator may be dressed in his usual Clothing or in his Priestly Robes as he may see fit. The meeting Should be opened by Prayer then the Administrator should Anoint the man A King & Priest unto the Most High God. Then he should Anoint his wife or wives Queens & Priestess unto her husband.[12]

Young indicated that "There should be but one man anointed at any one meeting. If more than one man is anointed in a day, They should Come together and open by Prayer as though their had not been any

---

10. Kenney, 5 (26 Nov. 1857): 124.

11. Ibid., 5 (18 Dec. 1857): 139.

12. Ibid., 6 (26 Dec. 1866): 307.

meeting before and thus Continue to the End."[13] Woodruff's journal continues:

> President Young said when a woman was Anointed a Queen to a good man and he died & the woman was sealed to another man for time it was not necessary for her to be anointed a Queen again but if she was Anointed a Queen to a man who was not worthy of a wife & she is sealed to another man she should be anointed a Queen unto him. When a good man dies & his wives have not been anointed Queens unto him they may be anointed Queens to him after his death without any Proxey.[14]

This last comment suggests that the second anointing was, at least during Young's administration, the only vicarious ordinance wherein a living proxy was not required.

The next day the First Presidency and most of the Twelve consecrated olive oil for second anointings. On 31 December 1866 Daniel H. Wells and his four wives received their second anointing from Young who had perfumed the consecrated oil for this ordinance. As Woodruff recorded, "The brethren rejoiced at the commencement again of the administration of these ordinances which had not been administered since they were in the Temple at Nauvoo."[15]

This marked the beginning of a new momentum in conferring the fullness of the priesthood. George Q. Cannon and his three wives received their second anointing the next day, 1 January 1867; Joseph A. Young on the second; Brigham Young, Jr., on the third; Joseph F. Smith and two wives on the fourth; and others from January through June 1867.[16]

---

13. Ibid.

14. Ibid.; a decade later Brigham Young repeated these instructions to Wilford Woodruff (ibid., 7 [15 Jan. 1877]: 322).

15. Ibid., 6 (30-31 Dec. 1866): 309-10; compare Elijah Larkin Journal, 31 Dec. 1866, Special Collections, Harold B. Lee Library, Brigham Young University, Provo, Utah.

16. The cited names are found in Wilford Woodruff's journal, 31 Dec. 1866, 1-4 Jan. 1867 (6:310-17). In addition to Woodruff's entries for 1867, other private journals and diaries of this period record the administration of second anointings. These include Elijah Larkin journal (31 Dec. 1866), Thomas Evans Jeremy journal (30 Apr. 1867), Jesse N. Smith journal (3 June 1867), John Lyman Smith diary (30 July 1867), L. John Nuttall journal (23 Sept. 1867), Lorenzo Brown diary (2 Oct. 1867), Sylvester H. Earl diary

Young's view on the number of people to receive the second anointing on a single day changed slightly during the initial week, for on 2 January 1867, "It was decided by Presidet Young that we dress & offer up the signs of the Holy Priesthood before we give the 2d anointing & ownly Anoint one man & his wives in one day at one place."[17] Eight weeks later, on 26 February, Young again reversed himself: "we should not anoint ownly one man & his family at one meeting. If any other women are to be anointed to another man it must be at a separate meeting. There may [be] two meetings in a day at one place."[18] A decade later, while standardizing the endowment in written form in 1877, Young reiterated to Woodruff that "their was No Necessity of dressing in the Temple Clothing while giving the second Anointing any more than in administering [the] first Anointing or Ordaining."[19]

One of those to receive her second anointing in the Endowment House was Fanny Stenhouse, who described her experience with her husband and a second wife in 1874 in *Tell It All: The Tyranny of Mormonism, or an Englishwoman in Utah*:

> Not long after this, my husband one day told me that a select few had been chosen to receive their Second Endowments, and that we were to be honoured with the same privilege. This I was told was one of the highest honours that could be conferred upon us, as the Second Endowments had never been given to any one since the Mormons left Nauvoo. . . .
>
> After preparing our Temple robes, we started for the Endowment House. . . . When we reached the Endowment House, we ladies were shown into one room and *our* husband into another. We then proceeded to array ourselves in our robes, caps, and aprons—the same as

---

(1867), John Lyman Smith diary (23 Oct. 1868), Henry Eyring journal (24 Feb. 1877), J. D. T. McAllister journal (10 Apr. 1877), Samuel H. Rogers journal (1 Feb. 1878), Oliver B. Huntington journal (12 Jan. 1881), Samuel Bateman diary (30 Nov. 1887), and Thomas Memmott journal (13 Dec. 1889 and 13 Feb. 1890); all of these are either at the Lee Library or LDS archives. An important published account of the second anointing is Mrs. T. B. H. (Fanny) Stenhouse, *An Englishwoman in Utah: The Story of a Life's Experience in Mormonism* (London: Sampson Low, Marston, Searle, & Rivington, 1880), 320-21.

17. Kenney, 6 (2 Jan. 1867): 316.

18. Ibid., 6 (26 Feb. 1867): 328.

19. Ibid., 7 (15 Jan. 1877): 322.

when we received our first Endowments—and when all was ready we were ushered into another room by one of the brethren, who was also dressed in his Temple robes. There we met *our* husband and several other brethren, all dressed in the same way. We sat down, and oil was then poured upon the head of *our* husband by two of the brethren— Daniel H. Wells and another—and he was then ordained a King and Priest to all eternity. After that, we two wives were anointed in like manner, and ordained Queens and Priestesses, to reign and rule with *our* husband over his kingdom in the celestial world.[20]

Samuel Hollister Rogers described in his journal the private ceremony between husband and wife which followed the Endowment House ritual: "Monday 22 September 1879 the eavening of the fifty second anniversary of the Angel delivering of the Plates of the Book of Mormon to Joseph Smith the Prophet of the Lord, I dedicated the house and room also blest the Oil after which my Ruth Anointed my feet and wiped them with the hair of her head, then kissed then [them] after the pattern as written in the Testament of the Lord Jesus Christ."[21]

Oliver Huntington, writing in 1883, captured the impact of the second anointing in the daily life of the Saints:

As I went to the neighbor[']s well for water, he asked me if I turned the water from the night previous. I said, "I guessed that I did," and without explanation where upon he kicked me in great wrath. Then I explained to him that as he only had a small stream to make mortar, as he was building a house and water through the night, and got permission. I had right to it and he had no right in the night.

He said that made no difference, and that I must never come on his lot again. That was the end of our neighborly acts and sociability. I sought no revenge but left him in the hands of God, and when at prayer that evening I told the Lord that his annointed one had been violated[,] that an enemy, without a cause, had committed violence upon xxx my body and I asked him to avenge me of my enemy.[22]

In 1873, as the St. George temple neared completion, Young had

---

20. Fanny Stenhouse, *Tell It All: The Tyranny of Mormonism, or an Englishwoman in Utah* (Hartford, CT: A. D. Worthington and Co., 1890), 320-21.

21. Journal of Samuel Hollister Rogers, 2:78, Special Collections, Lee Library.

22. Oliver B. Huntington Journal, 10 Sept. 1883, Special Collections, Lee Library.

summarized his understanding of which rituals could be performed in the Endowment House and which required completion of a temple:

> There are many of the ordinances of the house of God that must be performed in a Temple that is erected expressly for the purpose. There are other ordinances that we can administer without a Temple. . . . We can, at the present time, go into the Endowment House and be baptized for the dead, receive our washings and anointing, etc., for there we have a font that has been erected, dedicated expressly for baptizing people for the remission of sins, for their health and for their dead friends; in this the Saints have the privilege of being baptized for their friends. We also have the privilege of sealing women to men, without a Temple. This we can do in the Endowment House; but when we come to other sealing ordinances, ordinances pertaining to the holy Priesthood, to connect the chain of the Priesthood from father Adam until now, by sealing children to their parents, being sealed for our forefathers, etc., they cannot be done without a Temple. But we can seal women to men, but not men to men, without a Temple. When the ordinances are carried out in the Temples that will be erected, men will be sealed to their fathers, and those who have slept clear up to father Adam. This will have to be done, because of the chain of the Priesthood being broken upon the earth. The Priesthood has left the people, but in the first place the people left the Priesthood.[23]

The Endowment House was closed down in late 1876. Henry W. Bigler wrote in his diary, "President Young said, 'If the people wish to receive their endowments and sealings they must go to Saint George and receive them in a Temple.'"[24] However, after Young's death in August 1877, the Quorum of the Twelve, led by John Taylor, would vote to reopen it. On 15 November 1877 Taylor sent a letter to stake presidents explaining what cases justified use of the Endowment House rather than the temple. These included being sealed for time but not eternity as well as sealings or personal endowments for those who could not travel to southern Utah because of age or health.[25]

The lower portion of the St. George temple was dedicated on 1

---

23. JD 16:186.

24. "Journal of Henry W. Bigler," *Utah Historical Quarterly* 4:143.

25. John Taylor to All Stake Presidents, 15 Nov. 1877, LDS archives.

January 1877. Brigham Young was ill and had to be carried into the meeting, where he made the following remarks:

> I cannot consent in my feelings to retire from this house without exercising my strength, the strength of my lungs, stomach and speaking organs, in speaking to this people. I hardly dare say what is in my heart to say to this people. Perhaps it would not be prudent, but I will say a few encouraging things to the Latter Day Saints, that is they ought to be encouraging. We that are here are enjoying a privilege that we have no knowledge of any other people enjoying since the days of Adam. that is, to have a Temple completed, wherein all the ordinances of the House of God, can be bestowed upon His people. Brethren and Sisters, do you understand this! it seems that a great many of the people knew nothing about it. It is true that Solomon built a Temple for the purpose of giving Endowments, but from what we can learn of the history of that time, they gave very few, if any Endowments, and one of the High Priests was murdered by wicked and corrupt men, who had already begun to Apostatize, because he would not reveal those things Appertaining to the Priesthood, that were forbidden him to reveal until he came to the proper place. I will not say, but what Enoch had Temples and officiated therein, but we have no account of it. We knew that he raised up a people so pure and holy that they were not permitted to remain with the wicked inhabitants of the earth, but were taken to another place. We as Latter Day Saints have been laboring for over forty years, and the revelations given us in the first, were to establish the Kingdom, by gathering the Saints, building Temples, and organizing the people as the family of heaven here on the earth, We reared up a Temple in Kirtland, but we had no basement in it, nor a font, nor preparation to give Endowments for the living or the dead. It was left by the saints before it was completed, they going to Missouri; Joseph located the site for the Temple Block, in Jackson County Missouri, and pointed out the southeast corner of the Temple in the year 1831. also laid the corner stone for a Temple in Far West, Caldwell County, Missouri. These Temples were not built. We built one in Nauvoo, I could pick out several [people] before me now, that were there when it was built, and knew just how much was finished and what was done. It is true we left brethren there with instructions to finish it, and they got it nearly completed before it was burned, but the Saints did not enjoy it. Now we have a Temple which will be finished in a few days, and of which there is enough completed to commence work therein, which has not been done since the days of Adam, that we have any knowledge of. Now those that can see the Spiritual Atmosphere, can

see that many of the Saints are still glued to this earth, and lusting and longing after the things of this world, in which there is no profit. It is true we should look after the things of this world and devote all to the building up of the Kingdom of God. According to the present feelings of many of our brethren, they would arrogate to them-selves this world and all that pertains to it, and cease not day nor night to see that it was devoted to the building up of the Kingdom of the devil. and if they had the power, they would build a rail-road to carry it to Hell and establish themselves there! Where are the eyes and hearts of this people? Where is their interest in their own Salvation and that of their fore-fathers? We enjoy privileges that are enjoyed by no one else on the face of the earth. suppose we were awake to this thing, namely the salvation of the human family, this house would be crowded—as we hope it will be—from Monday Morning until Saturday night. This house was built here in this place purposely, where it is warm and pleasant in the winter time, and comfortable to work, also for the Lamanites and all those coming from the South and other places to receive their Endowments and other blessings. What do you suppose the fathers would say if they could speak from the dead! Would they not say, "We have lain here thousands of Years, here in this prison house, waiting for this dispen-sation to come. Here we are bound and fettered in the Association of those who are filthy." What would they whisper in our ears? Why! if they had the power the very thunders of heaven would be in our ears, if we could but realize the importance of the work we are engaged in. All the Angels of heaven are looking at this little handful of people, and stimulating them to the Salvation of the human family, so also are the devils in hell looking at this people too. and trying to overthrow us, and the people are still shaking hands with the servants of the devil. Instead of sanctifying themselves and calling upon the Lord and doing the work which he has commanded us, and put into our hands to do. When I think upon this subject, I want the tongues of Seven thunders to wake up the people. Can the fathers be saved without us? No. Can we be saved without them? No. and if we do not wake up and cease to long after the things of this earth, we will find that we as individuals will go down to hell, although the Lord will preserve a people unto Himself.

Now we are ready to give Endowments. Do you have any feelings for those who have died without having the Gospel? The Spirit was awakened in the people in the North. When we gave the word that we should do no more work in the Endowment House, they came to us crying and pleading to be baptized for their dead. What else could they do? They can come here and do the work for their dead. and put these poor prisoners on the ground where they will be free. Do we realize this? As long as we tarry here, we are subject to the world. But now go to, like men and women, and say, we will embrace the truth and enter into the covenants of God, and carry them out. Then the bonds are broken and the hearts of the people are united in the Father. Perhaps, brethren and sisters, you will not get my meaning, but now go to work and let these holes in the ground alone, and let the Gentiles alone, who would destroy us if they had the power. You are running after them, and some of our brethren are putting their wives and daughters into their society, and will go to the devil with them too, if they do not look out. I would not have a dollar on the earth if I had to get it there. It has been the Kingdom of God with me. What I have, I have got in this Kingdom. Well, now, some of the Elders are running after these holes in the ground, and I see men before me in this house, that have no right to be here, they are as corrupt in their hearts as they can be, and we take them by the hand and call them brother. You will go to hell [if you do not ?] repent. You may think this is plain talk, it is not as plain as you will find by and by. If you should ever go to the Gates of heaven, Jesus will say he never knew you, while you have been saying your prayers and going to your Meetings and are as corrupt in your hearts as men can be. You had better stop now and repent of your sins, and sin no more while there is yet time. and before the doors are Closed against you. I want to wake you up, and if I had the power to lift the Vail from your eyes, and let you see things as they are, you would be astonished. Not but what there are a great majority of the people as good as they know how to be. Now I will say, bless the people, that they may do better, but show some of the Elders of Israel according to their present conduct, a dollar on one side, and Eternal life on the other, and I fear they would choose the dollar.[26]

The first recorded endowments for the dead were performed in St. George on 11 January 1877, according to temple president David H. Cannon.[27] Shortly thereafter Wilford Woodruff, the new temple president, received a revelation about endowments and sealings for his dead, which he recorded in his journal:

Let my servant Wilford Call upon the virgins Maidens, Daughters, &

26. "St. George Temple. Account of Building and Dedication 1873-1877," LDS archives.

27. George Q. Cannon to George F. Richards, 18 July 1922, LDS archives.

Mothers in Zion and let them Enter into my /Holy/ Temple on the 1 day of March the day that my servant Wilford has seen the time alloted to man, Three score years and Ten, and there let them receive their washing and Anointing and Endowments for and behalf of the wives who are dead and have been sealed to my servant Wilford, or those who are to be Sealed to him, and this shall be acceptable unto me Saith the Lord, and the dead of my servant shall be redeemed in the spirit world and be prepared to meet my servant at the time of his Coming which shall be at the time appointed unto him, though not revealed to man in the flesh. Now go to and perform this work and all shall be accomplished according to the desire of your heart.[28]

Accordingly on 1 March 1877 Woodruff spent his seventieth birthday in the St. George temple with 154 women performing proxy endowments for deceased women who had been or were being sealed to Woodruff:

I arived at the Temple of the Lord in Saint George Washington County, Utah, at 8 oclok in the Morning. I was there Surrounded with one hundred and fifty four virgins, Maidens Daughters and Mothers in Zion from the age of fourteen to the Aged Mother leaning upon her Staff. . . . When they had all assembled to gether in the Creation Room I presented myself before them Clothed in my white Doe skin Temple dress. I there delivered unto them a short address. . . . You are to day in this Endowment without a man with you. But we shall furnish one Man as an Adam. . . . I went through the Endowments of the day more like being in vision than a reality. These *154* Sisters were led to three veils and three of us . . . all dressed in Temple Clothing[,] took them all through the three veils. . . . Presidet Young was present at the Temple in witnessing the Ceremonies.

At the Close of the labor at the temple I . . . [was] placed in the midst of a surprize Party Got up for the Occasion the Room decorated, and a Table set loaded with all the luxeries of life, Surrounded by nearly One hundred of those who had been receiving Endowments for my dead during the day.

Presidet Young sat at the head of the Table surrounded By his family and after Blessing was asked their was presented before me a present of a birth day Bridal Cake three Stories high adorned with the beasts of the field from the Elephant down, and Ornamented with two

---

28. Kenney, 7 (1 Mar. 1877): 331.

Satin Sheets Covered with *Printed Poetry* Composed for the occasion. . . . This scene this day is among the most wonderful Events of the last dispensation and fulness of times in which we live. And this door which is open for the redemption of the Dead in this manner will accomplish great and important Results, for it is now being Carried out in a great many instances in the Temple of the Lord, and will Continue to be more and more unto the end.[29]

Shortly after the dedication of the lower portion of the temple, Young decided it was necessary to commit the endowment ceremony to written form. On 14 January 1877 he "requested Brigham jr & W Woodruff to write out the Ceremony of the Endowments from Beginning to End," assisted by John D. T. McAllister and L. John Nuttall.[30] Daily drafts were submitted for Young's review and approval. The project took approximately two months to complete. On 21 March 1877 Woodruff recorded in his journal: "Presidet Young has been laboring all winter to get up a perfect form of Endowments as far as possible. They having been perfected I read them to the Company today."[31]

The St. George endowment included a revised thirty-minute "lecture at the veil" first delivered by Young. This summarized important theological concepts taught in the endowment and contained references to Young's Adam-God doctrine. In 1892 L. John Nuttall, one of those who transcribed Young's lecture, recalled how it came about:

> In January 1877, shortly after the lower portion of the St. George Temple was dedicated, President Young, in following up in the Endowments, became convinced that it was necessary to have the formula of the Endowments written, and he gave directions to have the same put in writing.
>
> Shortly afterwards he explained what the Lecture at the Veil should portray, and for this purpose appointed a day when he would personally deliver the Lecture at the Veil. Elders J. D. T. McAllister and L. John Nuttall prepared writing materials, and as the President spoke they took down his words. Elder Nuttall put the same into form and the writing was submitted to President Young on the same evening at his

---

29. Ibid., 330-33.

30. Ibid., 322.

31. Ibid., 340; see also 322-23, 325-27, 337, 340-41; entries from Jan.-Mar. 1877.

office in residence at St. George. He there made such changes as he deemed proper, and when he finally passed upon it [he] said: This is the Lecture at the Veil to be observed in the Temple.

A copy of the Lecture is kept at the St. George Temple, in which President Young refers to Adam in his creation and etc.[32]

On 1 February 1877, when Young's lecture was first given, Woodruff wrote in his journal: "W Woodruff Presided and Officiated as El[ohim]. I dressed in pure white Doe skin from head to foot to officiate in the Priest Office, white pants vest & C[oat?] the first Example in any Temple of the Lord in this last dispensation. Sister Lucy B Young also dressed in white in officiating as Eve. Pr[e]sident [Young] was present and deliverd a lecture at the veil some 30 Minuts."[33] The copy of the veil lecture which Nuttall describes is not presently available. But on 7 February Nuttall summarized in his diary additions to the lecture which Young made at his residence in Nuttall's presence:

> In the creation the Gods entered into an agreement about forming this earth, and putting Michael or Adam upon it. These things of which I have been speaking are what are termed the mysteries of godliness but they will enable you to understand the expression of Jesus, made while in jerusalem, "This is life eternal that they might know thee, the on[l]y true God and jesus Christ whom thou hast sent." We were once acquainted with the Gods and lived with them, but we had the privilege of taking upon us flesh that the spirit might have a house to dwell in. We did so and forgot all, and came into the world not recollecting anything of which we had previously learned. We have heard a great deal about Adam and Eve, how they were formed and etc. Some think he was made like an adobe and the Lord breathed into him the breath of life, for we read "from dust thou art and unto dust shalt thou return." Well he was made of the dust of the earth but not of this earth. He was made just the same way you and I are made but on another earth. Adam was an immortal being when he came on this earth; He had lived on an earth similar to ours; he had received the Priesthood and the keys thereof, and had been faithful in all things and gained his resurrection

---

32. L. John Nuttall, "Memoranda, For Presidents W. Woodruff, Geo. Q. Cannon, and Jos. F. Smith," 3 June 1892, Nuttall Papers, Special Collections, Lee Library.

33. Ibid., 325.

and his exaltation, and was crowned with glory, immortality and eternal lives, and was numbered with the Gods for such he became through his faithfulness, and had begotten all the spirit that was to come to this earth. And Eve our common mother who is the mother of all living bore those spirits in the celestial world. And when this earth was organized by Elohim, Jehovah and Michael, who is Adam our common father, Adam and Eve had the privilege to continue the work of progression, consequently came to this earth and commenced the great work of forming tabernacles for those spirits to dwell in, and when Adam and those that assi[s]ted him had completed this kingdom our earth[,] he came to it, and slept and forgot all and became like an infant child. It is said by Moses the historian that the Lord caused a deep sleep to come upon Adam and took from his side a rib and formed the woman that Adam called Eve—This should be interpreted that the Man Adam like all other men had the seed within him to propagate his species, but not the Woman; she conceives the seed but she does not produce it; consequently she was taken from the side or bowels of her father. This explains the mystery of Moses' dark sayings in regard to Adam and Eve. Adam and Eve when they were placed on this earth were immortal beings with flesh, bones and sinews. But upon partaking of the fruits of the earth while in the garden and cultivating the ground their bodies became changed from immortal to mortal beings with the blood cours- ing through their veins as the action of life—Adam was not under transgression until after he partook of the forbidden fruit; this was necessary that they might be together, that man might be. The woman was found in transgression not the man—Now in the law of Sacr[i]fice we have the promise of a Savior and Man had the privilege and showed forth his obedience by offering of the first fruits of the earth and the firstlings of the flocks; this as a showing that Jesus would come and shed his blood. . . . Father Adam's oldest son (Jesus the Saviour) who is the heir of the family, is father Adam's first begotten in the spirit world, who according to the flesh is the only begotten as it is written. (In his divinity he having gone back into the spirit world, and came in the spirit to Mary and she conceived, for when Adam and Eve got through with their work in this earth, they did not lay their bodies down in the dust, but returned to the spirit world from whence they came.)[34]

The veil lecture continued to the turn of the twentieth century, though

---

34. L. John Nuttall Journal, 7 Feb. 1877.

it is uncertain whether the St. George lecture with its Adam-God teaching was included in all temples.[35]

This probably was not the first time Adam-God had been mentioned in the endowment ceremony. Although official temple scripts do not exist prior to 1877, several unfriendly accounts of the Endowment House ceremony contain cast listings and dialogues of different characters during the creation scene for Elohim, Jehovah, Jesus, and Michael.[36] Their recounting of the concomitant presence of Jehovah and Jesus provides further evidence of the use of Young's doctrine.[37] Given that the doctrine achieved its fullest expression in Utah, it seems unlikely that similarly speculative ideas were advanced in the Nauvoo temple.

Although this material was clearly an innovation, official documentation on other developments during the Utah period is sparse. John Hyde, a disaffected Mormon, wrote in 1857 that "the whole affair is being constantly amended and corrected, and Kimball often says, 'We will get it perfect by-and-bye.'"[38]

One of the few known windows into LDS temple worship during this period is the late 1800s discussion about reconvening the School of the Prophets. On 28 April 1883 church president John Taylor announced a revelation reestablishing the school for "all such as are worthy" and thereby raised several interesting questions. At a

35. See also ibid., 5, 9, 10, 12, 14, 15, 16, 22, 25, 27 Jan., 1, 3, 10, 12, 13, 19, 21, 24, 27 Feb., 16, 17, 18, 20, 22 Mar., and 3 Apr. 1877; St. George Historical Record Minutes, 8 Nov., 13 Dec. 1890, 15, 22 May 1891, 11 June 1892, LDS archives; A. Carl Larson and Katharine Miles, eds., *Diary of Charles Lowell Walker*, 2 vols. (Logan: Utah State University Press, 1980), 2:740-41; David H. Cannon to Joseph F. Smith and Counselors, 21 Oct. 1916, LDS archives. For more on the Adam-God doctrine, see David John Buerger, "The Adam-God Doctrine," *Dialogue: A Journal of Mormon Thought* 15 (Spring 1982): 14-58; and Boyd Kirkland, "Jehovah as the Father," *Sunstone* 9 (Fall 1984): 36-44.

36. John Hyde, Jr., *Mormonism: Its Leaders and Designs* (New York: W. P. Fetridge & Co., 1857), 92-93; Jules Remy and Julius Brenchley, *A Journey to Great Salt Lake City,* 2 vols. (London: W. Jeffs, 1861), 2:67-68; Catherine Waite, *The Mormon Prophet and His Harem* (Cambridge, MA: Riverside Press, 1866), 246-49, 252; John H. Beadle, *Life in Utah: Or, the Mysteries and Crimes of Mormonism* (Philadelphia: National Publishing Co., 1870,) 486, 489-91; Ann Eliza Webb Young, *Wife No. 19: Or, The Story of a Life in Bondage* (Hartford, CT: Dustin, Gilman and Co., 1876), 357.

37. See Kirkland.

38. Hyde, 100.

preliminary organizational meeting on 25 July 1883, George Q. Cannon, counselor in the First Presidency, and George Reynolds, secretary to the First Presidency, were appointed to "get together all papers and information that they could obtain relating to the former Schools of the Prophets that were organized under the direction of the Presidents Joseph Smith and Brigham Young, so that the School might be properly organized in accordance with the designs of the Almighty."[39]

They presented their findings to the First Presidency and the Twelve on 2 August 1883.[40] Understandably, in view of the time elapsed and complexity of the intervening history, there was confusion about how all the previous initiation rites and ordinances fit together. The 2 August minutes taken by John Irvine record George Q. Cannon's remarks:

> Now, whether the washing of feet [at the original Kirtland school] was suspended by the Endowment or not is a question in my mind, and probably in all our minds. But it seems to be clear that after Peter, at least, had received an uncommon bestowal of power at the Transfiguration, that the Savior even after that washed his feet and the feet of the rest and commanded them that as they had seen him do, so should they do to one another. It was one of the last ordinances he performed in their midst. Brother Nuttall whispers to me a thing with which you are no doubt all familiar; that in the washing that takes place in the first endowment, they are washed that they might *become* clean from the blood of this generation–that is, I suppose, in the same way they are ordained *to be* Kings and Priests–that ordinance does not make them clean from the blood of this generation anymore than it makes them Kings and Priests. It requires another ordinance to make them Kings and Priests. If they fully receive of another endowment, a fulness of that power, and the promises are fulfilled in the bestowal of the power upon them.[41]

Further discussion led to the conclusion that the original Kirtland school had not used the "greeting" outlined in Doctrine and Covenants 88. Moreover, it was decided that the Kirtland school's washing

---

39. Salt Lake School of the Prophets Minute Book, 25 July 1883, LDS archives.
40. Ibid., 2 Aug. 1883.
41. Ibid.

ceremony was not intended to be a preparatory ordinance for the Kirtland temple. Apostle Erastus Snow recalled: "I did not understand [it] to be a preparatory work. . . . I understood it rather as a finishing work, and the words used in most cases according to the best of my recollection, were: 'I wash you and pronounce you clean from the blood of this generation.'"[42]

President Taylor decided that the ordinance of washing feet could be appropriately used to initiate individuals into the School of the Prophets. The "form of ceremony" decided upon by Taylor was to invoke proper authority, explain that the ritual was "an introductory ordinance," and pronounce blessings upon the recipient. The ordinance was strongly reminiscent of the ritual performed by Jesus with his apostles during the last supper. School minutes state that Taylor occasionally inserted "And I say unto thee thy sins are forgiven thee." He also specified that "the washing of feet is not the same ordinance associated with this as attended to administration of Endowments in the Kirtland temple. . . . This is a distinct thing and is introductory to the School of the prophets. The other was an Endowment."[43] The exact purpose of the washing of feet in this new context was primarily to be a reminder to be united and to provide selfless service.

Taylor asserted that the church in 1883 was operating on a "higher plane"[44] than in Kirtland half a century earlier. His decision to allow the washing of feet as initiation to the school suggests that members had probably already received their second anointing. The washing of feet would confirm their earlier "cleansing," or absolution, and renew blessings already pronounced. Members were required to be endowed, married in the temple, and polygamous.[45]

President Taylor, reflecting on uncertainties members of the

---

42. Ibid., 27 Sept. 1883.

43. Ibid., 12 Oct. 1883.

44. Ibid., 28 Sept. 1883.

45. Taylor presented a revelation on 13 October 1882 that all church leaders, both local and churchwide, were to obey "my law"—i.e., the law of plural marriage—or they would not "be considered worthy to hold my priesthood." "Revelation," cited in B. H. Roberts, *The Life of John Taylor* (Salt Lake City, 1892), 349-51. See also John Taylor in JD 25:309.

school had about the endowment, explained at a 12 October 1883 meeting:

> The reason why things are in the shape they are is because Joseph [Smith] felt called upon to confer all ordinances connected with the Priesthood. He felt in a hurry on account of certain premonition[s] that he had concerning his death, and was very desirous to impart the endowments and all the ordinances thereof to the Priesthood during his life time, and it would seem to be necessary that there should be more care taken in the administration of the ordinances to the Saints in order that those who had not proven themselves worthy might not partake of the fulness of the anointings until they had proven themselves worthy thereof, upon being faithful to the initiatory principles; as great carelessness and a lack of appreciation had been manifested by many who had partaken of those sacred ordinances.

The president concluded, "Had Joseph Smith lived he would have had much more to say on many of those points which he was prevented from doing by his death."[46]

This view of the unfinished temple ceremonies licensed innovations. Taylor expressed reservations about giving newly initiated people an endowment consisting of both the lower (Aaronic Priesthood) and higher (Melchizedek Priesthood):

> And I must say, too, that I have had serious misgivings about conferring all the blessings and powers of the Priesthood as we do in our Endowments at the present time, upon everybody indiscriminately, that is recommended to as worthy by men sometimes, who themselves are unworthy and who do not comprehend their position; I say I have serious misgivings as to whether it is proper to confer these blessings on so great a number of people who do not seem to comprehend them and who are not prepared to carry them out. And if we could only arrive at some form whereby a smaller degree or a portion of the Endowment could be given to parties first; . . . I have been, as I have stated, of the opinion that if our Endowments could only be given in part instead of as a whole, it would be much better and much safer, and we should thus avoid placing upon the heads of the incompetent people that which they are not prepared to receive and which they seldom live up to. It has seemed to me always to be tampering with sacred things to

---

46. Salt Lake School of the Prophets Minute Book, 12 Oct. 1883.

thus indiscriminately bestow all the blessings of the Priesthood upon all that come along.[47]

Concurring associates included Wilford Woodruff, George Q. Cannon, and Franklin D. Richards.[48] Previously on 11 June 1864 Brigham Young had expressed a similar view:

> Most of you, my brethren, are Elders, Seventies, or High Priests: perhaps there is not a Priest or Teacher present. The reason of this is that when we give the brethren their endowments, we are obliged to confer upon them the Melchisedec Priesthood; but I expect to see the day, when we shall be so situated that we can say to a company of brethren you can go and receive the ordinances pertaining to the Aaronic order of Priesthood, and then you can go into the world and preach the Gospel, or do something that will prove whether you will honor that Priesthood before you receive more. Now we pass them through the ordinances of both Priesthoods in one day, but this is not as it should be and would if we had a Temple wherein to administer these ordinances. But this is all right at present; we should not be satisfied in any other way, and consequently we do according to the circumstances we are placed in.[49]

This view must have been in wide circulation, since on 9 July 1877, Jans Christian Anderson Weib[y]e recorded in his journal that "Prs. E[rastus]. Snow said, when we can get time, we will give [the] Endowment for Each Priesthood separate, and after a while when Temples is built we will give [the] Endowment to each according to what Priesthood they hold; then we will give men the Endowment of the Aronic Priesthood and nothing else."[50]

David H. Cannon, present at the St. George temple dedication in 1877, later recalled such notions: "at that time it was thot that the endowment was to be administered in two degrees, the first degree to include the Aaronic Priesthood only and that when the second token of the Aaronic Priesthood was given the robe would be on the right shoul-

---

47. Ibid., 2 Aug. 1883.

48. Ibid. See also David H. Cannon to George F. Richards, 18 July 1922, LDS archives.

49. JD 10:309.

50. Jans Christian Anderson Weibe Daybooks, 9 July 1877, LDS archives.

der and that when the applicant had received the higher or Melkesedic Priesthood the robe would be on the left shoulder."[51] Despite apparent consensus, advocated by George Q. Cannon as late as 14 January 1894,[52] this two-stage endowment was never implemented.

Once the basic revised format was established, endowments and second anointings were regularly administered in the Utah temples at St. George and Logan and later at Salt Lake City and Manti. The second anointing typically was performed by the temple president, not the church president or apostle. Because of the proliferation of second anointings, the First Presidency issued, over the next few decades, several procedural requirements.

On 7 October 1889, six months after he was sustained as church president, Woodruff "spoke in regard to second anointing[s] and said the Presidents of Stakes were to be judges of who were worthy to receive them." He also indicated that "it was an ordinance of the eternal world which belonged particularly to old men."[53] Although stake presidents were shortly thereafter given final signatory authority for general temple recommends, a 6 November 1891 First Presidency directive indicated that second anointings still required final approval by the president of the church.[54]

In 1901 Lorenzo Snow, fourth church president, stated "that persons who are recommended for second anointings should be those who have made an exceptional record, that they are persons who will never apostatize."[55] Other early twentieth-century First Presidency writings and correspondence[56] indicate that at various times the following criteria of worthiness were applied:

51. David H. Cannon to George F. Richards, 18 July 1922.

52. In Jerreld L. Newquist, comp., *Gospel Truth: Discourses and Writings of President George Q. Cannon*, 2 vols. (Salt Lake City: Deseret Book Co., 1974), 1:227-28.

53. Abraham H. Cannon Journal, 7 Oct. 1889, Special Collections, Lee Library; see also Cannon's journal entry for 18 August 1893.

54. Wilford Woodruff, George Q. Cannon, and Joseph F. Smith to Presidents of Stakes and Bishops of Wards, 6 Nov. 1891, LDS archives; also cited in James R. Clark, ed., *Messages of the First Presidency of the Church of Jesus Christ of Latter-day Saints, 1833-1964*, 6 vols. (Salt Lake City: Bookcraft, 1965-75), 3:228 (hereafter MFP).

55. Anthony W. Ivins Journal, 8 Apr. 1901, Utah State Historical Society, Salt Lake City.

56. See, for example, Joseph F. Smith, John R. Winder, and Anthon H. Lund to C.

* Unquestionable and unshaken in one's integrity to the work of the Lord.

* "Valient in the defense of the truth," "active in all good works," able to bear "the heat and burden of the day," and endure "faithfully to the end."

* Obedient to commandments such as tithing, chastity, and honesty.

* Older but not necessarily "old"; typically over fifty years of age.

* A resident of the intermountain Mormon corridor, having "gathered with the body of the Church." Faithful "non-gatherers" were to be "dealt with by the authority on the other side of the veil."

* Innocent of any major sins—for example, a man who committed adultery after receiving his endowment would not be recommended, even after full repentance.[57]

* Previously endowed, especially candidates for posthumous second anointings who must have received their endowment during their lifetime.

* Married and sealed in the temple. Bachelors ordinarily were not allowed to have deceased women anointed to them.

* Church officers—apostles, stake presidents, high councilmen, bishops, and patriarchs—were expected to be worthy to receive the ordinance.

R. Hakes, 1 Aug. 1902; Smith, Winder, and Lund to S. L. Chipman, 16 June 1905; Smith and Winder to David John [and] Joseph B. Keeler, 18 Mar. 1902; Smith, Winder, and Lund to C. N. Winder, and Lund to Oleen N. Stohl, 22 May 1908; Smith, Winder, and Lund to Isaac Smith, 16 Feb. 1909; "Special Instructions to the Stake President," for 1901-21, all in LDS archives; and Joseph F. Smith, "Temple Instructions to the Bishops," 1918, in MFP, 5:112.

57. Isaac C. Haight, who, according to traditional sources, was excommunicated for authorizing the Mountain Meadows massacre, was later rebaptized and died en route to the temple to receive his second anointing.

These guidelines were perhaps best summarized by Joseph F. Smith's First Presidency to a stake president in 1911:

> [T]he second anointing is not intended for every male member of the Church, and goodness alone is not a sufficient recommendation to receive the higher blessings.
>
> Recommends for the second anointing should only be given to men and women who have lived together as husband and wife, and who through long years of faithfulness are still found to be worthy before the Lord and their brethren. They should be men of good report, men whose faith has never been shaken, whose integrity to the Lord and his servants has been beyond question, men who have been valiant for the truth, men who have either defended the servants of the Lord or would do so at all hazards should circumstances require it at their hands. They should be men who have done what they could whether in preaching or working or otherwise helping their file leaders in the building up of Zion, and who are ever ready and willing to labor in the interests of Zion at home or abroad. And all those thus recommended must be in harmony with the First Presidency and general authorities of the Church, also those immediately presiding over them. And this spirit also must characterize their wives in order to make them eligible to be associated with their husbands in receiving these blessings.
>
> . . . it is not for you to take your bishops into your confidence in having them recommend brethren to you for these blessings, because they are in no wise responsible for such recommends. It is you as stake president, and you alone, who are held responsible . . . all brethren recommended by you should be instructed to regard this matter in the utmost privacy. . . . neither should they take the liberty of advising any to ask you to be likewise recommended, as it is not for any man to seek for these blessings, but for those worthy of them to be sought out.
>
> You must be exceedingly careful in recommending for the second anointing, careful as to the character of the men recommended, also careful with a view to maintaining privacy, and in order to avoid attention being drawn to recommends of this character, we suggest that you do not recommend more than one couple at a time, and that not more than one couple from your stake come to the temple during any one week.
>
> . . . . Deceased men or women recommended by you must of course also be likewise worthy . . .

P.S. We take it for granted that you and your counselors have received higher blessings.[58]

Guidance on women's recommends varied. During Wilford Woodruff's administration, the rule was "not to permit a woman to be anointed to a man unless she had lived with him as his wife."[59] The First Presidency in 1900 decided to "restore the practice" as follows: "Any woman who has been sealed to a man in life or by proxy whether she has lived with him or not, shall have the privilege of being anointed to him inasmuch as he shall have had his second blessings."[60] Joseph F. Smith, fifth president of the church, followed this new rule in 1902,[61] but in 1907 he and his counselors John R. Winder and Anthon H. Lund wrote: "They must be, or have been, husband and wife . . . or one flesh, to use the scriptural expression."[62] One 1904 First Presidency letter denied the second anointing for a woman whose deceased husband had shown indifference toward temple work.[63]

---

58. Joseph F. Smith and Anthon H. Lund to William C. Partridge, 23 Oct. 1911, Joseph F. Smith Papers, LDS archives. See also the First Presidency to David Halls, 25 June 1913, Joseph F. Smith Papers: "During the early history of the Church, as well as the early settlement of Utah, second blessings were adminstered only to those chosen by the president of [the] Church, and this continued all through the administration of President Brigham Young, but later the authority vested in the stake presidents to recommend to the First Presidency such men presided over by them [and] deemed worthy by them to receive the second anointing, this for the reason that the Church had increased in numbers so that it had become a matter of impossibility for the President of the Church to be personally acquainted with every man suitable and worthy to be thus honored."

59. Lorenzo Snow, George Q. Cannon, and Joseph F. Smith to John D. T. McAllister, 14 Apr. 1900, Lorenzo Snow Letterpress Book, LDS archives; see also Wilford Woodruff to James H. Martineau, 26 Oct. 1887, LDS archives.

60. Snow, Cannon, and Smith to McAllister.

61. First Presidency letter of 11 June 1902, recorded in J. D. T. McAllister Journal, 31 Dec. 1902, Special Collections, Lee Library.

62. Joseph F. Smith, John R. Winder, and Anthon H. Lund to Lewis Anderson, 14 Mar. 1907, LDS archives.

63. Smith, Winder, and Lund to Thomas R. Bassett, 4 Nov. 1904, LDS archives. Other letters containing directives on second anointings for females are the First Presidency to Thomas E. Bassett, 5 Jan. 1902, 16 Nov. 1903; Smith, Winder, and Lund to C. N. Lund, 21 Nov. 1906; Smith, Winder, and Lund to William Budge, 22 May 1908, all in LDS archives. With respect to the rule that a man and wife were to have been endowed members during their lifetimes, the First Presidency counseled one stake

The recommend itself was usually initiated by a candidate's stake president, but some men and women themselves requested second anointings prior to the 1890s.[64] One letter from Wilford Woodruff to Salt Lake Stake president Angus M. Cannon suggests that local initiative was occasionally exercised by bishops[65] but not encouraged.[66] If a stake president felt a couple worthy of the ordinance, they filled out an ordinary temple recommend and submitted it, with short biographical summaries, directly to the church president. This was the procedure for both the living and the dead. If the church president returned the signed recommend, the stake president would then contact the candidates who usually knew nothing of their candidacy.[67]

Because of the strict confidentiality surrounding second anointings, it is unclear precisely what long-term effect they had on recipients nor, for that matter, the degree to which the conferral of godhood

---

president that persons who had died before the church was organized could be recommended, provided that adequate evidence was available to determine their worthiness. See Smith, Winder, and Lund to Oleen N. Stohl, 22 May 1908, LDS archives.

64. For example, see John Taylor to Eliza Perry Benson, 14 Mar. 1886, John Taylor Letterpress Book, 1886-87; John Hawkins to John Taylor, 6 June 1886, John Taylor Letter File; Benjamin F. Johnson to First Presidency, 9 Dec. 1886; Eliza R. Snow to First Presidency, 27 Dec. 1886; and Wilford Woodruff to M. W. Merrill, 29 Mar. 1888, all in LDS archives. One request from Benjamin F. Johnson to John Taylor, 29 Jan. 1887, LDS archives, "as[ked for] the Privilege of 2d anointing for my son James Fransis, who is the Present Bishop at Tempe. . . . He is over 30 years of age and appears really one of the comeing young men of Zion."

65. Wilford Woodruff to Angus M. Cannon, 24 Jan. 1889, LDS archives. See letter from Smith, Winder, and Lund to Moses W. Taylor, 4 Jan. 1902, LDS archvies: "We would say that it is not expected that people shall be found asking that this most sacred ordinance shall be administered to them, but you should take pains to seek out the worthy people under your jurisdiction, and this by means of your counselors and Bishops."

66. Abraham H. Cannon Journal, 18 Aug. 1893; Smith, Winder, and Lund to Moses W. Taylor, 4 Jan. 1902; George F. Gibbs (secretary to the First Presidency) to Ira W. Hinckley, 9 Dec. 1905; Smith, Winder, and Lund to Thomas E. Bassett, 4 Feb. 1902; George F. Gibbs to Alma Merrill, 14 Jan. 1908; Winder and Lund to Don C. Walker, 24 Mar. 1909; Joseph F. Smith, "Temple Instructions to the Bishops," 1918 (also in MFP, 5:112), all in LDS archives.

67. Smith, Winder, and Lund to Thomas E. Bassett, 4 Feb. 1902; Smith, Winder, and Lund to C. R. Hakes, 1 Aug. 1902; Smith, Winder, and Lund to J. S. Paige, Jr., 22 Sept. 1903; George F. Gibbs to Alma Merrill, 14 Jan. 1908; Winder and Lund to Don C. Walker, 24 Mar. 1909; and "Special Instructions to the Stake President," for 1901-21, all in LDS archives.

was held to be conditional or unconditional. Most early nineteenth-century statements imply that the ordinance was unconditional. As early as August 1843 Joseph Smith had expanded on the Calvinist doctrine of the elect in a sermon containing overtones of predestination. On 13 August Smith reportedly said, "When a seal is put upon the father and mother it secures their posterity so that they cannot be lost but will be saved by virtue of the covenant of their father." Another reported: "the Covenant sealed on the fore head of the Parents secured the children from falling that they shall all sit upon thrones as one with the God-head joint Heirs of God with Jesus Christ."[68] This promise was invoked in Heber Kimball's personal second anointing blessings given by Brigham Young on 8 January 1846.[69]

The promises of godhood outlined in Smith's revelation on celestial marriage (now D&C 132) seem unconditionally dependent upon having received the key ordinances of celestial marriage and being "sealed by the Holy spirit of promise, through him whom I have anointed and appointed unto this power" (v. 18), a reference to the second anointing. Smith equated this "sealing" with the "Holy spirit of promise" in a 10 March 1844 sermon as "i e *Elijah*." He then explained, "to obtain this sealing is to make our calling and election sure."[70] Indeed "the power of Elijah is sufficient to make our calling & Election sure."[71] This power was said to be bestowed "by revelation and commandment through the medium of mine anointed, whom I have appointed on the earth to hold this power (and I have appointed unto

68. William Clayton Diary, 13 Aug. 1843, and Franklin D. Richards's "Scriptural Items," cited in Andrew F. Ehat and Lyndon W. Cook, eds., *The Words of Joseph Smith* (Provo, UT: Brigham Young University Religious Studies Center, 1980), 241-42, originals in LDS archives. On p. 300, Ehat and Cook argue that this effect upon the posterity of parents was conditional. Their comment is based only on the Howard and Martha Coray Notebook, cited on p. 241. They assume that the "sealing" spoken of by Joseph Smith is that of marriage. The actual "seal" discussed, however, was that of the Holy spirit of Promise or the second anointing, not the marriage sealing. This, as well as the comments cited in the narrative, show that Smith intended that the sealing unconditionally affect a couple's posterity after this life.

69. Book of Anointings, 8 Jan. 1846, LDS archives.

70. Richards, "Scriptural Items," cited in Ehat and Cook, 335, emphasis in original.

71. Wilford Woodruff journal, same date, cited in Ehat and Cook, 330; see also D&C 124:124. This equation of the "Holy spirit of promise" with the "calling and election sure" doctrine, particularly with respect to its conferral by a human intermediary, has since undergone significant reinterpretation.

my servant Joseph to hold this power in the last days, and there is never but one on the earth at a time on whom this power and keys of the priesthood are conferred)" (D&C 132:7).[72]

As weighty as the unconditional promise of exaltation was, so was the sole postmortal alternative: banishment as sons and daughters of perdition with no chance of forgiveness in this life or in the hereafter.[73] Recipients of the second anointing were not eligible for the graded degrees of judgment outlined in Doctrine and Covenants 76: they would be either gods or devils.

Doctrine and Covenants 132:26-27 imply that such individuals would be deprived of godhood only if they committed the unpardonable sin: "murder wherein ye shed innocent blood, and assent unto my death."[74] This would seem to give license to commit a wide variety of sins including adultery, theft, extortion, and so on, and still be guaranteed godhood after "they shall be destroyed in the flesh, and shall be delivered unto the buffetings of Satan unto the day of redemption."[75]

The unconditional nature of the second anointing was occasionally preached in public sermons. On 7 April 1855 Orson Pratt stated,

> But we have no promise, unless we endure in faith unto the end. . . . In speaking of this, I will qualify my language by saying, that the Saint who has been sealed unto eternal life and falls in transgression and does not repent, but dies in his sin, will be afflicted and tormented after he

---

72. This powerful sealing authority residing in a sole human intermediary, Joseph Smith, represented a significant departure from Smith's earlier caution against papism and priestcraft.

73. See Brigham Young, JD 3 (8 Aug. 1852): 93.

74. John D. Lee's recollection of the deliberations preceding the 1857 Mountain Meadows massacre describes their concern that by killing the women and children, they might be guilty of shedding innocent blood. This task was left to the Indians so that "it would be certain that no Mormon would be guilty of shedding *innocent blood*—if it should happen that there was any innocent blood in the company that were to die." John D. Lee, *Mormonism Unveiled; or The Life and Confessions of the Late Mormon Bishop, John D. Lee* (St. Louis: Brand & Co., 1877), 237, emphasis in original. Lee received his second anointing on 17 January 1846 (John D. Lee diary, under date, LDS archives).

75. This may have provided a theoretical basis for the latter-day doctrine of blood atonement preached by several nineteenth-century church authorities.

leaves this vale of tears until the day of redemption; but having been sealed with the spirit of promise through the ordinances of the house of God, those things which have been sealed upon his head will be realized by him in the morning of the resurrection.[76]

Pratt's September 1860 comments were even more explicit: "This would seem to be as near an unconditional promise as can well be made to mortals. but this is not altogether unconditional, for there are some exceptions; but it would come as near as anything we have ever read of."[77] In November 1867 Brigham Young affirmed, "When men and women have travelled to a certain point in their labors in this life, God sets a seal upon them that they never can forsake their God or His kingdom; for, rather than they should do this, He will at once take them to Himself."[78]

Despite these affirmations, others indicated that the second anointing could be invalidated by actions less serious than the sin against the Holy Ghost. For example Heber Kimball graphically stated:

> Some will come with great zeal and anxiety, saying, "I want my endowments; I want my washings and anointings; I want my blessings; I wish to be sealed up to eternal lives; I wish to have my wife sealed and my children sealed to me;" in short, "I desire this and I wish that." What good would all this do you, if you do not live up to your profession and practise your religion? Not as much good as for me to take a bag of sand, and baptize it, lay hands upon it for the gift of the Holy Ghost, wash it and anoint, and then seal it up to eternal lives, for the sand will be saved, having filled the measure of its creation, but you will not, except through faith and obedience.[79]

---

76. JD 2:260.

77. Ibid., 8:311-12.

78. Ibid., 12:103. Also of interest are Heber C. Kimball's 2 April 1854 remarks: "What you have agreed to do, God will require you to perform, if it should be ten thousand years after this time. And when the servants of God speak to you, and require you to do a thing, the Lord God will fulfil His words, and make you fulfil His words he gave to you through His servants. Inasmuch as you have come into this Church, and made a covenant to forsake the world, and cleave unto the Lord, and keep His commandments, the Lord will compel you to do it, if it should be in ten thousand years from this time. These are my views, and I know it will be so" (ibid., 2:151).

79. Ibid., 3:124.

Eighteen months later Kimball further explained, "Now you say I believe in the principle of election. I do; I believe . . . if [the elected] . . . be faithful to the end of their days, they will be saved—every one of them. That is as far as I believe in election."[80] Brigham Young echoed this idea: "There are few who live for the blessings of Abraham, Isaac and Jacob after they are sealed upon them. No blessing that is sealed upon us will do us any good, unless we live for it."[81] This pragmatic emphasis on works over grace was also preached by George Q. Cannon:

> When he [Brigham Young] sealed a man up to eternal life, he bestowed upon him the blessings pertaining to eternity, and to the Godhead, or when he delegated others to do it in his stead, God in the eternal world recorded the act; the blessings that were sealed upon that man or that woman, they were sealed to be binding in this life, and in that life which is to come; they became part of the records of eternity, and would be fulfilled to the very letter upon the heads of those upon whom they were pronounced, provided they were faithful before God, and fulfilled their part of the covenant.[82]

The conditional nature of the second anointing would become even more pronounced in the twentieth century. The "Holy Spirit of promise" would come to be reinterpreted as a "divine censor" which both seals and unseals according to an individual's worthiness.[83] Given this view, it is unclear when the "destruction in the flesh" and "buffetings of Satan" would be applied other than for the unpardonable sin, or how the second anointing would differ from the promissory anointing received in the regular endowment.

In sum, the endowment and second anointing ceremonies un-

---

80. Ibid., 4:363-64; see also his comments on 6 April 1857, ibid., 5:18-19.

81. Ibid., 11:117.

82. Ibid., 24:274. See also Charles W. Penrose, ibid., 21:356.

83. See Joseph Fielding Smith's opinion on this question in *Doctrines of Salvation*, 3 vols., comp. Bruce R. McConkie (Salt Lake City: Bookcraft, 1954-56), 1:55, and 2:94-99. Bruce R. McConkie echoes this idea in *Mormon Doctrine* (Salt Lake City: Bookcraft, 1966), 362. McConkie's "The Seven Deadly Heresies," a fireside address at Brigham Young University, 1 June 1980, should also be understood in light of this question. See *BYU Devotional Speeches of the Year, 1980* (Provo, UT: Brigham Young University Press, 1981), 74-80, esp. 77.

derwent minimal structural change from their Nauvoo introduction through the end of the nineteenth century.[84] However an important change in emphasis would occur, resulting from a revelation announced by Wilford Woodruff in the April 1894 general conference.[85] Woodruff's action stopped the practice of sealing people to general authorities and other church members outside their family lineage and instead directed that they be sealed to their own parents. This change successfully accommodated a growing discomfort among Latter-day Saints with the former practice, and the number of living and dead sealings to parents surged in the following year.[86] In November 1894 the church established the Genealogical Society of Utah and ultimately awakened a heightened interest in systematic work for dead lineal ancestors.

Also during this period marriage sealings continued to be performed outside the temples. This practice in part responded to travel difficulties for members living outside Utah. Faithful members had moved to far-flung colonies in Arizona, Mexico, and Canada to continue practicing plural marriage. In 1891 church president Wilford Woodruff sent the following letter to John Henry Smith, a member of the Quorum of Twelve visiting members in Arizona:

> The condition of many of the saints in Arizona in connection with their marriages has been brought to the attention of the First Presidency. We understand that there are many couples in that Territory who are prevented by poverty and other circumstances from going to the Temple to have their sealings, and that many of the children are being born out of the covenant because of this.
>
> We feel to take some action upon this, as it is a great deprivation for Latter-day Saints to not have the privilege of marrying and bearing children in the covenant. In view of this, we have decided to authorize you, as one of the Apostles to dedicate rooms which are now used for prayer according to the holy order, and in those rooms solemnize

---

84. Bathsheba Smith, "A Notable Event—The Weber Stake Reunion," *Deseret Evening News*, 23 June 1903.

85. *Deseret Weekly News* 48 (1894): 541-44.

86. See Gordon Irving, "The Law of Adoption: One Phase of the Development of the Mormon Concept of Salvation, 1830-1900," *Brigham Young University Studies* 14 (Spring 1974): 313.

marriages such as are properly recommended, and which are of the
class referred to—that is, marriages of those who are unable, through
poverty or some other serious impediment, to go to the Temple of the
Lord to be sealed for time and for eternity. The authority is hereby
conferred upon you during this present visit to Arizona to attend to
cases of this kind, and perform the sealing ordinances for time and for
eternity. In doing this, we desire you to be very careful and make a
proper record of all such sealings, that every case may be reported here;
and in order that this may be done, we furnish you a book in which you
will have entry made of all these sealings.[87]

Shortly after the Salt Lake temple's dedication on 17 October
1893, Woodruff met with the Council of the Twelve and the church's
four temple presidents, spending "three hours in harmanizing the
Different M[odes] of Ceremonies in giving Endowments."[88] The following year the First Presidency sent a letter to all temple presidents,
portions of which read:

> In the placing of the girdle, it should be placed on the outside of
> the apron strings.
>   In the ceremonies at the veil, the practice has been to use the
> words, "this man Adam," while in the Logan Temple the words, "this
> man, representing Adam", are used. It was decided to drop the words,
> "this man representing," and say "Adam, &c." . . .
>   The words, "new name," were substituted for the pronoun 'it,'
> to avoid ambiguity, where it reads in the lecture, "You must remember
> 'it', that is, your new name". . . .
>   The words "that my tongue be torn from its roots in my mouth,"
> were substituted for "from the roof of my mouth."
>   In giving the sign and token of the Aaronic priesthood the Salt
> Lake Temple used the word, "index", meaning the fore-finger. It was
> decided to use the words, "fore finger," instead of "index finger," the
> former being more easily understood.
>   It has been the practice to mark the shirt, but we think this
> unnecessary as it is not strictly a part of the Temple clothing. The
> marking of the garment should be done in the washing room and not

87. Wilford Woodruff to John Henry Smith, 21 Sept. 1891, LDS archives.
88. Kenney, 9:267.

at the veil; and the greatest care should be taken to see that no person is permitted to leave that room wearing an unmarked garment.

In the Salt Lake Temple the practice in the Garden is for the couple at the altar to remain kneeling while the covenant relating to the first token of the Aaronic Priesthood is being administered, while the practice in the other Temples is for the couple to arise. The reason given by the Salt Lake Temple for not arising is that the couple would have to descend three steps, and as a matter of convenience they were permitted to remain on their knees. It was decided that the couples should rise.[89]

Not quite eight years later the First Presidency issued another set of instructions regarding admission to the temple and the regulation of temple work, including:

(2) A deceased female who has attained, in life, the age of 10 or 12 years, may be sealed to a male as a wife.

The same rule applies in the case of a male having a wife sealed to him.

(3) Males should possess the Melchizedek Priesthood before coming to the Temple to receive their Endowments. . . .

(5) Males under 21 [who do not hold the Melchizedek Priesthood] and females under 18 [who are unendowed] can be baptized for their health. They can also be baptized for the dead, and sealed to their parents. All over 8 years old must be properly recommended by the Bishop of the Ward and the President of the Stake in which they reside.

(6) A female who has a husband or marries a man not in the Church cannot be admitted to the Temple to receive her endowments. The same rule applies to a Man who marries a wife not in the Church. . . .

(8) If of a naturally ripe and early development, of mind and body, living children may receive endowments at the age of twelve years; but as a rule, fifteen years old is sufficiently early. . . .

(10) Children who die under the age of 8 years, not born in the covenant, should receive no other Temple Ordinances than to be sealed to their parents. . . .

(15) A woman who has been born out of the Covenant, and who

89. Wilford Woodruff, George Q. Cannon, and Joseph F. Smith to Lorenzo Snow, president of the Salt Lake temple, 31 Aug. 1894, LDS archives.

is married should be sealed to her parents, unless they yield up their right to her as a daughter and wish to surrender her to some other family.

(16) Where a woman has been sealed to two men and had children by both, and each of the men have a good standing in the Church the children go to their respective fathers. Why? Because the children were born under the covenant to their respective fathers and bear their respective names. . . .

(18) In cases where the heads of families (deceased) have had the necessary ordinance work done for them and they have been adopted into a family whose relationship in the covenant connects with the Prophet Joseph Smith, the children of said parents can be sealed to their own parents without annulling the ordinance first performed. This rule includes children in the Church and their parents [who] were not.

(19) Where a husband and wife are both members of the Church and they have children; the husband dies; the wife afterwards marries another man, is sealed to her deceased husband and has children by the second, all of the children should go to the first husband.

(20) No person, male or female, living or dead, can receive the highest blessings in the House of the Lord without a special recommend for this purpose, signed by the President of the Stake and endorsed by the President of the Church. The recommend, for dead as well as living, should be based on competent evidence of faithfulness, and, in cases of those who were not members of the church at their death, on evidence of their chaste and moral conduct in life. Any woman who has been sealed (in life or by proxy) to a worthy man, whether she has lived with him or not, may have the privilege of being anointed to him, provided he has had his second blessings.

Miscellaneous

(21) Persons who die without having been endowed may be buried (if their friends choose) with un-marked garments, but not with robes or other Temple clothing.

(22) Unmarried people, who have been endowed, can act in sealing for the dead. Those who have been endowed may act for the dead in any of the ordinances of the House of the Lord, except Second Anointings. . . .

(24) Words used in baptizing for the dead:

"Having been commissioned of Jesus Christ, I baptize you

for and in behalf of _____ who is dead, in the Name of the Father, and of the Son, and of the Holy Ghost. Amen." . . .

(26) All who come to the Temple to perform ordinance work are expected to make donations, according to their circumstances, to aid in meeting necessary expenses; but the poor who have nothing to give are equally welcome.[90]

These early efforts to resolve ambiguities in temple ceremonies and procedures no doubt served as precursors for the most extensive review of temple ceremonies which would begin a decade later. A numerical summary of endowments between 1877 and 1898 shows a total of 38,317 for the living and 486,198 for the dead in the St. George, Logan, Manti, and Salt Lake temples. There were 5,213 second anointings for the living and 3,411 for the dead performed during the same period.

90. In Manti Temple Historical Record, 24 Apr. 1902, LDS archives.

[Photograph 1.] Joseph Smith in Nauvoo, Illinois, ca. 1844, two years after introducing the endowment ceremony in the room above his store. (Drawing by Sutcliffe Maudsley.)

The Kirtland (Ohio) House of the Lord, where the ordinances of washings and anointings were first administered to elders in early 1836.

Brigham Young revised and institutionalized Joseph Smith's temple ceremonies beginning in late 1845 in Nauvoo. Note the Masonic square and compass pin on his shirt.

The Nauvoo temple, where 5,200 men and women received their endowments and 591 their second anointings from 10 December 1845 to 7 February 1846.

Architect's sketch of a proposed Nauvoo temple weathervane, ca. 1846. The angel is dressed in special temple clothes—robe, hat, and slippers—and carries a trumpet and open book. Note the Masonic square and compass on the pole. (Rendering probably by William Weeks.)

The Endowment House in Salt Lake City, built in 1854-55 in the northwest corner of the Temple Block as a "temporary temple." By the time the Endowment House was razed in 1889, more than 54,000 men and women had received their endowments, 694 their second anointings.

The Salt Lake temple, dedicated on 6 April 1893 after forty years of intermittent construction.

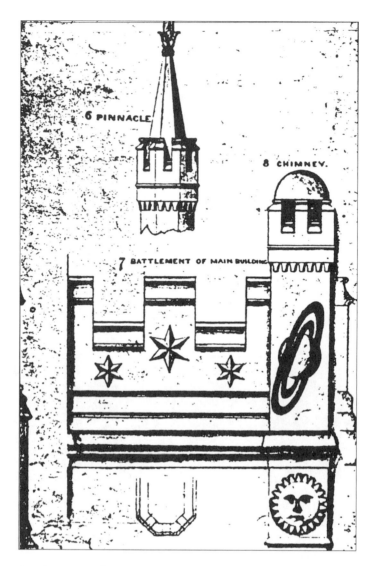

A rich source of cosmic symbolism, the Salt Lake Temple was to have featured Saturn-stones on each of its eighteen castellations. The decision to use granite in constructing the temple, however, meant that some details, such as the lateral views of Saturn's rings, were lost. Stone masons compensated for this by simplifying some of the symbolism. Also featured on the temple exterior are earth-stones, moon-stones, cloud-stones, star-stones, and sun-stones.

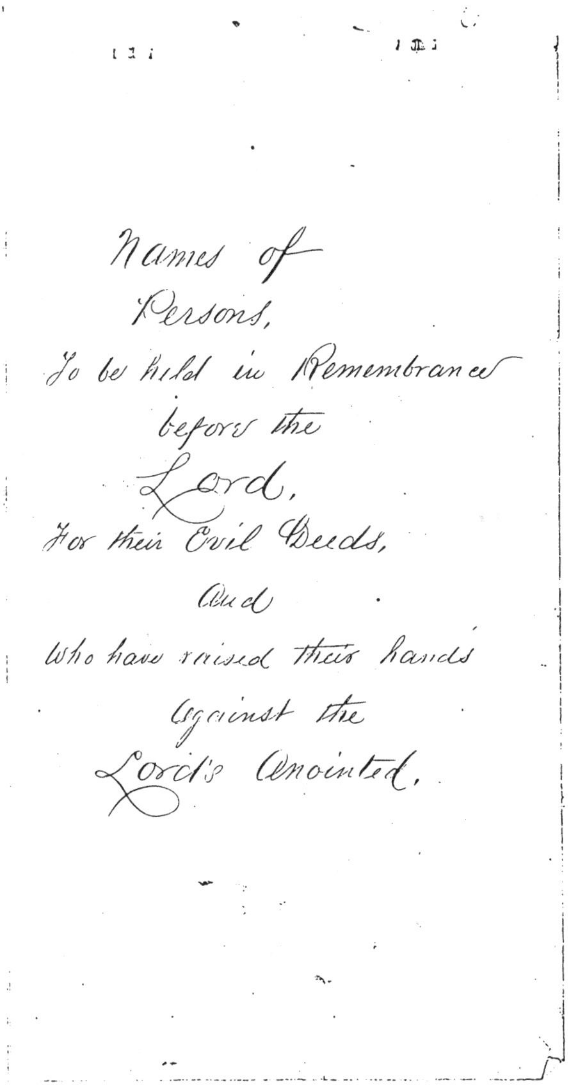

Names of

Persons,

To be held in Remembrance

before the

Lord,

For their Evil Deeds,

And

Who have raised their hands

against the

Lord's Anointed.

In 1880 Mormon leaders responded to efforts by the U.S. government to suppress plural marriage by convening a special temple prayer circle of general authorities to curse the church's enemies. Among the nearly 400 names listed on the prayer roll were those of Martin Van Buren, Ulysses S. Grant, Rutherford B. Hayes, and James Buchannan.

The Holy of Holies sealing room inside the Salt Lake temple (ca. 1911), where second anointings are performed.

Heber J. Grant, church president from 1918 to 1945, oversaw the modernizing of temple garments and the curtailing of second anointings.

George F. Richards, apostle from 1906 to 1950 and president of the Salt Lake temple from 1921 to 1937, spearheaded a progressive move to standardize and streamline all temple activities as well as liberalize the administering of second anointings.

CHAPTER 6

The Twentieth-century Temple

One of the most painful events in twentieth-century LDS history was the hearings of a United States Senate subcommittee to determine whether elected Utah senator and apostle Reed Smoot should be allowed to serve in the Senate. Among the many issues the committee heard testimony on were the "secret oaths" of the temple endowment ceremony. The committee's concern was whether the Mormon covenant of obedience to ecclesiastical authority conflicted with the senator's oath of loyalty to the Constitution. Not surprisingly, in the course of the Smoot hearings the oath or prayer of vengeance attracted the committee's sustained interest.

One witness, disaffected Mormon and recently resigned Brigham Young Academy professor Walter M. Wolfe, testified that this oath was worded: "You and each of you do covenant and promise that you will pray, and never cease to pray, Almighty God to avenge the blood of the prophets upon this nation, and that you will teach the same to your children and your children's children unto the third and fourth generations."[1] On 14 December 1904 the *Wash-*

---

1. Smoot Hearings, *Proceedings before the Committee on Privileges and Elections of the United States Senate in the Matter of the Protests against the Right of Hon. Reed Smoot, A Senator from the State of Utah, to Hold His Seat*, 4 vols. (Washington, D.C.: Government Printing Office, 1906), 4:6-7; see also 1:741-43, 791-92; 2:77-79, 148-49, 151-53, 160-62, 181-83, 189-90, 759, 762-64, 779; 4:68-69, and 495-97.

133

ington Times and the *New York Herald* featured front page photographs of a man in endowment clothing, depicting the signs and penalties. Testimony during this hearing as well as other previously published discussions of this oath indicate that, commencing with the Nauvoo temple ceremony, the oath of vengeance was in fact required of all initiates.[2]

Most Latter-day Saints today would be uncomfortable taking such an oath or prayer, and the same was true of the general public at the time of the Smoot Hearings. For Mormons in Nauvoo during the mid-1840s, the oath was a different matter. Encouraged perhaps by scriptural passages such as Revelation 6:9-11, many Latter-day Saints hoped for revenge. Allen Stout, a former Danite, recorded in his diary after he watched the bodies of Joseph and Hyrum Smith being returned to Nauvoo: "I [stood] there and then resolved in my mind that I would never let an opportunity slip unimproved of avenging their blood. . . . I knew not how to contain myself, and when I see one of the men who

---

2. See the following: Increase McGee and Maria Van Dusen, *The Mormon Endowment; A Secret Drama, or Conspiracy, in the Nauvoo-Temple, in 1846* (Syracuse, NY: N. M. D. Lathrop, 1847), 9; Catherine Lewis, *Narrative of Some of the Proceedings of the Mormons, etc.* (Lynn, MA: the Author, 1848), 9-10; William Hall, *The Abominations of Mormonism Exposed* (Sheffield, Eng.: M. Thomas & Son, 1852), 49-50; John Hyde, Jr., *Mormonism: Its Leaders and Designs* (New York: W. P. Fetridge & Co., 1857), 97; Jules Remy and Julius Brenchley, *A Journey to Great Salt Lake City*, 2 vols. (London: W. Jeffs, 1861), 72; Catherine Waite, *The Mormon Prophet and His Harem* (Cambridge, MA: Riverside Press, 1866), 257-58; John H. Beadle, *Life in Utah: Or, the Mysteries and Crimes of Mormonism* (Philadelphia: National Publishing Co., 1870), 496-97; Fanny Stenhouse, *Tell It All: The Tyranny of Mormonism, or an Englishwoman in Utah* (Hartford, CT: A. D. Worthington and Co., 1890), 365; Ann Eliza Webb Young, *Wife No. 19; Or, The Story of a Life in Bondage* (Hartford, CT: Dustin, Gilman and Co., 1876), 368; John D. Lee, *Mormonism Unveiled; or The Life and Confessions of the Late Mormon Bishop, John D. Lee* (St. Louis: Bryan, Brand & Co., 1877), 160; "Mrs. G. H. R." and James H. Wallis, Sr., "Mysteries of the Endowment House," *Salt Lake Tribune*, 28 Sept. 1879; Reorganized Church of Jesus Christ of Latter Day Saints, *Temple Lot Case* (Lamoni, IA: Herald Publishing House and Bindery, 1893), 453, 457-58; *The Inside of Mormonism* (Salt Lake City: Utah Americans, 1903), 13, 17, 29, 33, 42, 44, 47-49, 52-53, 65-66; and "The Mormon Temple Endowment Ceremony," *The World Today*, Feb. 1905, 170. A similar oath exists in the 30th degree of Scottish Rite Masonry ("Knight of Kadosh"); see Jabez Richardson, *Richardson's Monitor of Free-Masonry; Being a Practical Guide to the Ceremonies in All the Degrees Conferred in Masonic Lodges, Chapters, Encampments, etc.* (1860; rpt. ed. Chicago: Ezra Cook, 1975), 188.

persuaded them to give up to be tried, I feel like cutting their throats yet."[3]

Such feelings were institutionalized in the temple rites. On 21 December 1845 Heber C. Kimball recorded in his diary "seven to twelve persons who have met together every day to pray ever since Joseph's death . . . and I have covenanted, and never will rest . . . until those men who killed Joseph and Hyrum have been wiped out of the earth."[4] During an 1889 meeting George Q. Cannon's son recorded his father's reminiscence:

> Father said that he understood when he had his endowment in Nauvoo that he took an oath against the murderers of the Prophet Joseph as well as other prophets, and if he had ever met any of those who had taken a hand in that massacre he would undoubtedly have attempted to avenge the blood of the martyrs. The Prophet charged Stephen Markham to avenge his blood should he be slain; after the Prophet's death, Bro. Markham attempted to tell this to an assembly of Saints, but Willard Richards pulled him down from the stand, as he feared the effect on the enraged people. Bro. Joseph F. Smith was traveling some years ago near Carthage, when he met a man who said he had arrived just five minutes too late to see the Smiths killed. Instantly a dark cloud seemed to overshadow Bro. Smith and he asked how this man looked upon the deed. Bro. Smith was oppressed by a most horrible feeling as he waited for a reply. After a brief pause the man answered, "Just as I have always looked upon it—that it was a d——d cold-blooded murder." The cloud immediately lifted from Bro. Smith and he found that he had his open pocket knife grasped in his hand in his pocket, and he believes that had this man given his approval to that murder of the prophets, he would have immediately struck him to the heart.[5]

Negative publicity from the Smoot Hearings led to a deemphasis of this oath in the temple endowment. In 1912 David H. Cannon described the "law of retribution" as a prayer rather than an oath: "we

---

3. In Linda King Newell and Valeen Tippetts Avery, *Mormon Enigma: Emma Hale Smith* (New York: Doubleday & Co., 1984), 196.

4. George D. Smith, ed., *An Intimate Chronicle: The Journals of William Clayton* (Salt Lake City: Signature Books in association with Smith Research Associates, 1991), 224.

5. Abraham H. Cannon Diary, 6 Dec. 1889, Special Collections, Harold B. Lee Library, Brigham Young University, Provo, Utah.

importune our Father, not that we may, but that He, our Father, will avenge the blood of martyrs shed for the testimony of Jesus."[6]

This change in emphasis evolved along with other procedural revisions spearheaded by an apostolic committee organized in 1919 at the beginning of Heber J. Grant's presidential administration, under the direction of Grant's counselor and Salt Lake temple president Anthon H. Lund.[7] Following Lund's death in 1921, leadership of this committee went to the new Salt Lake temple president George F. Richards. From 1921 through 1927, Richards chaired the group which included Elders David O. McKay, Joseph Fielding Smith, Stephen L Richards, John A. Widtsoe, and later James E. Talmage. Under Richards's direction, the committee codified and simplified the temple ceremonies originally drafted in St. George in 1877, committing to paper for the first time those ceremonies informally known as the "unwritten ceremonies": "the covenants and the instructions given in forming the [prayer] circle and at the veil."[8]

Richards's work during these years is evident in the following excerpts from his diary:

[7 April 1921:] I attended and spoke at the 8 am. [Thursday] temple meeting. Attended regular council [of apostles] meeting from 10 am. to about 5 P.M. . . . At our council meeting it was decided that the old form of ordaining be used in the Temple and elsewhere. It was also decided that we disorganize the temple choir at once.

[8 April 1921:] Attended the [Friday] temple meeting as usual and after the meeting Elder Jos[eph]. F[ielding]. Smith and I met with the temple choir members, thanked them for their faithful services of the past and released them with our blessing. Congregational singing will be engaged in exclusively. Bro [illegible] will continue to lead without [illegible] after this month and Sister Davis will continue to be the organist. By instructions from the First Presidency given yesterday

6. St. George Temple Minute Book, 22 Feb. 1912, archives, historical department, Church of Jesus Christ of Latter-day Saints, Salt Lake City, Utah (hereafter LDS archives).

7. Thomas G. Alexander, *Mormonism in Transition: A History of the Latter-day Saints, 1890-1930* (Urbana: University of Illinois Press, 1986), 300.

8. George F. Richards Journal, 12 July 1924, LDS archives; see also entries for 7, 8, 12 Apr., 10, 27, 28 Dec. 1921; 3, 7 June, 30, 31 Aug. 1922; 14, 16, 17, 19, 20 Apr. 1923; 9, 16 Dec. 1926; 25, 27 Jan. 1927.

while in Council meeting, I instructed the brethren of the temple to eliminate from the ceremony of ordination ("We confer upon you the holy Melchesidek Priesthood") insisted by order of Pres. Jos. F. Smith. The old form is to be made uniform.

[12 April 1921:] We led our first temple [session] without a choir this morning [Tuesday]. Am working with Bro. D M McAllister on records trying to get uniformity of ordinances, decisions & with a view to having the [First] Presidency pass on our suggestions and have them go out to all the temples.

[3 June 1922:] I took 7:20 [a.m.] car for my work at the temple. This day [Saturday] I went before the [First] Presidency and presented to them an important change in the endowment ceremony by which the robes should be placed on the left shoulder first and then changed to the right shoulder once only before entering the Terrestrial room; also that Aaronic and Melchizedek be used instead of lower order of the Melchizedek and higher order of the Aaronic. I am to come back with a definite recommend of the Presidency of the Temple. This is my own suggestion. Other members not accessible today.

[7 June 1922:] I attended to my duties as usual at the Temple. . . . I presented the suggestions of a change in the order of robing and in the wording of the ordinances and lecture [at the veil] which were by vote approved. . . . The ceremonies and Lecture will be changed to conform. Full explanation will be given in Temple Historical Record. This will clarify some matters which at present are obscure and will shorten the services.[9]

---

9. In his "A MEMORANDUM OF SOME OF THE EVENTS AND OF SOME OF THE THINGS ACCOMPLISHED IN AND ABOUT THE SALT LAKE TEMPLE DURING THE PERIOD OF MY ADMINISTRATION AS PRESIDENT . . . FROM MARCH 14, 1921 to APRIL 30, 1937," LDS archives, Richards reported this change as follows:

"June 7, 1922—REGARDING THE ROBES OF THE HOLY PRIESTHOOD IN THE ENDOWMENTS

"CEREMONY: Taken from the minutes of a meeting at the office of the First Presidency. Presidents Grant, Penrose and Ivins being present. I represented having discussed with associates in the temple the advisability of instituting a change in the procedure of placing the Endowment Robes on the individuals receiving endowments the present method being to first place the robe on the right shoulder, subsequently change it to the left shoulder, and later again back to the right shoulder. The proposed change would be to place the robe first on the Left shoulder, and retain it there until

[14 April 1923:] I spent 1-1/2 hours with the [First] Presidency where I read to them the ceremonies connected with the giving of the 1st and 2nd lectures of the Aaronic Priesthood as I had written them after hearing them repeated and after I had revised them. I asked if all the ceremonies could not be written, revised and approved and go into the Presidents' Book held only by the Temple Presidents. The [First] Presidency were all present and thought favorably of these [suggestions]. The matter is to be submitted to the Council of the First Presidency, the Twelve & Patriarch. This would give us a standard to go by that these ceremonies might be kept uniform.

The subject of the garment was again brought up and considered and certain changes thought favorably of. The permisibility [sic] of dispensing with the collar, using buttons instead of strings, using the closed crotch and flop, and for the women wearing elbow[-length instead of wrist-length] sleeves and leg length legs just below the knee.

I spent about seven hours at the temple—President E. J. Wood was given a full set of Temple books to take home with him to Cardston for the Temple. [illegible] change.

[16 April 1923:] I spent at the temple writing what has heretofore been unwritten ceremonies of the temple. My son George assisted me all the afternoon.

[19 April 1923:] I was the speaker at the temple this morning [Thursday], prayed at the altar in Council—Our Council [of Twelve Apostles] meeting lasted from 10 am. to about 4 p.m. I read in the council meeting which is known as the unwritten ordinances of the temple prepared by me and it was decided to have copies made and one each entered inside the Presidents' Book of each Temple.

---

after the Second Token of the Aaronic Priesthood has been given, then to change it to the Right shoulder, in conformity with the giving of the Tokens of the Melchizedek Priesthood, thus obviating one of the changes heretofore made, and more effectively indicating transition from the lower to the higher orders of the Priesthood.

"After considering carefully the proposed change, the [First] Presidency decided unanimously that from that time on the Robe should first be placed on the Left shoulder, and be changed to the Right shoulder at the time the Endowment candidates are going to enter the Terrestrial World room. The necessary changes in the text, to conform with this decision, are to be made in the new books of rules, etc. that are to be issued to the Temple Presidents.

"(Announced to Temple workers in meeting held 14 Aug. 1922.)"

[12 July 1924:] . . . The Temple Committee have gone over the ceremonies of the Endowments with a view to more perfectly put them in proper form and we are still working on them and I am in hope that in due time these will be considered by the Presidency and as far as is right the suggestions will be approved and the ceremonies be re-written having all the written ceremonies appear in their most perfected form and regular order in the Presidents' Books and in the past books. I am delighted with what has been done thus far and am hopeful that the future will see the other changes made which are very much needed.

[9 December 1926:] Attended [Thursday] temple meeting at 8:15 am. and the Weekly Council meeting at 10:00 am. the latter continued until about 5 P.M. We had under consideration a revision of the Temple ordinances. The question of Retribution took considerable time.

[25 January 1927:] I went to the Temple as usual. Pres. Grant called me over to his office and the First Presidency then decided several important points pertaining to the Temple ordinances making a finish of the work which has been under consideration of a committee of five of the Twelve for several years. These points today decided will be reported to the Council for their approval next Thursday.

[27 January 1927:] At the [Thursday] Council meeting the last of the committees' recommendations concerning the endowment ceremonies was approved. There remains to have them written for all the temples.

Since 1893 St. George temple president David H. Cannon had maintained a certain degree of autonomy as president of the oldest temple. In 1911, he stated: "We are not controlled by [the] Salt Lake Temple. . . . This temple has the original of these endowments which was given by President Brigham Young and we have not nor will we change anything thereof unless dictated by the President of the Church."[10] Cannon balked at implementing the changes endorsed by Richards's special committee in 1924. In an assembly of local leaders on 19 June in the St. George temple, Cannon recounted that Richards had "criticized [him] very severely for not adhering to the unwritten

---

10. St. George Temple Minute Book, 14 Dec. 1911.

part of the ceremonies as he had been instructed to do," and said that Richards had instructed him to either burn the old rulings and instructions or send them to church headquarters in Salt Lake City. "If we want any information, not contained in the 'President's Book,'" Richard had ordered Cannon, "we will refer to the authorities of the Church for that information, but not refer to any of the old rulings."

St. George Stake president Edward H. Snow, who would become the temple president in 1926, thought he could approve of one of the recent changes: "no longer praying that the blood of the prophets and righteous men, might be atoned for, because this prayer has been answered and [is] no longer necessary." Cannon himself then recalled comments by First Presidency counselor Anthony W. Ivins at a conference in Enterprise, Utah, stating that Ivins "took exception to the way the Law of Retribution was worded, and said he [Ivins] thought the language was harsh and that the authorities [had] thought of changing that."[11]

As some resistance was being voiced to change, Richards sent a final letter in 1927 to all temple presidents:

> We have the Temple ordinances written into the books for the Presidents of Temples and are preparing the Part books and will get them to you in the near future, or at conference time.
>
> At request of President Grant we have already adopted some of the changes decided upon, and it will be in order for you to do the same.
>
> In sealing for the dead, whether one or both be dead, omit the kissing. Omit from the prayer in the circle all references to avenging the blood of the Prophets.
>
> Omit from the ordinance and lecture all reference to retribution. This last change can be made with a day's notice to those taking parts that contain such reference.
>
> This letter is written with the approval of the Presidency.[12]

Other changes during this period included:

Accommodating more patrons by streamlining the cere-

---

11. Ibid., 19 June 1924.

12. Richards to the President of the St. George Temple, 15 Feb. 1927, LDS archives.

mony. The length of the ceremony was reduced to roughly three hours (including initiatory ordinances).[13]

* The language of a number of penalties was tempered. For example, previously initiates had agreed that revealing endowment secrets would bring these penalties: "[Let] my throat . . . be cut from ear to ear, and my tongue torn out by its roots"; "our breasts . . . be torn open, our hearts and vitals torn out and given to the birds of the air and the beasts of the field"; and "your body . . . be cut asunder and all your bowels gush out." Now these penalties simply alluded to "different ways in which life may be taken."[14] The original penalties had clear antecedents in the first three Masonic ceremonies.

* For the first time dietary requirements—such as abstinence from tobacco, alcohol, tea, and coffee—became mandatory for admission to the temple. Apparently this had been encouraged prior to 1921, but exceptions had been made.[15]

* In 1920 the first night sessions started, beginning with one

---

13. Alexander, *Mormonism in Transition*, 300.

14. J. D. Stead, *Doctrines and Dogmas of Brighamism Exposed* (Independence, MO: Board of Publication of the Reorganized Church of Jesus Christ of Latter Day Saints, 1911), 113, 116-17; see Stuart Martin, *The Mystery of Mormonism* (London: Odhams Press Ltd., 1920), 256, 259-60; W. M. Paden, *Temple Mormonism* (New York: A. J. Montgomery, 1931), 18, 20; and Smoot hearings testimony cited above. Jerald and Sandra Tanner, *Mormonism: Shadow or Reality?* (Salt Lake City: Modern Microfilm Co., 1972), 468, 470-71; A. C. Lambert, "Notes of a Conversion with John A. Widtsoe," 24 Mar. 1950, A. C. Lambert Collection, Special Collections, Marriott Library, University of Utah; Tanner and Tanner, *Mormonism*, 462-73, contains a complete script of the pre-1990 endowment ceremony, which they first published in *The Mormon Kingdom* (Salt Lake City: Modern Microfilm Co., 1969), 1:123-34. More recent similar publications include Chuck Sackett, *What's Going on in There? The Verbatim Text of the Mormon Temple Rituals Annotated and Explained by a Former Temple Worker*, 2d ed. (Thousand Oaks, CA: Ministry to Mormons and Ex-Mormons for Jesus, 1982); Bob Witte and Gordon Fraser, *What's Going on in There? An Exposing of the Secret Mormon Temple Rituals* (Eugene, OR: Gordon Fraser Publishing, ca. 1983); and Jerald and Sandra Tanner, *Evolution of the Mormon Temple Ceremony: 1842-1990* (Salt Lake City: Utah Lighthouse Ministry, 1990).

15. Thomas G. Alexander, "The Word of Wisdom: From Principle to Requirement," *Dialogue: A Journal of Mormon Thought* 14 (Fall 1981): 82.

evening session per week and later expanded to three evening sessions per week.[16]

The final changes involved temple clothing worn during the
ceremonies and the undergarments worn continually by those who
had received their endowments. After learning that garments and
temple clothing were not originally designed solely by Joseph Smith,
the committee dramatically altered their styles. Joseph Smith left no
description of the temple garment. The earliest contemporary mention of the garment comes from John C. Bennett's 1842 book *The
History of the Saints*. Bennett includes a letter from George W.
Robinson, dated 8 August 1842:

> I have something new to communicate respecting ORDER LODGE,
> (though I do not expect it is new to *you*). After they are initiated into
> the lodge, they have oil poured on them, and then a mark or hole cut
> in the breast of their shirts, which shirts must not be worn any more,
> but laid up to keep the Destroying Angel from them and their families,
> and they should never die; but Knight's shirt would not save him. No
> one must have charge of their shirts but their wives.[17]

Many descriptions of garments have been passed down through
the families of Smith's acquaintances. One such recollection came
from the family of Elizabeth Warren Allred, wife of one of Smith's
bodyguards and, according to family tradition, the seamstress who
made the first garment: "The seamstress hired by Joseph Smith had to
cut out the garment three times to get it correct." According to the
account:

> It was while they were living in Nauvoo that the Prophet came
> to my mother, who was a seamstress by trade, and told her that he had
> seen the Angel Moroni with the garments on, and asked her to assist
> him in cutting out the garments. They spread unbleached muslin out
> on the table and he told her how to cut it out. She had to cut the third
> pair, however, before he said it was satisfactory. She told the prophet
> that there would be sufficient cloth from the knee to the ankle to make

---

16. Alexander, *Mormonism in Transition*, 299.

17. John C. Bennett, *The History of the Saints* (Boston: Leland & Whiting, 1842),
247-48.

a pair of sleeves, but he told her he wanted as few seams as possible and that there would be sufficient whole cloth to cut the sleeve without piecing. The first garments were made of unbleached muslin and bound with turkey red and were without collars. Later on the prophet decided he would rather have them bound with white. Sister Emma Smith, the Prophet's wife, proposed that they have a collar on as she thought they would look more finished, but at first the prophet did not have the collars on them. After Emma Smith had made the little collars which were not visible from the outside of the dress, Sister Eliza R. Snow made a large collar of fine white material which was worn on the outside of the dress. The garment was to reach to the ankle and the sleeves to the wrist. The marks were always the same.[18]

Another account is preserved in the family of Maria Jane Johnston, who lived with John Smith, uncle of Joseph:

Some people have denied that there was any such thing as endowments or endowment clothes before the time of Brigham Young, but I know there was. They were of the same pattern, had the same marks and were the same in every way as now. I was living with Father [John] Smith, the Prophet's uncle and on one occasion the Prophet wrote a letter to his uncle [asking] him to meet him the next morning in Nauvoo, [they lived] twenty-five miles from [Nauvoo]. Mother [Clarissa] Smith, . . . was sick and [since] I was the hired girl I had to get these clothes and fix them in time for Father Smith to meet the Prophet Joseph in Nauvoo. Mother Smith told Father Smith to explain to me about this clothing, what they were for and what they did with them, the reason he had to have them and have them in good condition, before I got them out, and he did so. That was the first I knew about endowment clothes but they were the same as they are now. Sister Smith told me where they were and how to prepare them for him. They were in a chest locked up, inside of a little cotton bag made for the purpose and were all together. Then I got the clothes and pressed them out and put them in good condition and he went to meet the Prophet. These clothes were never put out publicly, in the washing or in any other way. When we washed them we hung them out between sheets, because we were in the midst of the Gentiles.[19]

---

18. Taken from the history of Eliza Monson, LDS archives, whose great-grandmother, Elizabeth Warren Allred, was the wife of James Allred.

19. Transcript of testimony of Maria Jane Johnston Woodward, 21 Apr. 1902,

Jane E. Manning, a black woman who was sealed to Joseph Smith as a servant in the 1890s, also recalled her encounter with temple garments in Smith's household. She was employed to do the family laundry: "[Emma] brought the clothes down in the basement to wash. Among the clothes I found brother Josephs Robes. I looked at them and wondered. I had never seen any before, and I pondered over them and thought about them so earnestly that the spirit made manifest to me that they pertained to the new name given the saints that the world knows not of."[20]

Elizabeth Tyler later told her son of a vision her mother had received about the garments whose content had been confirmed by Smith:

> A short time prior to his [Smith's] arrival at my father's house my mother, Elizabeth Comins Tyler, had a remarkable vision. Lest it might be attributed to the evil one, she related it to no person, except my father, Andrew Tyler, until the Prophet arrived, on his way to Canada, I think. She saw a man sitting upon a white cloud, clothed in white from head to foot. He had on a peculiar cap, different from any she had ever seen, with a white robe, underclothing, and moccasins. It was revealed to her that this person was Michael, the Archangel. She was sitting in the house drying peaches when she saw the heavenly vision, but the walls were no bar between her and the angel, who stood in the open space above her.
>
> The Prophet informed her that she had a true vision, and it was of the Lord. He had seen the same angel several times. It was Michael, the Archangel, as revealed to her.[21]

Later in Utah Heber C. Kimball recalled that Jesus, John the Baptist, and Peter, James and John had all been wearing the temple garment when they appeared to Joseph Smith:

> What a blessing it is to be able to supply ourselves with so many of the necessaries and comforts of life here in these mountains! Some

Huntington, Utah, LDS archives.

20. "Biography of Jane E. Manning James written from her own verbal statement and by her request. She also wishes it read at her funeral . . . written in the 1893 . . . by E. J. D. Roundy," LDS archives.

21. Daniel Tyler, "Recollections of the Prophet Joseph Smith," *Juvenile Instructor* 27 (1892): 93.

of you have got an idea that wool will not do; but let me inform you that when Peter came and sat in the Temple in Kirtland, he had on a neat woolen garment, nicely adjusted round the neck. What do sheep wear next [to] the skin? wool, of course. What do goats wear? hair, for that is their nature. These are facts that are apparent to all who will look.

To return to the subject of the garments of the Holy Priesthood, I will say that the one which Jesus had on when he appeared to the Prophet Joseph was neat and clean, and Peter had on the same kind, and he also had a key in his ha[n]d. John also came and administered unto Joseph Smith, and remember that Peter, James and John hold the keys pertaining to their dispensation and pertaining to this, and they came and conferred their Priesthood and authority upon Joseph the Seer, which is for the gathering together of all who seek the way of life.[22]

George A. Smith recalled that Jesus wore the garment when he appeared in the Kirtland temple: "On the first day of the dedication, President Frederick G. Williams, one of the Council of the Prophet, and who occupied the upper pulpit, bore testimony that the Savior, dressed in his vesture without seam, came into the stand and accepted of the dedication of the house, that he saw him, and gave a description of his clothing and all things pertaining to it."[23]

It is within this context that one can understand the question posed to Zebedee Coltrin at the 1883 meetings of the School of the prophets. He was asked "about the kind of clothing the Father ha[d] on" at the Kirtland temple epiphany.[24] Taylor, who presided over the 1883 school, corroborated:

He said it was the pattern of the garment given to Adam and Eve in the Garden of Eden, and it all had a sacred meaning. The collar: My yoke is easy and my burden is light. (Crown of the Priesthood) the strings on each side have a double meaning, the strings being long enough to tie in a neat double bow knot, representing the Trinity; the double bow knots the marriage covenant between man and wife. The Compass: a

---

22. *Journal of Discourses*, 26 vols. (Liverpool, Eng.: Latter-day Saints' Bookseller's Depot, 1854-86), 9:376 (hereafter JD).

23. Ibid., 11:10.

24. Salt Lake School of the Prophets Minute Book, 3 Oct. 1883, LDS archives.

guide to the wearer as the North Star is a guide in the night to those who do not know the way they should go. The Square: representing the justice and fairness of our Heavenly Father, that we will receive all the good that is coming to us or all that we earn, on a square deal; the navel mark: meaning strength in the navel and marrow in the bones. The Knee Mark: representing that every knee shall bow and every tongue confess that Jesus is the Christ. The whole garment to be a covering and a protection from the enemy. The sleeves reaching to the wrist, and the legs to the ankles. This pattern was given to Joseph Smith by two heavenly beings.[25]

Early on, the garments were seen as protecting those who wore them. This idea was underscored by the circumstances surrounding the deaths of Joseph and Hyrum Smith in the jail at Carthage, Illinois. Neither Joseph, Hyrum, nor John Taylor had been wearing his garment. Willard Richards, who had, escaped unscathed in the attack. The topic of the garment's protecting and healing powers became the subject of discussion during the winter months of 1845-46 when ordinances were performed in the Nauvoo temple. William Clayton recorded remarks about the garment made during the 21 December 1845 meeting of the Quorum of the Anointed. First George A. Smith spoke of the importance of wearing a properly made garment night and day:

[George A. Smith speaking:] When we pray to the Lord we ought to come together clad in proper garments and when we do so, and unite our hearts and hands together, and act as one mind, the Lord will hear us and will answer our prayers. Our garments should be properly marked and we should understand those marks and we should wear those garments continually, by night and by day, in prison or free and if the devils in hell cut us up, let them cut the garments to pieces also, if we have the garments upon us at all times we can at any time offer up the signs. He then related an instance of some children being healed and cured of the whooping cough in one night, through the prayers of himself and Elder Woodruff, in Michigan, while they were there on a mission. Said that whenever they could get an opportunity they retired to the wilderness or to an upper room, they did so and offered up the signs, and were always answered. It would be a good thing for us to

25. From the "Record Book" of S. B. Roundy, LDS archives.

put on our garments every day and pray to God, and in private circles, when we can do so with safety.[26]

Others followed with similar remarks. Heber Kimball began:

In the coming week we will take through 100 a day, we want no man to come in here unless he is invited, or on business. Let those having cloth to make up send it here and we will make it up and put it to good use. . . . We cannot rest day nor night until we put you in possession of the Priesthood. We want you now to make up garments for yourselves. I want my own robe back again. If we have made you clean every whit, now go to work and make others clean. We will have a screw put up before the vail, and will make an office of my room, and have a stairway leading down from it. No person will be allowed to take people through the vail but those appointed. . . .

Elder P. P. Pratt approved of what had been said and said a few words about the fashion of our robes, his own robe, which was like those first used, was not sewed up at the sides, neither was it of more than one breadth.

Elder Kimball showed the right fashion for a leaf, spoke of Elder [Willard] Richards being protected at Carthage Jail, having on the robe, while Joseph and Hyrum and Elder Taylor were shot to pieces, said the Twelve would have to leave shortly, for a charge of treason would be brought against them for swearing us to avenge the blood of the anointed ones, and some one would reveal it and we shall have to part some say between sundown and dark.

George Miller said that when near the camp of Gen[eral] Hardin, he was shot at, and the Sentinel who was near him was killed, but he escaped unhurt, having on his garment. He then spoke of the design and purpose for which all the Symbols in the garden were given &c. Paul said he bore in his body the marks of the Lord Jesus Christ, which was as plainly as he dare allude to these things in writing. But the marks Paul alluded to were just such as we now have on our garments. He spoke of the signs, tokens and penalties and of the work in general, said it was the work of God, by which he designs to reinstitute man into his presence &c.

Elder John Taylor confirmed the saying that Joseph and Hyrum and himself were without their robes in the jail at Carthage, while Doctor Richards had his on, but corrected the idea that some had, that

---

26. Smith, *An Intimate Chronicle*, 221.

they had taken them off through fear. W. W. Phelps said Joseph told him one day about that time, that he had laid aside his garment on account of the hot weather.

Elder Kimball said word came to him and to all the Twelve about that time to lay aside their garments, and take them to pieces, or cut them up so that they could not be found.[27]

In 1861 Brigham Young still emphasized the saving power of the garments for Willard Richards:

I recollect a promise Joseph gave to Willard at a certain time, when he clothed him with a priestly garment. Said he, "Willard never go without this garment on your body, for you will stand where the balls will fly around you like hail, and men will fall dead by your side and if you will never part with this garment, there never shall a ball injure you." I heard him say this [voice in the stand "So did I"] It is true. When the mob shot Joseph, Willard was there and Br Taylor was in the room. I have nothing to say about the rest, you know about it. Willard obeyed the word of the prophet. He said, "I will die before I part with this garment." The balls flew around him, riddled his clothes, and shaved a passage through one of his whiskers.[28]

And fifteen years after this, Oliver B. Huntington recorded in his journal that John Taylor was still recounting this experience:

The prophet Joseph Smith pulled off his garments just before starting to Carthage to be slain and he advised Hyrum and John Taylor to do the same, which they did; and Brother Taylor told Brother Willard Richards what they had done and advised him to take off his also, but Brother Richards said that he would not take his off, and did not; said he was not harmed.

Joseph said before taking his garments off, that he was going to be killed. . . . "was going as a lamb to the slaughter" and he did not want his garments to be exposed to the sneers and jeers of his enemies.

These facts all came from President John Taylor's lips after he was president of the Church.

Elder John Morgan had told them to me as stated to him by Brother Taylor. Sister Lucy B. Young said that Brother John Taylor told

27. Ibid., 222-24.
28. Brigham Young, unpublished discourse, 14 July 1861, LDS archives.

her in answer to direct questions, the same, all except with regard to Willard Richards.[29]

Years later Ebenezer Robinson recalled what he had heard in Nauvoo before Smith's death:

> We here state a few facts which came under our personal obser-vation. As early as 1843 a secret order was established in Nauvoo, called the HOLY ORDER, the members of which were of both sexes, in which, we were credibly informed, scenes were enacted representing the garden of Eden, and that the members of that order were provided with a peculiar under garment called a robe. "It was made in one piece. On the right breast is a square, on the left a compass, in the center a small hole, and on the knee a large hole." This was the description of that garment as given to the writer in Nauvoo, in Joseph Smith's life time. It was claimed that while they wore this "robe" no harm could befall them.
>
> In confirmation of this idea, we quote the 2nd verse of the 113th section of the Doctrine and Covenants, Plano Edition, speaking of the Providential escape of Willard Richards, who was in the jail with Joseph and Hyrum Smith at the time they were murdered.
>
> "John Taylor and William (Willard) Richards, two of the Twelve, were the only persons in the room at the time; the former was wounded in a savage manner with four balls, but has since recovered: the latter, through the promises of God escaped without even a hole in his robe."
>
> It was stated that Willard Richards was the only one of the four, who had on his "robe" at the time, therefore the statement that he escaped through the promise of God, "without a hole in his robe."[30]

As late as 1916 President Joseph F. Smith emphasized the heav-enly origin of the garment:

> The garments worn by those who receive endowments must be white and of the approved pattern. They must not be altered and

---

29. In Oliver B. Huntington diary, 22 Apr. 1877, Special Collections, Lee Library.

30. *Return* 2 (Apr. 1890): 252. Robinson had been editor of the *Times and Seasons* and was well informed on the secret practices of the leading brethren of the church. In later years he drifted, refusing to go west with Brigham Young. He became disgusted with some Missouri Mormons who insisted Joseph Smith had never introduced the temple ritual in Nauvoo. In reply to these critics, he published a periodical called the *Return*.

mutilated and are to be worn as intended, down to the wrist and ankle, and around the neck. Admission to the temple will be refused those who do not comply with these requirements. The Saints should know that the pattern of endowment garments was revealed from heaven, and the blessings promised in connection with wearing them will not be realized if any unauthorized change is made in their form or in the manner of wearing them.[31]

Still, in June 1923, prompted by recommendations by the Richards temple committee, the First Presidency sent the following directive to stake and temple presidents:

For some time past the First Presidency and Council of Twelve have had under consideration the propriety of permitting certain modification in the temple garment, with the following result:

After careful and prayerful consideration it was unanimously decided that the following modifications may be permitted, and a garment of the following style be worn by those Church members who wish to adopt it, namely:

(1) Sleeve to elbow.
(2) Leg just below knee.
(3) Buttons instead of strings.
(4) Collar eliminated.
(5) Crotch closed.

It may be observed that no fixed pattern of Temple garment has ever been given, and that the present style of garment differs very materially from that in use in the early history of the Church, at which time a garment without collar and with buttons was frequently used.

It is the mind of the First Presidency and the Council of Twelve that this modified garment may be used by those who desire to adopt it, without violating any covenant they make in the House of the Lord, and with a clear conscience, so long as they keep the covenants which they have made and remember that the garment is the emblem of the Holy Priesthood designed by the Lord as a covering for the body, and that it should be carefully preserved from mutilation and unnecessary exposure, and be properly marked.

It should be clearly understood that this modified garment does not supercede the approved garment now in use, that either of these patterns may be worn, as Church members prefer, without being

31. *Improvement Era* 9 (June 1916): 812.

considered unorthodox, and those using either will not be out of harmony with the order of the Church.[32]

The introduction of this new style garment caused considerable unrest among some church members. On 4 June an article appeared in the *Salt Lake Tribune* which captured the various responses:

> Coming not as an order, nor as a rule to be rigidly enforced, but rather permissive in character, is a recent outgiving of the First Presidency of the Church of Jesus Christ of Latter-day Saints. It concerns the garments worn by members of the church who have been married in the temple, or who have participated in other ceremonies performed or rites observed therein.

> While minor modifications of the temple garment, it is said, have been made at various times during past years, the latest order in permission is regarded by younger members of the church as most liberal and acceptable. Among the older membership the optional change is variously received. Some of the pioneer stock look upon any deviation from the old order as a departure from what they had always regarded as an inviolable rule. Others of long standing in the church accept the change as a progressive move intended to add to personal comfort.

OLD STYLE UNCOMFORTABLE

> In the old days the temple garment was made of plain, unbleached cotton cloth. Unbleached linen was as far afield in "finery" as the devotee was permitted to go. No buttons were used on the garment. Tape tie-strings took their place. The garment itself was uncomfortably large and baggy. But despite these imperfections, the old-style garment is faithfully adhered to by many of the older and sincerely devout members of the church. These regard the garment as a safeguard against disease and bodily harm, and they believe that to alter either the texture of cloth or style, or to abandon the garment altogether would bring evil upon them.

> One good woman of long membership in the church, hearing of the change that has recently come about, went to the church offices and uttered fervid objection. "I shall not alter my garments, even if President Grant has ordered me to do so. My garments now are made as they were when I was married in the endowment house long before

---

32. Heber J. Grant Letter Books, 14 June 1923, LDS archives.

the temple was built. The pattern was revealed to the Prophet Joseph and Brother Grant has no right to change it," she said.

Explanation was made that the first presidency had merely issued permission to those who so desired to make the modifying change; that any member of the church who preferred to adhere to the original style was at perfect liberty to do so.

President Charles W. Penrose says that modification of the garment is elective with each individual member of the church who has gone through the temple. The change in style is permitted for various good reasons, chief among which are promotion of freedom of movement in the body and cleanliness. Formerly the sleeves were long, reaching to the wrists. While doing housework the women would roll up the sleeves. If sleeves were to be rolled up they might as well be made short in the first place for convenience, it was argued. Permission to abbreviate is now given, but it is not an order and is not compulsory, it is explained.

IS GENERALLY WELCOMED

Encasing the lower limbs the old-style garment reaches to the ankles and is looked upon by young members as baggy, uncomfortable and ungainly. The young of the gentler sex complained that to wear the old style with the new and finer hosiery gave the limbs a knotty appearance. It was embarrassing in view of the generally accepted sanitary shorter skirt. Permission is therefore granted by the first presidency to shorten the lower garment. Also buttons are permitted to take the place of the tie-strings.

Young men of the church, especially those who take exercise or play games at gymnasiums, favor the shorter garment. The permission granted is hailed by them as a most acceptable and progressive one. Altogether, and except in few instances, the permissive modification is welcomed as a sanitary move and a change looking to the comfort and health of those who wear temple garments.

Instead of the old style, coarse, unbleached, irritating material of which temple garments were once made, the finer knitted goods, and even silks, are now used. These materials and modified styles are officially approved, but such alterations are optional with each individual, and by no means compulsory, church officials desire it understood.[33]

---

33. "Temple Garments Greatly Modified, Church Presidency Gives Permission,

Additional recommendations were made by George F. Richards and the temple committee to the First Presidency nearly thirteen years later. Three members of the committee recommended, and one opposed, allowing the modified street garment to be worn in the temple and authorizing a sleeveless garment. The latter recommendation was made

> somewhat reluctantly and with deference only because we have convinced ourselves that it will . . . obviate undesirable exposure of the garment which now so frequently occurs through the wearing of present-day patterns of clothing. We feel sure that such a modification will greatly please many good women throughout the Church, and we have not been able to see that we are yielding any vital thing in this slight change.

The committee further recommended and received approval

that a definition be given in the temple of the symbolism and significance of the various marks in the garment. We believe that an understanding on the part of those entitled to wear the garment of these sacred makings will tend greatly to bring about more reverence for the garment itself. The best interpretation which has come to us up to this time has been supplied by President David O. McKay. It is as follows:

A. The square: Honor, integrity, loyalty, trustworthiness.

B. The compass: An undeviating course in relation to truth. Desires should be kept within proper bounds.

C. The navel: That the spiritual life needs constant sustenance.

D. The knee: Reverance [sic] for God, the source of divine guidance and inspiration.

To this last one might be added that which is now in use: That every knee shall bow and every tongue confess that Jesus is the Christ.

All concur in this recommendation.

4. We recommend that there be an understanding that when occasions arise that necessitate the exposing of the garment to the gaze of the curious, the unbeliever or the scoffer, the wearer is justified in laying it aside temporarily and that the wearer must be the judge as to what circumstances warrant this action.

5. We recommend that an effort be made to collect immediately

---

Style Change Optional With Wearer," *Salt Lake Tribune*, 4 June 1923.

all trademark labels signifying official approval of garments manufactured, and that hereafter we endeavor to prohibit their use entirely. We recommend also that an attempt be made to dissuade merchants and manufacturers from advertising L.D.S. garments.

6. We recommend that an effort be made, through selected agencies of the Church, to dissuade all members of the Church from asking for L.D.S. garments when purchasing from mercantile institutions, and that the people be instructed never to have the markings placed on the garments at such places; that all markings be placed on garments either by those entitled to wear them, the Relief Society, or other persons specially authorized to do this work, and then an understanding be had that no underwear becomes a temple garment until after it has been properly marked by those having authority to do the marking.

One member of the committee does not favor the restriction against mercantile institutions marking garments.[34]

The old style, pre-1923 style garment continued to be required use in the temple until 1975 when it became optional. It has now been almost entirely abandoned.[35] Mormons today wear garments manufactured by the church's Beehive Clothing Mills, which at various times has consulted non-Mormon fashion designers for pattern considerations. Members are permitted to make their own temple clothing provided it follows the approved design, although this is not encouraged. Upon approval of the stake or mission president, a handbook is loaned to worthy members who must make the clothing under the supervision or direction of the stake Relief Society president or mission president.[36] An additional policy change allows guests at temple

34. George F. Richards, Joseph Fielding Smith, Stephen L Richards, Melvin J. Ballard to the First Presidency and Council of Twelve Apostles, 22 Apr. 1936, LDS archives.

35. Spencer W. Kimball, N. Eldon Tanner, and Marion G. Romney to All Temple Presidents, 10 Nov. 1975.

36. Rose Marie Reid, Oral History, interviewed by William G. Hartley, 1973, James H. Moyle Oral History Project, LDS archives; Ron Priddis, "The Development of the Garment," *Seventh East Press,* 11 Nov. 1981, 5; *Instructions for Making Temple Clothing and Clothing for the Dead* (Salt Lake City: Church of Jesus Christ of Latter-day Saints, 1972), 1.

wedding ceremonies to attend in street clothes, provided they have donned white slippers.

One practice during the Depression was to pay people to perform endowments for the dead. Members who did not have time to perform ordinances for deceased ancestors customarily paid 75 cents for men and 50 cents for women per ordinance. Typically money was left on deposit with clerks at the temple who would disburse it as each vicarious endowment was performed. It is not clear when this practice ended, but it was probably difficult for temples to administer collection and distribution of cash.[37]

The greatest twentieth-century catalyst to vicarious endowments was Heber J. Grant's emphasis on temple work.[38] Endowments performed per member during Grant's administration increased substantially. From 1898 to 1912 vicarious endowments averaged .11 endowments per member per year (see Table 1). From 1912 to 1930 the average increased to .38. The decade of the 1930s saw the annual average again jump to .62. Perhaps partially resulting from the combination of World War II and Grant's lessening influence due to advanced age and death in 1945, this average dropped to .34 by 1945 and remained there through the end of 1950. Second anointings, however, decreased dramatically during Grant's administration, becoming practically non-existent by 1930 (see Table 2).

At the turn of the twentieth century the church had 264,000 members and about fifty stakes; by 1920 there were 508,000 members. In 1928 the one hundredth stake was organized.[39] By the time Heber J. Grant became church president late in 1918, over 14,000 second anointings had been performed for both living and deceased mem-

---

37. George F. Richards, Oral History, interviewed by William G. Hartley, 1973, 58, James H. Moyle Oral History Project; L. Garrett Myers, Oral History, interviewed by Bruce D. Blumell, 1976, 21-22, James H. Moyle Oral History Project; Joseph F. Smith, Anthon H. Lund, and Charles W. Penrose, "Temple Work for Church Members Abroad," *Improvement Era* 17 (Mar. 1915): 451-52. Richards was the son of apostle George F. Richards; Myers was formerly superintendent of the Genealogical Society, released in 1961.

38. See *Conference Report of the Church of Jesus Christ of Latter-day Saints, April 1928* (Salt Lake City: Church of Jesus Christ of Latter-day Saints, 1928), 8-9.

39. James B. Allen and Richard O. Cowan, *Mormonism in the Twentieth Century*, rev. ed. (Provo, UT: Brigham Young University Press, 1969), 52, 54.

Table 1. Temple Work for Living and Dead (And Other Vital Statistics), 1846 - 1985

Period Ending	Total Membership	Net Increase	Operating Temples	Endowments for Living	Endowments for Dead	2nd Anointings–Living	2nd Anointings–Dead	Avg. Vic. End. per Mem. p/yr.
1846	33,993	0	1.0	5,200	0	591	0	0.00
1884	158,242	124,249	1.1	54,170	0	694	0	0.00
1898	267,251	109,009	3.2	38,317	486,198	5,213	3,411	0.17
1912	417,555	150,304	4.0	56,752	536,309	6,367	2,216	0.11
1930	670,017	252,462	5.3	90,071	3,785,634	2,048	601	0.38
1940	862,664	192,647	7.0	67,479	4,716,556	8	3	0.62
1945	979,454	116,790	7.2	36,429	1,592,856	NA	NA	0.34
1950	1,111,314	131,860	8.0	60,457	1,927,806	NA	NA	0.37
1955	1,357,274	245,960	8.2	69,953	2,802,938	NA	NA	0.45
1960	1,693,180	335,906	11.2	88,408	4,681,781	NA	NA	0.60
1965	2,395,932	702,752	12.4	134,054	5,132,669	NA	NA	0.49
1970	2,930,810	534,878	13.0	141,778	7,557,458	NA	NA	0.56
1975	3,572,202	641,392	15.0	188,226	12,018,105	NA	NA	0.72
1980	4,644,768	1,072,566	16.4	244,682	18,568,811	NA	NA	0.89
1985	5,910,496	1,265,728	26.2	259,268	22,136,404	NA	NA	0.82
TOTALS:				1,535,244	85,943,525	14,921	6,231	0.43

bers.[40] In the midst of this growth, Grant issued a policy change which has affected the frequency of second-anointing administrations to this day.

On 30 January 1926, Grant wrote: "Second Blessings are only given by the President of the Church upon recommendation of a member of the Council of the Twelve." In response to a stake president's inquiry, Grant continued: "At some time when one of the Apostles is in your Stake, if he feels to properly recommend Brother . . . the matter will [be] taken under advisement."[41] This was reiterated by Grant on 6 April 1927: "It is not customary now for presidents of Stakes, as you know, to recommend people for higher blessings. That matter should be taken up by the visiting apostle at your quarterly conference, and all recommendations of this kind should come direct from the apostles."[42]

The policy change dramatically curtailed second anointings. According to Apostle George F. Richards, the policy was a result of an incident in which a

> brother had received his Second Blessings, [and] while speaking in a priesthood meeting in one of the Idaho stakes, told the brethren that they all should have their Second Blessings. Of course that was a serious infraction of the charge which he received when he had his Second Anointings; but I have never learned of any serious consequences to follow, except the action on the part of the Authorities, discontinuing the administration of these blessings in the Church.[43]

Averages proportioned to the dates each church president was in office would indicate that Wilford Woodruff probably authorized

---

40. This figure is based on the Salt Lake Temple Ordinance Book, LDS archives, as well as J. D. T. McAllister's "Totals to year ending Dec. 31, 1898" for the St. George, Logan, Manti, and Salt Lake temples, LDS archives. At the time, McAllister was president of the Manti temple.

41. Heber J. Grant to S. L. Chipman, 30 Jan. 1926, Heber J. Grant Letter Books, LDS archives.

42. Heber J. Grant to Levi S. Udall, 6 Apr. 1927, First Presidency Letterpress Copybooks, LDS archives.

43. George F. Richards to Members of the First Presidency and the Quorum of the Twelve [18 Aug. 1949; cf. Richards Journal, 18 Aug. 1949], George F. Richards Collection, LDS archives.

Table 2. Annual Second Anointing Data for All Temples, 1846 - 1941

Year	Second Anointings for the Living:						Second Anointings for the Dead:					
	St. George	Logan	Manti	S.L.	Other	Total	St. George	Logan	Manti	S.L.	Other	Total
1846	–	–	–	–	591	591	–	–	–	–	–	–
1847-95	1,312	1,325	810	817	694	4,958	1,387	681	403	405	0	2,876
1896	9	76	152	190	0	427	15	30	75	104	0	224
1897	5	99	41	136	0	281	4	41	32	88	0	165
1898	16	30	16	179	0	241	19	15	16	96	0	146
1899	53	69	51	328	0	501	25	29	22	135	0	211
1900	104	274	141	632	0	1,151	28	51	63	181	0	323
1901	43	188	376	529	0	1,136	13	49	166	113	0	341
1902	24	58	161	309	0	552	19	29	64	114	0	226
1903	15	70	71	234	0	390	8	25	37	107	0	177
1904	15	62	29	209	0	315	6	30	23	90	0	149
1905	23	35	32	172	0	262	11	23	24	55	0	113
1906	16	26	25	172	0	239	5	22	14	48	0	89
1907	5	23	60	269	0	357	9	7	33	66	0	115
1908	14	96	41	258	0	409	5	25	22	70	0	122
1909	9	30	20	160	0	219	3	11	2	75	0	91
1910	6	73	56	162	0	297	7	17	12	35	0	71
1911	3	68	38	195	0	304	2	19	23	42	0	86
1912	12	49	30	144	0	235	1	18	26	57	0	102
1913	14	46	11	138	0	209	6	21	6	54	0	87
1914	1	27	35	157	0	220	8	14	15	58	0	95
1915	24	25	36	116	0	201	6	9	4	28	0	47
1916	20	48	58	115	0	241	2	21	10	32	0	65

Year											
1917	10	44	23	135	0	212	6	7	10	42	0	65
1918	5	13	20	117	0	155	2	13	7	21	0	43
1919	7	41	17	86	0	151	1	7	12	19	0	39
1920	8	43	7	96	0	154	4	9	3	23	0	39
1921	17	24	28	106	0	175	5	10	9	24	0	48
1922	13	28	6	52	0	99	3	3	0	38	0	44
1923	2	10	5	47	13	77	1	1	0	5	1	8
1924	5	35	2	19	0	61	0	3	0	1	0	4
1925	2	3	2	34	0	41	0	1	0	2	0	3
1926	3	0	0	18	0	21	1	1	0	1	0	3
1927	0	2	0	13	0	15	0	0	0	8	0	8
1928	2	0	0	4	0	6	0	0	0	1	0	1
1929	0	0	2	8	0	10	0	0	1	1	0	2
1930	0	0	0	0	0	0	0	0	0	0	0	0
1931	0	0	0	2	0	2	0	1	0	0	0	1
1932	0	0	0	0	0	0	0	0	0	0	0	0
1933	0	0	0	0	0	0	0	0	0	0	0	0
1934	0	0	0	2	0	2	0	0	0	1	0	1
1935	0	0	0	0	0	0	0	0	0	0	0	0
1936	0	0	0	0	0	0	0	0	0	0	0	0
1937	0	0	0	2	0	2	0	0	0	1	0	1
1938	0	0	0	2	0	2	0	0	0	0	0	0
1939	0	0	0	0	0	0	0	0	0	0	0	0
1940	0	0	0	0	0	0	0	0	0	0	0	0
1941	0	0	0	0	0	0	0	0	0	0	0	0
TOTALS:	1,817	3,040	2,402	6,364	1,298	14,921	1,612	1,243	1,134	2,241	1	6,231

about 2,000 second anointings, or an average of just over 300 each year during his administration. Lorenzo Snow apparently authorized about 2,000, roughly twice as many per year as Woodruff. Joseph F. Smith seems to have authorized about 4,000 anointings, or less than half as many per year as his predecessor. And Heber J. Grant apparently authorized only a few hundred for an annual average of one-tenth that of his predecessor. After 1928 the average was less than two per year for at least the next decade and a half. Data after 1941 are not presently available. By 1941 a total of 6,000 second anointings for the living and over 2,000 for the dead had been administered in the Salt Lake temple during the late nineteenth and early twentieth centuries. Three-fourths of these were for the living; three-fifths were for women. Counting all temples, just under 15,000 second anointings had been performed for the living by 1941 and just over 6,000 for the dead.[44]

During the period of declining ordinances, George F. Richards singlehandedly labored to revive this practice. In a 1934 letter to President Grant, he listed five living general authorities who had not received second anointings and then wrote: "I understand that it is in order for a member of the council of the Twelve to recommend worthy members to the President of the Church to receive their Second

---

44. See n41 and the statistical reports in *Genealogical and Historical Magazine of the Arizona Temple District* 14 (Apr. 1938): 10-11, and 15 (Apr. 1939): 10-11. These statistics were published under the direction of Franklin T. Pomeroy. Interestingly the same type of statistics were included in George F. Richards's letter (see n43), but his totals are significantly different from those cited in the text. Richards claimed that just over 22,000 second anointings had been performed for the living by the end of 1942, with over 10,000 for the dead. His statistics for second anointings in the Nauvoo temple are almost 150 short of the number recorded in the Book of Anointings, and his Salt Lake temple statistics were dramatically inflated above those officially recorded in the Salt Lake Temple Ordinance Book.

It should be noted that although a great number of vicarious second anointings were performed, church officials seemed somewhat reluctant to permit a wholesale rash of these ordinances. President Lorenzo Snow was quoted as saying, "Many faithful people have gone into the spirit world without those blessings [i.e., the second anointing], and they will lose nothing by it," and that he preferred "to refer [them] to the future than to undertake to endorse recommends for persons who cannot be regularly recommended" (George F. Gibbs to D. H. Cannon, 22 Dec. 1900). On 19 October 1926 Heber J. Grant, Anthony W. Ivins, and Charles W. Nibley wrote Joseph W. McMurrin, saying it "has been some years since ordinances bestowing second blessings [i.e. second anointings] have been performed in cases where both parties are dead."

blessings. Accordingly, I recommend that these brethren and their wives be invited to receive their blessings."[45]

Action on the request was evidently slow, for eight years later Richards recorded:

> I attended regular Thu[rsday]. meetings. At the 10:a.m. meeting of the [First] Presidency, the Twelve and the Patriarch held in the Temple, the matter of allowing the administration of second blessings was considered. I brought up the subject at our last Quarterly meeting of the Twelve held in the Temple Sept. 29*th* last [1942]. I made quite an extended talk on the subject at that time at the conclusion of which it was decided by vote to present the question to the Council of the First Presidency, the Twelve and the Patriarch. Today all were present except Geo. Albert Smith, Richard R. Lyman and Sylvester Q. Cannon and I suggested to Pres. [Rudger] Clawson that he bring the question forward, which he did. I had a chance to explain, and it was decided that the four members of the Council, viz. J. Reuben Clark Jr., Albert E. Bowen, Harold B. Lee and the Patriarch Jos. F. Smith should be privileged to receive theirs and others whom the members of this council may recommend and the Council sustain. Pres. Grant appointed me to administer these blessings. I suggested that Jos. Fielding Smith be appointed to assist me in this work. We are to make the appointment, i.e. Jos. Fielding & I, for the brethren. I have anxiously looked forward to this action.
>
> The records show that there have been 32,495 such blessings administered in the Church and that during the last 12 years there have been but 8 administrations. Thirteen of the 32 General Authorities had not had theirs and at least two others who have had them with their first wives have later wives not yet anointed to their husbands.[46]

By the end of the month a much happier Richards noted:

> I obtained permission of Pres. Grant to see him at his home. I found him in bed and his condition seemed worse than I had expected to find. I gave him a blessing, and recommended that he issue recommends to all the General Authorities and their wives who have not received their second blessings and give it [to] them for Christmas which he approved and authorized[,] also approved Stephen L. Chipman & Wife whom I

---

45. George F. Richards Journal, 19 Apr. 1934.
46. Ibid., 10 Dec. 1942.

recommended. I reported to Joseph Anderson, who had recommends made. These I took to the President and he signed them. I returned the signed recommends to Joseph Anderson, the President's Secretary, for distribution. I feel that this day's accomplishments has been inspired and is a wonderful accomplishment. May the Lord be praised for ever. This is one of the most happy days of my life. I am sure it will endure over Christmas.[47]

The following year he again recorded: "Attended 10:00 A.M. meeting of the First Presidency, the Twelve & the Patriarch. The council approved my recommendation that 2nds be offered the following: Harold S. Snow of St. George Temple, El Ray Christiansen Pres. of Logan Temple, and David Smith, Pres. of Idaho Falls Temple."[48]

Judging from his remarks six years later, however, Richards was still frustrated that change was not more forthcoming, a situation he described as "deploring":

[12 August 1949:] I attended quarterly meeting of the Twelve where I presided and presented my views respecting the non admini-stration of seconds, which received approval with the request by motion made by Stephen L Richards that I present the matter to the [First] Presidency if I could get a hearing, either to them alone or in the Council of the First Presidency & the Twelve.[49]

Six days later he delivered a communication to the First Presidency and Twelve arguing for these *"ordinances without which we cannot obtain Celestial thrones."* He explained:

The following tabulation of Second Blessings administered in the temples where such blessings were administered will no doubt be of interest to you:

Temple	Period	Living	Dead	Total
Salt Lake	To Dec. 10, 1942	14,847	6,226	21,073
Logan	To Oct. 13, 1931	3,139	1,229	4,368
St. George	To Jan. 13, 1938	1,885	1,619	3,504

---

47. Ibid., 24, 31 Dec. 1942.
48. Ibid., 14 Oct. 1943.
49. Ibid., 12 Aug. 1949.

Manti	To Dec. 12, 1929	2,407	1,143	3,550
Nauvoo	In Jan. & Feb. 1846			406
	Totals	22,278	10,217	32,901

Richards noted that from 1930 to 1942 only "eight such blessings were administered in the Church. Only EIGHT blessings in twelve years!" Consequently he recommended that "Temples under construction now and in the future should be provided with a room for the administration of these blessings alone, to be known as the Holy of Holies, for if we do not move in the matter before us, some others coming after us will do so *for it must be done*, and temples should be designed and constructed with that thought in mind."[50] Later that day Richards noted: "At the 10:00 A.M. council meeting of the [First] Presidency and Twelve I read a paper of 5 or 6 pages deploring the neglect on our part in not administering Second blessings as formerly. The paper and other statements made by me in connection therewith were accepted 100%."[51] Entries in Richards's journal over the next two years include mention of several second anointings:

[7 December 1949:] I went to the temple at 11:00 a.m. and assisted Elder Jos. Fielding Smith, administered Seconds to Preston D. Richards and wife Barbara, and the members of Emigration Stake Presidency and their wives.

[6 January 1950:] I went to the Temple by appointment, and administered Second blessings to three of the general authorities and their wives, Elders Eldred G. Smith, Milton R. Hunter, and B[isho]p. Thorp[e] B. Isaacson. Bro. T[horpe]. B. Isaacson stood as proxy for Samuel F. Ball who is dead & Betsy Hollings Richards for Adena Christena Anderson Ball.

[20 April 1950:] I obtained permission from President Geo. Albert Smith for my Sons Oliver and Ray and their wives to receive their Second Anointings.[52]

---

50. George F. Richards to the First Presidency and Quorum of Twelve Apostles, ca. 18 Aug. 1949, LDS archives.
51. Ibid., 18 Aug. 1949.
52. Ibid., 7 Dec. 1949, 6 Jan., 20 Apr. 1950.

Aside from a few letters and other bits of information, little is known of recent LDS practice regarding second anointings. One person recalled that when he was a small boy in a rural Utah town early this century, "second endowments *were spoken of* rather frequently."[53] Today, most Mormons do not know of the ordinance at all. Nonetheless, it is still performed, as are vicarious second anointings, though less frequently.[54] Usually the church president performs or is present at the ceremony, although this is not always possible, especially when the president is physically or mentally incapacitated. The policy of the president calling up candidates to receive the second anointing still continues. In the past the ordinance was held in the Holy of Holies, but today any room in a temple set apart for the purpose suffices.[55]

The current official policy initiated by Heber J. Grant suggests that church authorities now feel that the second anointing is not required for exaltation.[56] The fact that the ordinance continues to be performed—albeit on a small scale—seems to signal some importance. But when the ordinance came to be interpreted as conditional, it became a "special blessing" for a limited number of proven, trustwor-

---

53. A. C. Lambert, from holograph notes titled "Second Endowments," which recount an interview with Howard S. McDonald, located in Lambert Papers.

54. For example, see Carrel H. Sheldon's letter in *Dialogue: A Journal of Mormon Thought* 14 (Winter 1981): 15, where she tells of knowing one couple who received the second anointing during David O. McKay's administration and two couples during Spencer W. Kimball's administration.

55. This procedural information was related to me by Provo temple president Orville Gunther in March 1978 and was reiterated by Oakland temple president Richard B. Sonne on 14 November 1981 and by Idaho Falls temple president Devier Harris on 29 December 1982. A picture of the Holy of Holies in the Salt Lake temple was published in James E. Talmage's original edition of *House of the Lord*; more recent "reprints" have removed the picture. The same picture was reprinted in *Improvement Era* 39 (Nov. 1936): 241; and later in *The Salt Lake Temple: A Monument to a People* (Salt Lake City: University Services, 1983), 128-29.

56. When John A. Tvedtnes, for example, asked Apostle Harold B. Lee in a Salt Lake temple missionary question-and-answer session if the "second endowment" existed and, "if so, what connection does it have with the Holy Spirit of Promise, and who receives it and why and how," Lee answered, "You don't have to worry. You've received all the ordinances necessary for exaltation. . . . It is a special blessing given by the President of the Church to men who have been called. It is not necessary to receive it, however. You have all the endowment you need to be exalted" (John A. Tvedtnes Journal, 30 June 1961, recounted by permission).

thy older men and women and the upper levels of an elite, insular hierarchy. In such a light the significance of the ordinance was reduced.[57]

Early Mormons who received the second anointing recorded the event with great joy. Abraham O. Smoot wrote that it "was a day of great enjoyment for me, it gave birth to the greatest blessings and an higher exaltation in the Priesthood than ever had been anticipated by me."[58] John D. Lee, called by Brigham Young to keep records of the anointings, wrote in his diary: "[W]e received our anointings yea, Holy anointings in the Temple of the Lord under the hands of Elder Orson Hyde[.] this certainly produced more joy comfort and pleasure & reconciliation of feeling—than could possibly have been imagined."[59] For them the event clearly had theological significance as well.

Theoretically the blessing of the fullness of the priesthood is still attainable. As future apostle Bruce R. McConkie noted:

> Holders of the Melchizedek Priesthood have power to press forward in righteousness, living by every word that proceedeth forth from the mouth of God, magnifying their callings, going from grace to grace,

57. In an interview with one temple president, I was told the second anointing was merely a "special blessing" and is not essential to exaltation. He said he was not sure why people were called to receive second anointings and for that reason had "put the subject out of his mind." During his remarks he defined "fulness of the priesthood" as having received the Melchizedek priesthood, the temple endowment, and the marriage sealing for eternity. "By receiving the temple marriage sealing," he stated, "you will receive the 'fulness of the priesthood' in the sense that it is the final ordinance for exaltation." In talking with him later, I mentioned it was my understanding the phrase "fulness of the priesthood" referred to the second anointing. He disagreed and reaffirmed his statement. I asked him if he had received precise instruction from higher sources regarding his statement on "fulness of the priesthood." He replied he had not; that "I researched it out on my own, and if you read Joseph Fielding Smith and Bruce R. McConkie, they say the same thing." Another interview with a different temple president drew similar comments. This president, however, not only described the second anointing as a "special blessing" but stated: "The second anointing doesn't do anything more for you than the first anointing and endowment; no special ordination is performed in the second anointing." If this information is correct, the ceremony's structure may have been altered in recent years to reflect church leaders' concerns about ordaining members to godhood. This would help explain present-day leaders' uniform, widespread use of the descriptive term "special blessing" when referring to the second anointing.

58. Abraham O. Smoot Journal, 17 Jan. 1846, Special Collections, Lee Library.

59. John D. Lee Diary, 17 Jan. 1846, LDS archives.

until through the fulness of the ordinances of the temple they receive
the fulness of the priesthood and are ordained *kings and priests.* Those
so attaining shall have exaltation and be kings, priests, rulers, and lords
in their respective spheres in the eternal kingdoms of the great King
who is God our Father.[60]

Elder Joseph Fielding Smith asserted, "There is no exaltation in the
kingdom of God without the fulness of the priesthood."[61] Whether
this is confirmed in a special ordinance was not specified.

Since its introduction in 1842, the endowment has been presented within a theatrical setting. The earliest known comment by the
First Presidency regarding the use of motion pictures in the ceremony
came in 1927, when they affirmed that they had no intention of using
them.[62] This attitude changed by late 1953, however, when President
David O. McKay asked Gordon B. Hinckley to chair a committee to
create an endowment presentation for the new one-room Swiss temple.[63] Other committee members included Richard L. Evans, Edward
O. Anderson, and Joseph Fielding Smith.[64] The outgrowth was a
16-millimeter film directed by Harold I. Hansen, filmed mostly in the
upper room of the Salt Lake temple, and shot over a period of one year.
Due to inclement Utah weather, outside photography was done in the
southern United States, while lava-flowing scenes accompanying the
Creation portion came from Walt Disney Studios which granted permission to use 350 feet from the film *Fantasia.*[65]

---

60. Bruce R. McConkie, *Mormon Doctrine*, 2d ed. (Salt Lake City: Bookcraft,
1966), 425.

61. Joseph Fielding Smith, *Doctrines of Salvation*, comp. Bruce R. McConkie, 3
vols. (Salt Lake City: Bookcraft, 1954-56), 3:132.

62. Heber J. Grant, Anthony W. Ivins, and Charles W. Nibley to Pearl W. Peterson,
27 Aug. 1927, First Presidency Letterpress Copybooks, LDS archives.

63. Unless otherwise noted, information concerning the history of endowment
movies is based on Frank S. Wise, Oral History, interviewed by Gordon Irving, 1980-81,
James H. Moyle Oral History Project, and Frank S. Wise, "A New Concept in Temple
Building and Operation," 18 Feb. 1983, attached to Wise's oral history. Wise edited all
endowment films.

64. David O. McKay Diary, 29 Oct. 1953, in Francis M. Gibbons, *David O. McKay:
Apostle to the World, Prophet of God* (Salt Lake City: Deseret Book Co., 1986), 329.

65. See relevant correspondence of the First Presidency, BYU president Ernest L.
Wilkinson, and Wetzel O. Whitaker in Richard L. Evans Collection, LDS archives.

Different casts were used for versions in English, German, French, Dutch, Danish, Swedish, Norwegian, and Finnish. A year later additional casts produced Samoan, Tahitian, Tongan, and Maori films for use in the New Zealand temple. In these early films, there was no real acting, no scenery, and no attempt at sophistication; the temple workers simply enacted a live endowment session. This conservative use of the technology was not an effort to produce an art form but a means of efficiently allowing sessions to take place in a single room rather than moving from one room to another.[66]

The wide-screen concept introduced in early 1960s American movies influenced architect Harold Burton in designing the Oakland temple's two endowment rooms. He planned huge projection areas that required the use of 35-millimeter film, although curtains reduced the total screen size. After the temple was dedicated in 1964, 4" x 5" slide projectors were used to produce photo murals depicting room changes found in live endowment presentations.

The second film of the endowment ceremony was produced in 1966.[67] Due to space limitations in the Salt Lake temple, the First Presidency authorized this production (known as Project #100) to take place in the motion pictures studio on the campus of Brigham Young University.[68] A new studio stage constructed for this purpose was formally opened on 24 April 1966 with a prayer by Gordon B. Hinckley. This film was used for several years in Oakland; 16-millimeter reduction prints were prepared for English-speaking patrons in foreign temples.

In a successful effort to condense the presentation to about ninety minutes, a third motion picture was filmed at the BYU studio

---

66. Spencer Palmer, interview, 1 Aug. 1979; Wise, Oral History, 53. Palmer was an actor in the third endowment movie, 1969.

67. The cast for this film was Adam: Max Mason Brown; Eve: Marielen Wadley Christensen; Lucifer: Lael Woodbury; Minister: Morris Clinger; Peter: Harold I. Hansen; James: Douglas Clawson; John: Max Golightly; Elohim: unknown; Elohim voice: Dan Keeler; Jehovah: unknown; Jehovah voice: Carl Pope; Narrator: Glen Shaw. The production crew was Camera: Robert Stum and Dalvin Williams; Lighting: Grant Williams and R. Steven Clawson; Casting: Keith Atkinson, David Jacobs and Judd Pierson; Sound: Kenneth Hansen and Sharrol Felt; Set Design: Douglas Johnson and Robert Stum; Research: Scott Whitaker and Douglas Johnson; Script Girl: Marilyn Finch; Editing: Frank S. Wise; and Director: Wetzel O. Whitaker.

68. See relevant correspondence in Evans Collection.

during October and November 1969. Like the second film, this professional effort (known as Project #134) was directed by Wetzel O. Whitaker. The cast included both professional and amateur actors,[69] as well as elaborate scenery. Much of the outside scenery was filmed on the West Coast. Actors and production staff had to have temple recommends and received prior worthiness clearance through their bishops before being asked to participate. The portions filmed in studio were shot between ten at night and midnight to ensure privacy. Actors were required to memorize their lines in a room just off the set and could not take the script home for study. Prompt cards were used.[70] This film was completed by November 1971 when the Provo and Ogden temples opened. Due to its shorter playing time, it replaced the second film originally used in the Oakland temple.

Primarily because of President Harold B. Lee's discomfort with the long hair and beards of a few cast members in the third film, a fourth endowment movie (Project #198) was produced at BYU during the early to mid-1970s. Again directed by Wetzel Whitaker, this film used a predominantly new cast.[71] A major goal for this production was to create foreign sound tracks without refilming that did not look obviously dubbed. Since some languages such as Finnish and Japanese require substantially more time than the English equivalents, this aspect was challenging. Moreover, theological concerns required

---

69. The cast for this film was Adam: Hank Kester; Eve: Lena Tuluanen Rogers; Lucifer: Ron Fredrickson; Minister: Spencer Palmer; Peter: Gordon Jump; James: Charles Metten; John: R. LeRoi Nelson; Elohim: Jesse Stay; Elohim voice: Lael Woodbury; Jehovah: Bryce Chamberlain; Jehovah voice: Robert Peterson; Narrator: Glen Shaw. The production crew was Camera: Robert Stum; Lighting: Grant Williams; Casting: Keith Atkinson; Sound: Don Fisk and Sharrol Felt; Set Design: Douglas Johnson; Production Manager: Dalvin Williams; Editing: Frank S. Wise; and Director: Wetzel O. Whitaker.

70. Palmer interview.

71. Wise, Oral History, 57, and Wise, "A New Concept," 16. The cast for this film was Adam: James Adamson; Eve: Laurel Pugmire; Lucifer: Sterling VanWagenen; Minister: Keith Engar; Peter: Craig Costello; James: Ivan Crosland; John: Bruce Moffit; Elohim: Jesse Stay; Elohim voice: Lael Woodbury; Jehovah: Bryce Chamberlain; Jehovah voice: unknown; Narrator: Glen Shaw. The production crew was Camera: Robert Stum and Ted VanHorn; Lighting: Reed Smoot and Grant Williams; Casting: Peter Johnson; Sound: Don Fisk, Steve Aubrey and Kent Pendleton; Set Design: Douglas Johnson; Script Girl: Francine (last name unknown); Editing: Frank S. Wise; Director: Wetzel O. Whitaker; and Assistant Director: Dave Jacobs.

translations to be literal in nature, and not merely approximate as they often are in general entertainment films. This synchronization was partially accomplished through techniques such as speeded up sound track playback and step-printing every third frame twice to expand film length. Voice actors for the dubbings were local nationals. Production crews recorded audio sequences for European nationals in the London Temple in June 1972 and for Pacific nationals in a secured sound room at the BYU-Hawaii campus in June 1973.

In early 1976 the church's Temple Committee transferred all endowment film and sound operations from BYU to new facilities in the Salt Lake temple basement. While the film continues to be processed in a California lab, all sound tracks are now produced in this basement facility. Sound track duplication facilities also exist in some other temples.

Because of recommendations made by Harold B. Lee, of the First Presidency, and a committee including Howard W. Hunter (president of the Genealogical Society) working from 1968 to 1972 to investigate endowment procedures, several phrases used in ceremony film scripts were subsequently dubbed out in the mid-1970s.[72]

According to the actor who portrayed the minister in the third filmed version,[73] the role of Satan was to have originally been filled by an African-American, but due to protests by LDS Polynesians, a Caucasian filled the role. Although this film was intended as an interim production, both the third and fourth films remained in use for nearly two decades. Reportedly, the third film was not phased out as soon as expected because people preferred it over the fourth film.[74] Film two

72. Henry E. Christiansen, Oral History, interviewed by Bruce D. Blumell, 1975-76, James H. Moyle Oral History Project, 68; George H. Fudge, Oral History, interviewed by Bruce D. Blumel, 1976, James H. Moyle Oral History Project, 71; and Harold B. Lee Diary, 31 Jan., 6 Feb. 1971, in L. Brent Goates, *Harold B. Lee: Prophet & Seer* (Salt Lake City: Bookcraft, 1985), 427-28. For example, the preacher's reference to Satan having black skin was omitted; compare Witte and Fraser, *What's Going on in There?*, 23, with Sackett, *What's Going on in There?*, 38. Another omission was the preacher leading the audience in a Protestant hymn. Satan and the preacher no longer fixed a specific salary to proselytize the audience for converts (Tanner and Tanner, *Mormonism*, 468-49; Witte and Fraser, 21).

73. Palmer interview.

74. Ibid.

was cut down to the same length as that of films three and four to provide diversity for frequent temple-goers.[75]

The most recent modifications to the temple ceremony occurred in April 1990. Following several in-house studies, including a national survey of some 3,400 members, a number of changes was implemented to soften the ritual's treatment of women, non-Mormon clergy, use of Masonic elements, and violence of the penalties. According to the *Los Angeles Times*:

> [T]he central temple ceremony has been altered to eliminate the woman's vow to obey her husband. . . . Two other features dropped were a dramatization suggesting that Satan beguiles Christian clergy to teach false doctrine and the requirement that members make throat-slitting and disemboweling gestures as signs that they will not reveal the ceremony's contents . . . Also dropped is an "embrace" of a man representing God, who stands behind a ceiling-to-floor veil. Reaching through a slit in the veil, the church member puts his or her hand to the back of the deity and presses against him at the cheek, shoulders, knees and feet with the veil between them. The contact at "five points of fellowship," including the hand to his back, has been omitted, although the member must still give a secret handshake and repeat a lengthy password.[76]

Perhaps one of the most significant effects of modern technology on temple work has stemmed from the church's widespread use of electronic data processing. In 1961 a growing shortage of names provided by members for vicarious ordinance work forced church officials to decide among closing some temples, decreasing the number of endowment sessions, or taking institutional responsibility for providing names. President David O. McKay opted to have the Genealogical Society provide names for vicarious ordinances. Since the start of its name extraction program, the society has provided about 75 percent of all names.[77]

The church's computer planning committee realized during the late 1950s and early 1960s that given the estimated 70 billion people

75. Wise, "A New Concept."

76. "Mormons Modify Temple Rites," *Los Angeles Times*, 5 May 1990, F20.

77. Fudge, Oral History, 15-19.

who have been born on the earth, all LDS adults working in temples eight hours a day, seven days a week would not be able to keep up with world population growth, much less complete ordinance work for deceased ancestors. This concern has not disappeared.[78] Accordingly, a number of procedural changes were implemented. Despite some initial opposition by Harold B. Lee and Joseph Fielding Smith to what they perceived as "doctrinal tampering," vicarious ordinances were permitted to be performed out of their traditional order, with new data processing systems collating the results. Thus deceased persons could be sealed or endowed before they were baptized, washed, anointed, or confirmed.[79]

Since the Genealogical Society initiated the computer-based name extraction program in 1965, computers have been used to track the administration of both living and vicarious temple ordinances ranging from initiatory work to marriage sealings. While some have balked at the introduction of "mammon's world" in the temple, computerization clearly has augmented efficiency.[80]

---

78. *Church News*, 20 July 1986, 16.

79. Fudge, Oral History, 17-19; Gary Carlson, Oral History, interviewed by James B. Allen, 1980, 8-21, James H. Moyle Oral History Project. Carlson was on the LDS church Data Processing Committee and the board of directors of Management Systems Corporation—a Mormon-owned company which provided the church with data processing services.

80. James B. Allen, "Testimony and Technology: A Phase of the Modernization of Mormonism since 1950," in Thomas G. Alexander and Jessie L. Embry, eds., *After 150 Years: The Latter-day Saints in Sesquicentennial Perspective* (Provo, UT: Charles Redd Center for Western Studies, 1983), 173-207.

CONCLUSION

In 1980 LDS church president Spencer W. Kimball stated: "We feel an urgency for this great work to be accomplished and wish to encourage the Saints to accept their responsibility of performing temple ordinances."[1] From outward appearances, Mormons have embraced vicarious temple work with more vigor than ever before. Many older temples have been renovated and have replaced live actors with the more efficient movie format. The number of operating temples has increased dramatically, from thirteen in 1970 to forty-four in 1990.

An analysis of ordinance data, however, suggests that at the most temple work has remained relatively flat over the last few decades. Based on figures from this period, an average of one out of every three converts actually receives his or her own endowment. Since 1971 the difference between total live endowments and the number of new converts has steadily widened. This trend clearly began after World War II. New missionaries, most at age 19-21, are endowed, and they average almost one-third of all live endowments since 1971. Thus the actual percentage of new members receiving their own endowment is much smaller. Since the church does not release geographic annual totals of new converts, it is not possible to determine sociological factors which may account for the widening gap between total new converts and total live endowments. Since 1971 vicarious endowments have been performed at an average rate of .81 per member per

---

1. Spencer W. Kimball, edited version of a speech given 4 Apr. 1980 to regional representatives, in *Ensign* 10 (Aug. 1980): 2.

173

Annual Endowment Data, 1971 - 85

Year	Total Membership	Convert Baptisms	Operating Temples	Endowments for Living	Endowments for Dead	Living Endowments as a Percentage of Total Converts	Vicarious Endowments per Member per year	Missionaries Set Apart	Percentage of Total Live Endowments
1971	3,090,953	83,514	13	31,685	1,701,907	0.38	0.55	8,344	0.26
1972	3,218,908	91,237	15	35,003	2,275,192	0.38	0.71	7,874	0.22
1973	3,306,658	79,603	15	36,964	2,477,532	0.46	0.75	9,471	0.26
1974	3,409,987	69,018	16	37,432	2,535,518	0.54	0.74	9,811	0.26
1975	3,572,202	95,412	16	47,142	3,027,956	0.49	0.85	14,446	0.31
1976	3,742,749	133,959	16	43,645	3,421,793	0.33	0.91	13,928	0.32
1977	3,969,220	167,939	14	47,037	3,555,118	0.28	0.90	14,561	0.31
1978	4,166,854	152,000	16	50,400	3,756,600	0.33	0.90	15,860	0.31
1979	4,404,121	193,000	17	51,600	3,873,300	0.27	0.88	16,590	0.32
1980	4,644,768	211,000	19	52,000	3,962,000	0.25	0.85	16,600	0.32
1981	4,920,449	224,000	19	49,800	4,101,000	0.22	0.83	17,800	0.36
1982	5,162,619	207,000	19	48,800	4,418,000	0.24	0.86	18,260	0.37
1983	5,351,724	189,419	25	52,116	4,364,928	0.28	0.82	19,450	0.37
1984	5,641,054	192,983	31	53,998	4,395,424	0.28	0.78	19,720	0.37
1985	5,910,496	197,640	37	54,554	4,857,052	0.28	0.82	19,890	0.36
						0.33	0.81		0.32

FIGURE 1.

Avg. Net Member Increase vs. Avg. Live Endowments: 1846 - 1985

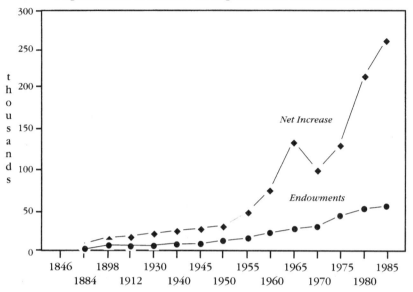

FIGURE 2.

Avg. Vicarious Endowments per Member per Year: 1846 - 1985

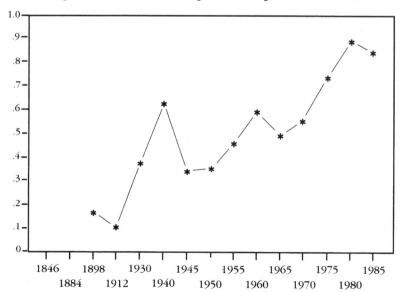

year. These per-member levels have declined slightly during the past fifteen years despite the impressive number of new temple dedications.

It is not possible to give full confidence to these figures or their interpretation since church administrators have not released detailed endowment data arranged by year.[2] Other unavailable data critical to a reliable statistical analysis include annual totals of temple recommend holders and parallel information on temple work in regions outside the United States. The only statistics available indicate that in 1985 at least 75 percent of all live and vicarious endowments were performed in United States temples.[3]

U.S. membership in 1990 constituted about 54 percent of total membership. The disproportionate amount of U.S. endowments may indicate that the temple—or that vicarious work for the dead—has lower priority overseas, a condition that could change as new generations abroad grow up with their own temples. It also could indicate that foreign converts may be economically disadvantaged and cannot often attend, even when temples are relatively close. Only time will tell what effect the large number of new foreign temples will have on the number of endowments performed.

There is no way to quantitatively evaluate the spiritual benefit of temple work for either the living or the dead. Certainly no spiritual benefits can be realized without participation. Waning individual temple activity has no doubt led to an increased effort among church leaders to try to stimulate renewed interest among temple-goers.[4]

------

2. A telling example of the increasing reticence to share operating statistics is that in 1987 for the first time in thirty-one years, the official *Conference Report of The Church of Jesus Christ of Latter-day Saints* (first appearing in *The Ensign*) omitted all figures related to temple work, including the number of operating temples and number of live and vicarious endowments performed during the prior year (*Ensign* 17 [May 1987]: 21). This practice has continued to the present.

3. *Deseret News 1987 Church Almanac* (Salt Lake City: Deseret News Press, 1987), 304. Carrie A. Miles has gathered evidence that an average of 90 percent of all temple work takes place within the United States. She also found evidence that most conversions to Mormonism during the past twenty years have occurred outside the United States (privately circulated manuscript, 1982, 62-65, 119-22, 215-16). If her data are accurate (the church will not release any figures), it has great bearing on the relative symbolic and social significance of the temple.

4. An analysis of the ratio of general conference talk references to temple work

During the late 1970s many stakes were issued endowment quotas. While less emphasis is now placed on quotas, expectations remain high. For example, active recommend holders living close to a temple usually are expected to perform an average of one vicarious endowment per month.

The church has already begun addressing the economic problem of attending the temple by constructing numerous scaled-down temples strategically placed in areas of high member densities. Although temples have traditionally been separate structures with the sole function of temple work, it would be possible to create special rooms in stake centers for endowments and sealings. This would reduce temple construction and operating expenses, even though the ordinances may lose something of their "special" character by being associated with a multi-use building. Similarly, the wearing of temple undergarments could be restricted to temple work. This would help address the question of financial demands made of members in less economically-advantaged countries.

Another consideration is the appeal of the ceremony. If new converts and maturing youth have become less likely to seek their own endowments, the ordinance may be seen as less meaningful or have a different meaning. Allen Roberts, tracing the decline of church architectural symbolism, suggests that today's Saints are no longer comfortable with symbolism of any sort.[5] Contemporary Saints may understand it much less than they once did. They recognize, for instance, an all-seeing eye, but unlike nineteenth-century Saints who saw it on doorknobs, carved on the lintels of doors, and printed on the letterheads of stationery and newspapers, modern Mormons see it only on the temple. Joseph Smith and contemporaries would have understood certain symbols from the richness of at least two contexts—Masonry as well as Mormonism.

(compared to other themes, counting paragraphs) from 1830 to 1979 indicates resulting scores ranging from .023 to .027 through 1919; since 1920 the scores have ranged from .001 to .011, a dramatic drop (Gordon Shepherd and Gary Shepherd, *A Kingdom Transformed: Themes in the Development of Mormonism* [Salt Lake City: University of Utah Press, 1984], 255).

5. Allen D. Roberts, "Where Are the All-Seeing Eyes? The Origin, Use, and Decline of Early Mormon Symbolism," *Sunstone* 4 (May-June 1979): 28-29.

The feelings contemporary Saints have for the temple merit continued analysis by social scientists. Prior to the 1990 changes, I heard from many people about the discomfort they felt in one degree or another with elements of the temple ceremony. Although such reports are anecdotal, they represent areas that could be explored in attempting to understand the place of the temple in the lives of modern Saints.

Another area that may influence feelings about the temple comes from the increasing impact of technology and rationalism on our culture as a whole. The idea of a "lodge" may itself have an old-fashioned ring to it. Probably in no other settings except college organizations, with their attendant associations of youthfulness and possible immaturity, do people encounter secret ceremonies with code handshakes, special signs and tokens, and unusual clothing.

Despite the 1990 changes, the endowment still depicts women as subservient to men, not as equals in their right. For example, while women now covenant to obey God and their husbands in righteousness, it is the man who acts as intermediary with God. Women are promised ordination in future states as queens and priestesses to their husbands and are required to veil their faces at one point in the ceremony. Eve does not speak in the narrative portion once she and Adam are expelled from the garden. Such elements seem at odds with other aspects of New Testament Christianity and Mormon teachings.

Some individuals find that the filmed presentations have a dulling effect on response. The freshness of live-session interpretation brings new insights in subtle details. While some people enjoy the more rapid pace of the filmed versions, others worry about being "programmed" by repetition and find themselves unable to imagine other faces, other voices, and other interpretations than those being impressed upon them by repetition.

In short, at least some Saints perceive the temple as incongruent with other important elements of their religious life. Some find it irrelevant to the deeper currents of Christian service and worship. Some admit to boredom. Others describe motivation for continued and regular temple attendance as feelings of hope and patience—the faith that by continuing to participate they will develop more positive feelings and even the joy that others sometimes report. Often they feel unworthy or guilty because the temple is so unanimously presented as the pinnacle of spiritual experience for Latter-day Saints.

To suggest that all Latter-day Saints are deeply troubled by such elements would be incorrect. For many the temple experience is one of selfless service, peaceful communion with God, a refreshing retreat from the world, and a promise of future union with departed loved ones. Reports of spiritual enlightenment, personal revelation, and grateful contact with those for whom vicarious work is being done are not infrequent.

Certainly the social value of the temple has expanded and become more far-reaching as more and more people have gained access and as more Latter-day Saints retire with economic means and health to spend years of service there. Non-Mormon anthropologist Mark P. Leone has suggested that temple worship is a key institution by which Mormons resolve the conflict of being "in the world but not of it" and spiritually and psychologically reinforce their unique purpose in life.[6] The value of the temple experience clearly manifests itself in a renewed individual commitment to values and goals due in part to strict requirements of worthiness one must adhere to for permission to attend. It follows that Latter-day Saints receive satisfaction belonging to a select group of devout members qualified to perform this sacred work.

Reviewing the historical development of any important institution in a community's life raises questions about its future. Temple ritual has changed a great deal in response to community needs over time. Obviously it has the capability of changing still further as the need arises. If one were to set aside questions of spiritual, emotional, and social significance and examine the ritual strictly from a functional perspective, some suggestive conclusions emerge.

For instance, it is interesting that vicarious endowments remain the only portion of the total temple sequence (baptism, confirmation, washing, anointing, ordination, endowment, and sealing) which has not been "batch processed" to increase efficiency. Through 1985 a cumulative total of over 1.5 million endowments for the living and

6. Mark P. Leone, "The Mormon Temple Experience," *Sunstone* 3 (Sept.-Oct. 1978): 10-13.

almost 86 million endowments for the dead have been performed. From a strictly functional perspective, the amount of time required to complete a vicarious endowment seems excessive. If patrons do not need to hear baptismal and confirmation speeches prior to performing these proxy ordinances or talks on how to have a good marriage before vicarious sealings (as all living people traditionally receive before their own ceremonies), it seems inconsistent that they must hear about events in the Garden of Eden or the lone and dreary world before vicariously receiving the signs, tokens, and key words which form the apparent essence of the endowment ceremony. If increasing the number of endowments were the primary objective, these elements could be performed in a few minutes instead of two hours. Baptisms for the dead and sealings already occur with accelerated routines.

If the vicarious elements were detached from the endowment or performed in another sequence, then the balance of temple activities devoted to instructing members in theological matters and allowing time for meditation, inspiration, and worship might be done under a different, less mechanical setting. Refocusing attention on the temple's function as a house of prayer and personal revelation might draw more individuals who genuinely wish for a worshipful experience in community and then quietly, alone. At the present time most temples do not have the facilities for solitary meditation and discourage lingering in the celestial room after passing through the veil. A reversion to the live presentation might also augment attentiveness and rediscovery as participants review fundamental concepts.

Such strategies suggest ways of meeting the need for effectively and efficiently carrying out the mission of salvation for the dead while providing a holy setting for spiritual healing. The richness and centrality of the endowment ceremony in the late twentieth century, as throughout the nineteenth, roots Latter-day Saints in a tradition of spiritual power that promises equal abundance in the future, provided that the essential can be sorted from the non-essential and that relevance can be grounded in contemporary experience, divorced from claims of unchanging, mysterious transcendence and unconditional guarantees of salvation.

APPENDIX 1

The 7, 14, 21, and 28 December 1845 Meetings
of the Nauvoo, Illinois, Holy Order

[Unless otherwise indicated, all manuscript sources are housed in archives, historical department, Church of Jesus Christ of Latter-day Saints, Salt Lake City, Utah.]

I. 7 December 1845; Sunday

Joseph Smith, Jr., *History of the Church of Jesus Christ of Latter-day Saints,* 7 vols., ed. B. H. Roberts, 2d ed., rev. (Salt Lake City: Deseret Book Co., 1973), 7:538:

Sunday, 7.–I met with the Twelve and others in the Temple. We partook of the sacrament, exhorted each other and prayed.

Heber C. Kimball Diary, date, in Stanley B. Kimball, ed., *On the Potter's Wheel: The Diaries of Heber C. Kimball* (Salt Lake City: Signature Books in association with Smith Research Associates, 1987), 163-65 (italicized portions indicate words not included in Helen Mar Whitney's publication of her father's diary in "Scenes in Nauvoo, and Incidents from H. C. Kimball's Journal," *Woman's Exponent* 12 [15 June 1883], 2:10):

Sunday, De. the 7, 1845. Snow falling. The weather more mild. *After Brexfast I went to Br. Hills and got my Watch. From thence I* went to David Fulmers and Sealled two Sisters to him fore time and Eternity. Gave some council and then returned to the Temple whare I found my wife. Bishop Whitney and wife *went in with me. I arived*

181

at 10 found 6 or Eight present. O. Spencer come in my room and read my procclamation to me and my wife.

Present B. Young, Mary Ann [Young]; Heber C. Kimball, Vilate Kimball; Orson Hide, Marinda Hide; O. P. Pratt, Mary Ann Pratt; John Tailor, Leonora Tailor; G. A. Smith, Barshebe [Bathsheba] Smith; Willard Richards.

High Preas [and wives] present John Smith, Clarrisa; A. Cutler, Lois; R[eynolds] Cahoon, Thirza; N. K. Whitney, Elizebeth Ann; Cornelius Lott, Permila; I. Morly, Lucy, O. Spencer, Catherine; Wm. Claton, Agness Smith; George Miller, Mary Cathrine; Joseph Young, Sister Tomson, Levi Richards, Mary Smith, Joseph Fielding, W. W. Phelps, Sally; Joseph Kingsburay, L. Woodworth, Phebe; John Berunisel [Bernhisel].

The following Persons are members of the Holy Order of the Holy Preasthood having Recieved it in the Life time of Joseph and Hirum, the Prophets. *Elder B. Young went and gave the Brethren and Sisters present a view of the Seprate rooms, and the object of them, then pute up the Veil and choe [showed] the Order of it.* The Brethren and Sisters clothed *half past one*, commenced our meeting at two Oclock. Meeting [opened] by prair by Joseph Fielding, sung humn and Elder John Tailor spoke a chort time then H. C. Kimball spoke. Elder B. was sick and had to retire to his room and lay down on his couch. Then Elder O. Hide gave a chort exortation. After he closed, him [hymn] sung. Then H. C. K. [Heber C. Kimball], N. K. [Newell K. Whitney] brock [broke] Bread. Blessed by H. C. K. Elder B. Young come in pertaock [partook], *carid around by N. K.* Wine, blest by Joseph Young, Carrid round by N. K. Singing while the wine going round. Then El. P. P. Pratt rose and spoke *on a simeler object before the pople.* W. W. Phelps spoke. *It was 3 Oclock when we partoock of sacrement.* Great Solemnity rested on the Breth and sisters, great union in our meeting. *Seven present have not had thare Last [or second] Anointing. L. Woodworth and wife, Sister Tomson, Wm. Claton, Joseph Kingsbury, John Benhisel, Sister Marinda Hide, Agness Smith, the wife of Don [Carlos] Smith [deceased].* John Smith our Patriarch spoke a chort time them Elder B. Young Said this quorum should meet heare evry Sabath and take of the Sacrament. *The Br. and Sisters ware completly clothed. Elder B. Young gave us good council. We offerd up the Signs Little after fore, got through at five. G. A. Smith mouth.*

When he got through all went home in good spirrits. *My wife spent part of the Eve with J. Kingsbury.*

Willard Richards Diary, date:

Sunday Decr. 7. I went to the Temple at eleven o clock and remained until dusk had the sacrament for the first time in the Temple

II. 14 December 1845; Sunday

Joseph Smith, *History of the Church*, 7:545-46:

The Twelve and others with our wives met in the attic story of the Temple.

After prayer and singing, Elders Isaac Morley and Charles C. Rich administered, and we partook of the sacrament.

I introduced the subject of establishing rules for the preservation of order in the House of the Lord which were agreed to and ordered to be printed.

There is too much covetousness in the church, and too much disposition amongst the brethren to seek after power and has been from the beginning, but this feeling is diminishing and the brethren begin to know better. In consequence of such feelings Joseph [Smith] left the people in the dark on many subjects of importance and they still remain in dark. We have got to rid such principles from our hearts.

I referred to the manner in which the corner stones of this Temple were laid as published in the *Times and Seasons*, and said that the perfect order would have been for the presidency of the stake to lay the first or southeast corner; the high council the second or southwest corner; the bishops the northeast corner; but the high priests laid the southwest corner, though they had no right to do it. I spoke of the brethren making objections to persons being permitted to receive the ordinances, and added, that when objections were made I should feel bound to determine whether the person making the objections was a responsible person, and if he is not, I should do as I pleased about listening to the objections; but if he was a responsible person I should listen to them.

To constitute a man responsible he must have the power and

ability not only to save himself but save others; but there are those who are not capable of saving themselves and will have to be saved by others.

When a man objects to another receiving the ordinances he becomes responsible to answer to God for that man's salvation; and who can tell but if he received the ordinances he would be saved, but if we refuse to give him the means he cannot be saved and we are responsible for it.

There is no law to prevent any man from obtaining all the blessings of the priesthood if he will walk according to the commandments, pay his tithes and seek after salvation, but he may deprive himself of them.

After much profitable instruction we united in prayer, Orson Hyde being mouth.

Meeting adjourned for one week.

Heber C. Kimball/William Clayton Diary, date, in George D. Smith, ed., *An Intimate Chronicle: The Journals of William Clayton* (Salt Lake City: Signature Books in association with Smith Research Associates, 1991), 211-15 (note: Helen Mar Whitney did not include this entry in "Scenes in Nauvoo, and Incidents from H. C. Kimball's Journal"):

The following brethren and sisters assembled to the Attic Story of the Temple according to appointment viz., Pres Brigham Young & Mary Ann Young, Heber C. Kimball & Vilate Kimball, Parley P Pratt & Mary Ann Pratt, Orson Hyde [sic]. Orson Pratt & Nancy M. Pratt, George A. Smith & Barsheba W. Smith, Amasa Lyman & Loisa M. Lyman, John Taylor & Leonora A [sic] Taylor, John Smith & Clarissa Smith, Newel K. Whitney & Elizabeth A. Whitney, George Miller & Mary C. Miller, Alpheus Cutler [sic] Isaac Morley & Lucy Morley, Wm W. Phelps & Sally Phelps, John M. Bernhisel, William Clayton, Joseph C. Kingsbury, Franklin D. Richards, Samuel Bent & Lettice Bent, Agness M. Smith & Mary [Fielding] Smith, Mercy R. Thompson & Tirzah Cahoon, Lucian Woodworth & Phebe Woodworth, Orson Spencer & Catherine C. Spencer, Cornelius P. Lott & Joseph Fielding, Joseph Young.

Soon after 11 o clock those who were present were ordered by the president to clothe themselves, which being done and seated at 20 minutes after 11 oclock sang, "Adam Ondi Ahman" &c. After which we bowed before the Lord and President Young offered up prayers. We next sang "Glorious things of thee are spoken" &c. When bread and wine having been provided by Bishop N. K. Whitney Elders Isaac Morley and Charles C. Rich were called upon to administer the sacrament. They broke the bread which was then blessed by Isaac Morley and passed round by Charles C. Rich, who also blessed the wine and passed it round likewise.

We then sang, "O happy souls who pray" &c. and "Come all ye sons of Zion." After which President Young introduced the subject of having rules of order to govern all who come here and to regulate our works, printed. He wished to know the minds of the quorum whether they thought it best. It was voted unanimously that we think it wisdom to have some rules printed for that purpose.

It was also unanimously voted that President Young introduce the rules.

He then explained that he had some rules draughted [drafted] last evening, but they were now at the office to be printed ready for tomorrow, he however explained the majority of them explaining also the order he wished carried out, and then took a vote whether this quorum will sustain him in this regulation.

The vote was unanimous in the affirmative.

He then observed that he should henceforth have all the cloth which was intended for robes, garments and aprons, brought and either cut or made in this Temple under the superintendance of those who know how to do it right. There are now scarcely two Aprons alike nor two garments cut or marked right, and it is necessary to observe perfect order in this thing and it never can be done unless we take this course.

A conversation then ensued on the distinction of office or power, between a president of Seventies, and a member of the High Council or a High Priest. It arose in consequence of some of the High Council having been washed and anointed by some of the presidents of Seventies and inasmuch as there had been some considerable differ-ence in the views of the brethren in regard to the difference of authority between the High Council and Seventies, President Young concluded it would be wisdom to have the subject understood at this early stage of business so as to prevent any feelings or dispute arising on the subject hereafter.

He stated that the Seventies are ordained Apostles, and when they go forth into the ministry, they are sent with power to build up the Kingdom in all the world, and consequently they have power to ordain High Priests, and also to ordain and organize a High Council.

Some of the High Priests have been ready to quarrel on the subject, supposing they had power and authority above the Seventies, and some in their zeal for power, have abused and trampled on the feelings of some of the Seventies.

There is too much covetousness in the Church and too much disposition amongst the brethren to seek after power and has been from the beginning, but this feeling is diminishing and the brethren begin to know better. In consequence of such feelings Joseph left the people in the dark on many subjects of importance and they still remain in the dark. We have got to rid such principles from our hearts.

He then referred to the manner in which the corner stones of this Temple were laid as published in the Times and Seasons and then stated that the perfect order would have been for the presidency of the Stake to lay the first or South East corner. The High Council the 2nd or South West corner. The Bishops the North West corner and the Priests the North East corner, but added the High Priests laid the South West corner, but they had no right to do it.

He then introduced the subject of the brethren making objections to any person being permitted to receive the ordinances, and added that when the objections were made he should feel bound to determine whether the person making the objections was a responsible person, if he was not he should do as he pleased about listening to the objections, but if he was a responsible person he should then listen to the objections.

To make a man a responsible man he must have the power and ability not only to save himself but to save others, but there are those who are not capable of saving themselves and will have to be saved if they are saved at all by those who are capable of doing it. An objection from such would have no weight on his mind.

When a man objects to another receiving the ordinances, he becomes responsible to answer to God for that mans salvation. And who knows but if he received the ordinances he would be saved, but if we refuse to give him the means he cannot be saved and we are responsible for it.

There is no law to prevent any man from obtaining all the blessings of the priesthood if he will walk according to the commandments, pay his tithes and seek after salvation, but he may deprive himself of them.

After much important instruction from the president the signs of the Holy Priesthood were offered up and prayers. Elder Orson Hyde being mouth after which the company were dismissed till next Sunday with strict orders to be here and dressed precisely at 11 o clock.

At 2 o clock P.M. agreeable to appointment nearly all those new members [of the Holy Order] who have received the ordinances the past week assembled in the upper department to receive instructions in regard to the ordinances and their duty to be observed henceforth and forever.

At the same hour President Young, H. C. Kimball, P. Pratt, O. Pratt, O. Hyde, J. Taylor, G. A. Smith, A. Lyman, N. K. Whitney, G. Miller, W. W. Phelps, Wm. Clayton and P[hineas] H. Young retired into President Young's Room. The President appointed W. W. Phelps and P. P. Pratt to instruct the brethren and sisters now waiting, which was done and much good instruction given by them. They were especially instructed more fully into the nature and importance of the blessings and powers of the Holy Priesthood which they have received, and it was enjoined upon them not to talk out of doors, but to be wise and prudent in all things.

They were also informed that no one will be admitted into these rooms during the time we are to work except those who are called to assist, unless they are invited by those who have authority.

At a quarter to 5 they were dismissed by blessing from Elder Taylor.

At the same time this was going on those who were in President Youngs room were listening to a number of letters which were read together with the report of the trial of J. B. Backenstos as published in the Peoria Register.

About 5 o clock nearly all the company having left the house President Young and others of the Twelve went down to the lower story of the Temple to council together on the arrangements of the Pulpits. The following persons remained and slept in the Temple over night, viz. President Young, A[lbert]. P. Rockwood, J[ohn]. D. Lee and David Candland.

Brigham Young Journal, date:

. . . about 11. 0. the breth. met for service & I presented the rules of order after singing & prayer accepted. We then partook of the sacrament spent the rest of the day with the brethren in giving them instruction and offering prayer's to the most High

III. 21 December 1845; Sunday

Heber C. Kimball Diary, date (note: italics indicate material not included in Helen Mar Whitney's "Scenes from Nauvoo, and Incidents from H. C. Kimball's Journal"):

According to appointment on Sunday last, a meeting was held in the east room *this day of all those who could clothe themselves in the garments of Priesthood,* 75 persons were present, Elder H. C. Kimball presiding. *The names of those present so far as the clerks could ascertain them are as follows H. C. Kimball, Vilate Kimball John Taylor Leonora Taylor–P. P. Pratt, Mary Ann Pratt Orson Pratt, Sarah M. Pratt–Amasa Lyman Maria Louisa Lyman George A. Smith, Bathsheba W. Smith, John Smith, Patriarch, Clarissa Smith Alpheus Cutler, Lois Cutler Reynolds Cahoon, Tirzah Cahoon, George Miller, Clarissa Miller C. C. Rich Sarah D. Rich W. W. Phelps Sally Phelps Samuel Bent, Theodore Turley F. D. Richards Jane S. Richards.–David Fullmer, Rhoda Ann Fullmer Reuben Miller F. Nickerson Simeon Carter–Lydia Carter Thomas Grover Caroline E. Grover G. W. Harris Lucinda Harris William Felshaw, Mary H. Felshaw, James Allred–Elizabeth Allred Elizabeth Taylor Steven Markham Levi Richards–Wm A Sanger, Mary Sanger Louisa Sanger William Crosby, Sally Crosby, Joseph Fielding & wife (Hannah Fielding) Elijah Fordham, Anna B. Fordham William Weeks Caroline Weeks David Candland L. R. Foster, Mary Smith Mercy R. Thompson John M. Bernhisel Erastus Snow Ezra T. Benson & wife John Pack & wife–Cynthia Durfee, Eliza R. Snow–James Taylor, Joseph L. Heywood & wife William Cahoon & wife and 2 others whose names were not obtained. –*

At 5 minutes before 11, the song "Glorious things of thee are

Spoken" was sung. Father John Smith then made a few remarks, blessed the bread and it [was] handed round by Bishop Geo. Miller, the Wine was blessed by Geo. Miller and handed round by him. While the wine was passing round, Elder George A. Smith arose and addressed the congregation. He thanked God for the privileges this day enjoyed and spoke of the difficulties under which the church had labored to attain the blessings we now enjoy. Another thing he thanked God for, already had more than 500 persons passed through [the endowment], and therefore if half of them should be like the foolish virgins, and turn away from the truth, the principles of the Holy Priesthood, would be beyond the reach of mobs and all the assaults of the adversaries of the Church. Order was one of the laws of Heaven, *there ought to be no whispering here, no difficulty ought to be mentioned, whatever transpires here ought not to be mentioned any where else.*

When we *pray to the Lord we ought to* come together *clad in proper garments and when we do so*, and unite our hearts *and hands together*, and act as one mind, the Lord will hear us and will answer our prayers. *Our garments should be properly marked and we should understand those marks and we should wear those garments continually, by night and by day, in prison or free and if the devils in hell cut us up, let them cut the garments to pieces also, if we have the garments upon us at all times we can at any time offer up the signs* [and tokens]. He *then* related an instance of some children being healed & cured of the whooping cough in one night, through the prayers of himself and Elder Woodruff, in Michigan, while they were there on a mission. Said that whenever they could get an opportunity they retired to the wilderness or to an upper room they, did so *and offered up the signs*, and were always answered. It would be a good thing for us *to put on our garments* every day and pray to God, and in private circles, *when we can do so with safety*.

We are *now* different from what we were before we entered into this quorum. Speedy vengeance will now overtake the transgressor. When a man and *his* wife are united in feeling, and act in union, I believe they can hold their children by prayer and faith and will not be obliged to give them up to death until they are fourscore years old.

Sometimes mere trifles destroy the confidence which each ought to have in the other. This prevents a union of faith and feeling. The

apostacy of Thomas B. Marsh was caused by so small a thing as a pint
of strippings and his oaths brought the exterminating order which
drove us all out of Missouri. The woman ought to be in subjection to
the man be careful to guard against loud laughter, *against whispering*,
levity, talebearing. He expressed his unfeigned love for his brethren,
and his confidence in their endeavors to keep these rules.

"The Spirit of God" was then sung.

Elder Kimball next addressed the meeting. He concurred in all
that had been said, the observation of these things is most essential.
About 4 years ago next May nine persons were admitted into the Holy
order 5 are now living. B. Young W. Richards George Miller N. K.
Whitney & H. C. Kimball two are dead [James Adams and Hyrum
Smith], and two are worse than dead [William Law and William Marks].
You have not got all you will have if you are faithful *and keep your
tongue in your mouth. You are pronounced clean, but were you
pronounced clean from the blood of this generation? NO! not all of
you, only some few who have deserved it. Females were not received
when we first received the Holy order. Men apostatized, being led by
their wives, if any such cases occur again, no more women will be
admitted.* He spoke of the Necessity of Women being in subjection to
their husbands. I am subject to my God, my wife is in subjection to me
and will reverence me in my place and I will make her happy. I do not
want her to step forward and dictate to me any more than I dictate to
President Young. In his absence I take his place according to his
request. Shall we cease from loud laughter *and mirth*? Will you never
slander your brother or sister? I will refer your minds to the covenants
you have made by an observance of these things, you will have dreams
and visions. *In the coming week we will take through 100 a day, we
want no man to come in here unless he is invited, or on business.
Let those having cloth to make up send it here and we will make it
up and put it to good use. Women should be appointed to attend to
the washing and anointings of the High Priests wives. There is a large
lot ahead. You are not yet ordained to any thing, but we have the
clay here, it is mellow and we shall soon put it on the wheel. If any
brother divulges any thing we shall cut him off.* We shall not be with
you long. We cannot rest day nor night until we put you in possession
of the Priesthood. *We want you now to make up garments for
yourselves. I want my own robe back again.* If we have made you

clean every whit, now go to work and make others clean. *We will have a screw [screen?] put up before the vail, and will make an office of my room, and have a stairway leading down from it. No person will be allowed to take people through the vail but those appointed.*

Let women wait upon women and let men wait upon men, then no jealousies will arise. He closed at 5 m[inutes]. before one.

Elder P. P. Pratt approved of what had been said & said a few words about the fashion of our robes, his own robe, which was like those first used, was not sewed up at the sides, neither was it of more than one breadth.

Elder Kimball showed the right fashion for a leaf, spoke of Elder Richards being protected at Carthage Jail, having on the robe, while Joseph and Hyrum and Elder Taylor were shot to pieces, said the Twelve would have to leave shortly, for a charge of treason would be brought against them for swearing us to avenge the blood of the anointed ones, and some one would reveal it and we shall have to part some day between sundown and dark.

George Miller said that when near the camp of General Hardin, he was shot at, and the Sentinel who was near him was killed, but he escaped unhurt, having on his garments. He then spoke of the design and purpose for which all the [signs and tokens] Symbols in the garden were given &c. Paul said he bore in his body the marks of the Lord Jesus Christ [Gal. 6: 17], which was as plainly as he dare allude to these things in writing. But the marks Paul alluded to were just such as we now have on our garments. He spoke of the signs, tokens and penalties, and of the work in general, said it was the work of God, by which he designs to reinstitute man into his presence &c.

Elder John Taylor confirmed the saying that Joseph and Hyrum and himself were without their robes in the jail at Carthage, while Doct Richards had his on, but corrected the idea that some had, that they had taken them off through fear. W. W. Phelps said Joseph told him one day about that time, that he had laid aside his garment on account of the hot weather. Elder Kimball said word came to him and to all the Twelve about that time to lay aside their garments, and take them to pieces, or cut them up so they could not be found.

The Sisters ought not to gather together in schools to pray unless their husbands, or some man be with them, every evening at 5 o clock the High Priests meet for prayer by themselves Clothed in their robes of Priesthood. Also the High Council, and the Seventies.

There are from seven to twelve persons who have met together every day to pray ever since Joseph's death, and this people have been sustained upon this principle. Here is brother [Theodore] Turley [he] has been liberated by the power of God and not of man, *and I have covenanted, and never will rest nor my posterity after me until those men who killed Joseph and Hyrum have been wiped out of the earth.*

Elder [Reynolds] Cahoon *had permission to speak at 20 m[inutes]. past one. He* bore testimony of the importance of those things which had been spoken. *He* rejoiced in the idea that the things he was taught in the beginning, were the same things now taught and remembered, and it is so because they are eternal things.

The whole assembly were then formed *into 2 circles one within the other, the signs and tokens were given, the proper attitude* for prayer *assumed,* and Elder Taylor being mouth, the whole congregation united with him in prayer *to God,* at 10 minutes past 2 the meeting was dismissed *and all unclothed themselves of their robes* and another congregation *which had been waiting in the vestibule of the temple was admitted into the east room, not being clothed in the garments of Priesthood.*

At 3 oclock sung Hosanna. Prayer by Elder Orson Hyde, after which by invitation of E[lder] Kimball who presided (President Young not having been at the Temple today, and the duty of presiding having devolved upon Elder Kimball as the next in succession) Amasa Lyman, addressed the assembly. He said Doubtless with the most of the present assembly it is the beginning of a new era, in their lives, they have come to a time they never saw before. They have come to the commencement of a knowledge of things, and it [is] necessary they should be riveted on their minds, one important thing to be understood is this, that those portions of the priesthood which you have received are all essential matters, it is not merely that you may see these things, but it is matter of fact, a matter that has to do directly with your salvation, for which you have talked and labored many years. It is not for amusement you are brought to receive these things but to put you in possession of the means of salvation and be brot [brought] into a proper relationship to God. Hence a man becomes responsible for his own conduct, and that of his wife, if he has one. It is not designed that the things that are presented today should be forgotten tomorrow but [they should be] remembered and practiced through all [your] coming life. Hence it [is] a stepstone to approach to the favor of God. Having descended to the lowest state of degradation, it is the beginning of a homeward journey. It is like a man lost in a wilderness and the means with which we are invested here are to direct us in our homeward journey. You then see the reason why you are required to put away your vain ties, cease to talk of all those things which are not conducive to eternal life.

This is why you are required to be sober, to be honest, that you could ask and receive, knock and it should be opened, and that when you sought for things you would find them. *It is putting you in possession of those keys by which you can ask for things you need and obtain them. This is the Key by which to obtain all the glory and felicity of eternal life.* It is the key by which you approach God. No impression which you receive here should be lost. It was to rivet the recollection of the *tokens and covenants* in your memory like a nail in a sure place, never to be forgotten.

The scenery through which you have passed is actually laying before you a picture or map by which you are to travel through life, and obtain an entrance into the celestial kingdom hereafter. If you are tempted in regard to these things here, you will be tempted when you approach the presence of God hereafter. You have, by being faithful been brought to this point, by maintaining the things which have been entrusted to you. *This is a representation of the Celestial Kingdom.* It is not merely for the sake of talking over these things that they are given to you, but for your benefit, and for your triumph over the powers of darkness hereafter.

We want the man to remember that he has covenanted to keep the law of God, and the Woman to obey her husband and if you keep your covenants you will not be guilty of transgressions. The line [that is] drawn is for you to maintain your covenants and you will always be found in the path of obedience, after that which is virtuous and holy and good and will never be swallowed up by unhallowed feelings and passions.

If you are found worthy and maintain your integrity, and do not run away and think you have got all your endowment you will be found worthy after a while [to receive your Second Anointing], which will make you honorable with God. You have not yet been ordained to any thing, but will be by and by. You have received these things because of your compliance *with all the requisitions* of the law, and if faithful you will receive more.

You have now learned how to pray. You have been taught how to approach God and be recognized. This is the principle by which the Church has been kept together, and not the power of arms. A few individuals have asked for your preservation, and their prayers have been heard, and it is this which has preserved you from being scattered to the four winds.

Those who have learned to approach God and receive these blessings, are they better than you? The difference is, they have been permitted to have these things revealed unto them. The principles which have been opened to you are the things which ought to occupy your attention all your lives. They are not second to any thing. You have the key by which if you are faithful, you will claim on you and on your posterity, all the blessings of the Priesthood.

Elder H. C. Kimball said, The ideas advanced by brother Lyman are good and true. *We have been taken as it were from the earth, and have travelled until we have entered the Celestial Kingdom, and what is it for, it is to personify Adam. And you discover that our* God is like one of us, for he created us in his own image. Every man that ever came upon this earth, or any other earth will take the course we have taken. Another thing, it is to bring us to an organization and just as quick as we can get into that order and government, we have the Celestial Kingdom here. You have got to *honor and reverence* your brethren, for *if you do not* you never can honor God. The man was created, and God gave him dominion over the whole earth, but he saw that he never could multiply, and replenish the earth, without a woman. And he made one [viz., a woman] and gave her to him. He did not make the man for the woman; but the woman for the man, *and it is just as unlawful for you to rise up and rebel against your husband, as it would be for man to rebel against God.*

When the man came to the vail, God gave the key word to the man, and the man gave it to the woman. But if a man dont use a woman well and take good care of her, God will take her away from him, and give her to another.

Perfect order and consistency makes Heaven but we are now deranged, and the tail has become the head.

We have now come to this place, and all your former covenants are of no account, and here is the place where we have to enter into a new covenant, and be sealed, and have it recorded. One reason why we bring our wives with us, is, that they may make a covenant with us to keep these things sacred. *You have been anointed to be kings and priests, but you have not been ordained to it yet, and you have got to get it by being faithful.* You can't sin so cheap now as you could before you came to this order. It is not for you to reproach the Lord's anointed nor to speak evil of him. You have covenanted not to do it.

One other thing. You all want to get garments, and you need not wait to get fine linen or bleached cotton for your garments. Shirting or sheeting will do for garments. The women can cut theirs from the cuts on their husbands. We dont want you to come here and take up the time to cut your garments. Go to a good faithful sister, and secret yourselves, and make your garments. We have been crowded too much and we have got to stop it. And if you have cloth, and come here to get your cloth cut we shall keep it here to make use of till we get through. We dont want one person that has come into the order the week past, to come into this room during the coming week except those who are to work. If you want any thing let it come in writing . . .

David Sessions, Gilbert D. Gouldsmith and Elam Ludington volunteered to draw water from the river in barrels for the use of the Temple. . . .

Elder George A. Smith made a few remarks. He spoke principlly in relation to the importance of keeping sacred those Signs and tokens and principles we had received while passing along through the different degrees.

He was followed by Elder Orson Hyde *who said a few words in approbation of what had been said by Elder Smith and followed up in the same matters.*

The congregation was dismissed by prayer by Elder John Taylor *and soon departed from the Temple to their respective homes.*

IV. 28 December 1845; Sunday

Joseph Smith, *History of the Church*, 7:555-56:

About two hundred of the brethren and sisters met at ten-thirty a. m. in the attic story of the Temple, some of the side rooms were filled, and the curtains withdrawn.

After singing and prayer, I addressed the meeting.

The sacrament was administered. Elder Kimball made a few remarks. After prayer the meeting was dismissed by benediction from Elder Orson Hyde.

Heber C. Kimball Diary, date, in Smith, *An Intimate Chronicle,* 238-241 (note: italics indicate material not included in Helen Mar Whitney's "Scenes from Nauvoo"):

Meeting at half past 10 oclock this day in the attic Story of the Temple, *for those who could clothe themselves in the garments of Priesthood.* A very large congregation was present, the side rooms were some of them filled, *the curtain was withdrawn and the other rooms besides the east room were filled.* About 200 persons were present, clothed in priestly garments. President Young addressed the meeting, it having been opened by prayer by P. P. Pratt, and singing the songs of Zion, "The morning breaks the shadows flee" & "Come to me" &c. *President Young came into the room at 1/4 before 12 [A.]M. He said he supposed those present were a part of those who had received their endowment, that they were those who* desired to be wise and do honor to the cause they have espoused, and bring no reproach upon the character of him who has given us of the things of his Kingdom liberally. The keys *or signs* of the Priesthood are for the purpose of impressing on the mind the order of the Creation. *In the first place the name of the man is given, a new name, Adam, signifying the first man, or Eve, the first Woman.* Adam's name was more ancient than he was. It was the name of a man long before him, who enjoyed the Priesthood. *The new name should be after some ancient man. Thus with your ancient name, your modern name and the name that was last given you, you enquire concerning things past present and future.*

After his fall, another name was given to Adam, *and being full of integrity, and not disposed to follow the woman nor listen to her was permitted to receive the tokens of the priesthood.*

I wish you to cease talking about what you see and hear in this place. No man or woman has a right to mention a work of the appearance of this building in the least; nor to give the signs and tokens except when assembled together, according to the order of the Priesthood, which is in an upper room. There are not a dozen persons that can give the signs and token[s] correct, and the reason is that person would run to that vail, one of the most sacred places on the face of the earth, that had not understood the right manner of giving the signs and tokens.

The order and ordinances passed through here prove the principles taught in the Bible. First men should love their God supremely. *Woman will never get back, unless she follows the man back, if the man had followed the woman he would have followed her down until this time.* Light, liberty and happiness will never shine upon men until they learn these principles. The man must love his God and the woman must love her husband. The love which David and Jonathan had for each other was the love of the priesthood. God is a personage of tabernacle, the Son is a personage of tabernacle, the Spirit or Holy Ghost is also a personage, but not a personage of tabernacle, but is a personage of Spirit. God dwells in eternal burnings puts his hand through the vail and writes on the wall. Any persons that goes through these ordinances, unless they cleanse their hearts and sanctify themselves and sanctify the Lord, it will damn them. *When we begin again I shall select those that are worthy.* We shall not be able to have another public meeting here on account of the weight on the floor, it has already caused the walls to crack prevents the doors from shutting, and will injure the roof. I see here 200 persons, *all clothed in their garments, tomorrow I suppose we cannot find half enough to work with, unless we lay an embargo on your garments, and forbid any of you carrying away your garments. When we began we could dress a company of 30. Now we cannot dress 18. For my right arm I would not say that every body is honest, for I do not believe they are.*

The names of those who would volunteer to furnish a suit of garments, to be used by those who were yet to go through the ordinances was then taken, they are as follows, viz W. W. Major, John Lytle, James Harman, Daniel Carter, John D. Lee, L. R. Foster, M. D. Hambleton, Vernon H. Bruce, Sidney A. Knowlton, Charles C. Rich, J. L. Heywood, Elijah Fordham, Norton Jacobs, Daniel Spencer, Joshua S. Holman, Willmer B. Benson, Hiram Spencer, L. O. Littlefield, J. M. Bernhisel Zimri H. Baxter, Andrew Whitlock, William A Sanger, J. S. Hovey, Stephen Winchester Jr, Wm S. Covert, John S Hatfield, Joseph Kain P. G. Sessions Ezra T. Benson Wm Matthews, Abraham Palmer & wife, 32 in all, each of these agreed to furnish one suit of garments for Temple use.

It was decided that when the High Priests were washed and anointed they should find the oil, and the lights, and the Seventies do the same when they occupied the rooms, and the wood is to [be] supplied as follows: 1000 men, or as many as can be obtained, to go to the islands and cut wood, and teams to go and draw it to the Temple until 1000 cords have been obtained.

Sung the hymn "Glorious things of thee are Spoken." Prayer by Amasa Lyman asking a blessing on the bread. Bread passed round by Charles C. Rich and George Miller. Blessing on the wine [was] asked by P. P. Pratt While the wine was passing, sung the hymn Adam ondi Ahman.

Elder H. C. Kimball cautioned the brethren and sisters against telling that the Twelve were in the Temple. *P. P. Pratt said a few words to the same point.*

Elder Kimball moved that no man tell his wife what he has seen. President Young said "all that are in favor of this signify it by holding your tongues when you go away from here." P. P. Pratt, "Contrary mind by the same sign."

Elder Kimball continued his remarks, alluded to the stories in circulation that several persons had been killed on their way through the ordinances, *and that men and women were stripped naked here. Joseph said that for men and women to hold their tongues, was their Salvation.*

A circle was formed, composed of about 20 persons, most of whom had received the ordinances, and been admitted to the first quorum at a previous time. They united in prayer. Elder John Taylor being mouth. A hymn was sung, being led by Goddard, Kay and Cahoon. notice was given that no more meetings would be held in the

Attic story, for the present, and the congregation dismissed after prayer by Elder Orson Hyde.

William Clayton, *rough draft of 28 December 1845 meeting* (final version in Heber C. Kimball Diary, date):

The keys or signs of the Priesthood is for the purpose of impressing on the mind on the creation. Penal Signs. In the first place the name of the man is given. A New name Adam signifies the first man or Eve the woman. Adam name was more Ancient than he was it was a man long before him who enjoyed the priesthood New name should be after some Ancient Man whereby you are enabled to ask for present future & past after his fall another name was given he being full of integrity & not to listen to the woman he was permitted to receive the tokens of the priesthood I wish you to learn one lesson you will find one lesson that you hold your tongues you will never be extricated unless you go to hell, you learn you will be damned we let no person assemble except in an upper room according to the priesthood. I have been saluted by the grips & tokens I have felt to slap their faces. look at the result of persons rushing to the vail one of the most sacred places on the earth. The two key words were received in the Garden. the first was his new name. the other is our name all such should be Ancient —the Aaronic is for helps and to assist the Melchisedec priesthood or Temporal things are entitled to those two signs the man having the Mel. priesthood. I will there are 4 token 4 Signs 4 Penal signs the ancient name will enable to ask for blessings or views of ancient things. I will use the very first token sign & penal David Let my arm forget not the order done of the Lord & thee O Jehovah if about Modern. my own name thus is the things of present now what about future events. my last name. In prayer you use the (fir) tokens in your own name This quorum is the more important. you are washed it is trifling. no —

John D. Lee, *"General Record of the Seventies. Book B Commencing Nauvoo, 1844. Record of Endowments commences on page 147, concluded [on] p 271. Copied into Nauvoo Temple Record,"* date:

the name that was given to Adam was more ancient than he was—

The name Adam was given him because he was the first man—but his New Name pertained to the Holy Priesthood & as I before stated is more ancient than he was—there are 4 Penal Signs & 4 Penal Tokens and should I want to address the Thorone [sic] to enquire after ancient things which transpired on Plannets that roled away before this Plannet came into existance, I should use my New Name which is Ancient & refers to Ancient things—Should I wish to Enquire for Present things I should use my own Name which refers to present things & should I want to Enquire for Future things I would use the 3rd Name which refers to the first token of the Melchizedek Priesthood—or is the 3rd token that is given—& refers to the son—the 2nd Token of the M. Priesthood is to be given only in one place and nowhere else—but these signs & tokens that pertain to the Priesthood should never be given any where only in such places as belong to the P.H. & that too by none but such as belong to the order of the Priesthood.

John D. Lee Journal, date:

He spoke in reference to the order of the Priesthood—the signs and tokens connected therewith—he observed that there were 4 penal signs & 4 penal tokens and each one of them aludes to certain names—the first aludes to your New or 1st name the 2nd to the 2nd & so on & should I or any of you want to enquire of the Lord—for anything ancient that transpired on Plannetts that roled into existence long after [before] this world or theater of action was organized—I would use my New Name because it is more ancient than my self & refers to ancient times—and should I want to enquire for things that are modern I would use my own name and to enquire for things that are future I would use the name which refers to things in the future—using the signs that are connected the 3 names.

Heber C. Kimball Journal, date:

The following High Priests met at 6 o'clock for prayer in their room No. 8—viz; George Miller Robert Pierce Gardner Clark L. Woodworth = Winslow Farr. Addison Everett Wm. Felshaw, Erastus Snow. Daniel Carn, Elizur G. Terrill John M. Bernhisel and Albert Petty Erastus Snow mouth. They adjourned at 8 o'clock

Also the following high Priests met in room No. 6. for prayer Viz; Joseph C. Kingsbury. George P. Dykes Ormus E. Bates, Benjn. Brown Daniel Carter. Joshua S. Holman David H. Redfield William Crosby Joseph C. Kingsbury mouth, closed at 8.–

The High Council met for Prayer at the usual time, about 6 o'clock President Isaac Morley David Fullmer William Huntington James Allred Alpheus Cutler George W. Harris Aaron Johnson. Thomas Grover Ezra T. Benson & Newel Knight Prayed for the health of H. G. Sherwood Wm. Huntington James Allred's wife and a boy in his family & for all the sick among the saints. For Pres. B. Young, that he might have wisdom, & bodily & mental strength, & be able to lead this people.

APPENDIX 2

Published Descriptions of the Temple Ceremony (with the assistance of Art deHoyos)

The following titles are listed chronologically, the author appearing first, then title, then publisher. Reprints and/or revisions by same author are listed after the first title. Pertinent commentaries on the first title are listed under same number; some of these comments are taken from Chad Flake, comp., *A Mormon Bibliography* (Salt Lake City: University of Utah Press, 1978). Reprints of first title by other authors are listed under separate, chronologically sequenced numbers, with bibliographic reference to original source. Bracketed trailer numbers refer to Flake's identifying number in *A Mormon Bibliography*. Most titles contain only a partial depiction of the endowment ceremony. Photocopies of most titles are in the David J. Buerger Papers, Ms. 622, Manuscripts Division, Special Collections, Marriott Library, University of Utah, Salt Lake City, Utah.

1. Bennett, John C. *The History of the Latter-day Saints; or, an exposé of Joe Smith and Mormonism.* (Boston: Leland & Whiting, 1842), pp. 217-25 and 272-78. [403]

2. "Ceremony of the endowment," *Warsaw Signal* (18 Feb. 1846), ii, no. 48, p. 2; and "Mormon endowments," *Warsaw Signal* (15 Apr. 1846), iii, no. 3, p. 2.
   _____. (same) in Tanner, *Evolution of the Mormon Temple Ceremony: 1942-1990.* (Salt Lake City: Utah Lighthouse ministry, 1990), pp. 3-4.
   3.Van Dusen (sometimes spelled "Van Deusen"), Increase McGee and Maria. *The Mormon endowment; a secret drama, or conspiracy, in the Nauvoo-temple, in 1846; in which process Mr. &*

Mrs. McGee, (the authors of this work,) were made king and queen, to which is added a sketch of the life of Joseph Smith, the circumstances of his finding the Mormon bible; his last revelation in the appointment of his successor; the angel's appearance to him; his finding another bible; his revelation concerning Polk and the Mexican war; baptism for the dead—Mormon faith—spiritual-wife-doctrine; description of Nauvoo and the temple, &c., &c. (Syracuse, NY: N.M.D. Lathrop, printer, 1847). [9422]

_____. (same) in Tanner, *Evolution of the Mormon Temple Ceremony: 1942-1990.* (Salt Lake City: Utah Lighthouse Ministry, 1990), pp. 3-4.

_____. *Positively true. A dialogue between Adam and Eve, the Lord and the devil, called the endowment: As was acted by twelve or fifteen thousand, in secret, in the Nauvoo Temple, said to be revealed from God, as a reward for building that splendid edifice, and the express object for which it was built.* (Albany, NY: C. Killmer, 1847). [9423]

_____. (same, under title) *The sublime and ridiculous blended; called, the endowment: as was acted, by upwards of twelve thousand, in secret, in the Nauvoo Temple, said to be revealed from God as a reward for building that splendid edifice, and the express object for which it was built.* (New York: Published by the author, 1848 [c. 1847]. [New introduction and text somewhat revised and sensationalized. Omission of Strangite material.] [9424]

_____. (same, under title) *Startling disclosures of the great Mormon conspiracy against the liberties of this country: being the celebrated "endowment," as it was acted by upwards of twelve thousand men and women in secret, in the Nauvoo Temple, in 1846, and said to have been revealed from God. By I. M'Gee Van Dusen and Maria his wife, who were initiated into these dreadful mysteries.* (New York: Published by Mr. and Mrs. Van Dusen, 1849). [Also published in 1849 in John Thomas's *A sketch of the rise, progress and dispersion of the Mormons.*] [9425]

_____. (same) (New York: Published by Mr. and Mrs. Van

Dusen, 1849). [Added illustrations and a different arrangement of some of the pages, Lacks pagination of prior edition.] [9426]

_____. (same) (New York: Blake & Jackson, 1849). [9427]

_____. (same) (New York: Blake & Jackson, 1849). [9428]

_____. (same) (New York: Blake & Jackson, 1850). [9429]

_____. *Startling disclosures of the wonderful ceremonies of the Mormon spiritual wife system. Being the celebrated "endowment," as it was acted by upwards of twelve thousand men and women in secret in the Nauvoo Temple in 1846, and said to have been revealed from God, By I. M'Gee Van Dusen and Maria his wife, who initiated into these dreadful mysteries.* (New York: n.p., 1850). [9430]

_____. (same) (New York: Blake & Jackson, 1852). [Reprint of 1850 ed.] [9431]

_____. (same) (New York: n.p., 1852). [Variant printing.] [9432]

_____. (same) (New York: n.p., 1855). [9433]

_____. (same) (New York: n.p., 1857). [9429]

_____. (same, under title) *Mormonism exposed . . . New York, For sale at all book and periodical stores* [1853?] [Copyrighted by the Van Dusens, 1848; "Preface to the sixth edition."] [9434]

_____. (same, under title) *Spiritual delusions being a key to the mysteries of Mormonism, exposing the particulars of that astounding heresy, the spiritual wife system, as practiced by Brigham Young of Utah, By Increase Van Deusen and Maria his wife, seceders from that singular sect who were personally initiated into those dreadful mysteries.* (New York: Moulton and Tuttle, 1854). [Frequently reprinted under this title and with a slightly varying title, which is enlarged from the previous copy; has a second recital of the ceremony and an allegorical description of its various degrees and ceremonies. Some copies have the fold-out sheet of plates.] [9435]

_____.(same) (New York: Published by the authors, 1854). [Variant printing.] [9436]

_____. (same) (New York: A. Ranney; . . . Chicago: Rufus Blanchard [etc., etc.,] 1855). [9437]

_____. (same) (New York: A. Ranney, 1856). [9438]

_____. (same) (New York: A. Ranney, 1857). [9439]

_____. (same) (New York: A. Ranney, 1859). [9440]

_____. (same, under title) *Startling disclosures of the Mormon spiritual wife system, and wonderful ceremonies of the celebrated "endowment" as it is acted by upwards of fifty thousand men and women in secret, in the temple in Utah, and said to have been revealed from god, By I. M'Gee Van Dusen, and Maria, his wife who were initiated and participators in these dreadful mysteries.* (New York: n.p., 1864). [9441]

_____. (same) (New York: n.p., 1864). [Variant printing.] [9442]

_____. *Misteries [sic] of Mormonism.* (New York: I. Van Deusen, [c] 1850). [Plates for their books. Scenes from the endowment ceremony.] [9443]

4. Lewis, Catherine. *Narrative of some of the proceedings of the Mormons giving an account of their iniquities, with particulars concerning the training of the Indians by them, description of the mode of endowment, plurality of wives, &c., &c,* (Lynn, MA: The author, 1848), pp. 6-24. [4885]

_____. (same) (Lynn, MA: The author, 1853). [4886]

5. *An authentic history of remarkable persons, who have attracted public attention, in various parts of the world; including a full exposure of the iniquities of the pretended prophet, Joe Smith, and of the seven degrees of the Mormon temple; also an account of the frauds practiced by Matthias the prophet, and other religious importers.* (New York: Wilson and Co., 1849, pp. 8-17. [233]

6. Thomas, John. *A sketch of the rise, progress, and dispersion of the Mormons, by John Thomas, M.D., President of the S. and E. Medical College of Virginia, United States, America; to which is added an account of the Nauvoo temple mysteries, and other abominations practiced by this impious sect previous to their emigration for California, by Increase McGee Van Dusen, formerly one of the initiated.* (London: Arthur Hall and Co., 1849), pp. 11-24. [8907]

7. Bowes, John. *Mormonism exposed, in its swindling and licentious abominations, refuted in its principles, and in the claims of its*

head, the modern Mohammed Joseph Smith, who is proved to have been a deceiver, and no prophet of God. (London, E. Ward, 1850[?]), pp. 17-22. [763]

8. White, Thomas. *The Mormon mysteries; being an exposition of the ceremonies of "The Endowment" and of the seven degrees of the temple. A new and improved edition By Thomas White.* (New York: Edmund K. Knowlton, 1851). [9737]

9. [Anon.] *A Confession of the awful and bloody transactions in the life of Charles Wallace etc. Unrecorded Barclays Fiction at its Best with a Destructive Visit to the Mormon Temple at Nauvoo. We visited Joe Smith's temple, one night, and smashed the windows in with bricks. Great fun it gave us, for we could not bear to see him humbug the easy fools around him out of their wives and property. He had a right we are told, to walk into a married man's bed-chamber, kick out her husband and lay himself down beside the pure and virtuous wife. We were very much tempted to murder him for the sole benefit of mankind. But we heard of two police officers from St. Louis who had also arrived at the Mormon city . . .* (New Orleans: Barclay, 1851), 1st ed., 8 vols., 32 pp., 4 illustrated.

10. Hall, William. *The abominations of Mormonism exposed. Containing many facts and doctrines concerning that singular people during seven years' membership with them, from 1840 to 1847.* (Cincinnati: I. Hart & Co,, 1852), pp. 4562. [3801]

11. Hepburn, Andrew Balfour. *An exposition of the blasphemous doctrines and delusions of the so-called Latter-day Saints, or Mormons, containing an authentic account of the impositions, spiritual wife doctrine, and the other abominable practices of Joseph Smith, the American Mahomet, and his twelve apostle, elders, and followers to the present time.* (Sheffield: M. Thomas & Son, 1852), pp. 60-61. [3960]

_____. *The doctrines, rites and ceremonies of Latter Day Saints, or Mormons, exposed; showing from their own books, &c, that they are, without exception, the most depraved, immoral, blasphemous, and ridiculous sect that ever polluted this earth. The extracts furnished by Mr. A. B. Hepburn, anti-Mor-*

mon lecturer. (London: Partridge and Oakey. . . and the Anti-Mormon Tract Depot, [c] 1853). [3959]

_____. *Mormonism exploded or the religion of the Latter-day Saints. Proved to be a system of imposture, blasphemy, and immorality; with the autobiography and portrait of the author. In two parts. Pt. I. By A. B. Hepburn. Anti-Mormon lecturer. Edited by Rev. Charles Short, A.M.* (London: Swansea, Simkin, Marshall and Co., 1855). [3961]

12. Pratt, Orson. *The Seer* 1 (Feb. 1853), no. 2, pp. 31-32. [Description of the temple wedding ceremony text; a similar description was published in the *Millennial Star* 15:214.]

13. *The secrets of Mormonism disclosed; an authentic exposure of the immorality and licentious abominations of the apostles, prophets, high-priests, and elders of the Latter-day Saints, and their spiritual wives; founded on their own quoted writings, doctrines, and official records, and the confessions of male and female members of their church; showing their obscene practices in the temple devoted to public worship, and the profligacy of a Mormon harem, composed of married and single females. Also the adulteries and seductions carried on at the celebration of their spiritual marriages, under the mask of having received divine sanction in visions! Including the horrors of the "agapemone," or abode of love.* (London: R, Bulman, 1854 [?]). [7608]

14. Taylder, T. W. P. *The Mormon's own book; or, Mormonism tried by its own standards, reason, and scripture.* (London: Partridge, Oakey, and Co., 1855), pp. 135-47. [8796]

_____. (same) *With an account of its present condition. Also a life of Joseph Smith. New edition.* (London: Partridge and Co., 1857). [8797]

15. Gunnison, John Williams. *The Mormons, or Latter day Saints, in the valley of the Great Salt Lake: a history of their rise and progress, peculiar doctrines, present condition, and prospects, derived from personal observation during a residence among them.* (Philadelphia: J.B. Lippincott, Grambo & Co., 1852). [3746]

_____. (same) (London: Sampson Low, 1852). [3747]

_____. (same) (Philadelphia: Lippincott, Grambo & Co., 1853). [3748]

_____. (same) (Toronto: T. Maclear, 1853). [3749]

_____. (same, in German) *Die Mormonen im Thale des grossen Salzee's nach personlicher Beobachtung geschildert von J. W. Gunnison. Deutsch von M. R. Lindau.* (Hamburg und Leipzig: Verlag von Rudolf Kuntze, 1855). [3756]

_____. (same) (Philadelphia: J. B. Lippincott & Co., 1855), pp, 58-61. [3750]

_____. (same) (Philadelphia: J. B. Lippincott & Co., 1857 [c 1852]. [3751]

_____. (same) (Philadelphia: J. B. Lippincott & Co., 1860). [3752]

_____. (same) (Philadelphia: J. B. Lippincott & Co., 1862). [3753]

_____. (same) (New York: J. W. Lovell Co., 1884). [3754]

_____. (same) (New York: G. Munro, 1890). [3755]

16. Hood, Edwin Paxton. *The lamps of the temple. Crayon sketches of the men of the modern pulpit.* (London: John Snow, 1856). [4078]

17. Cook, William. *The Mormons. The dream and the reality; or, leaves from the sketch book of experience of one who left England to join the Mormons in the city of Zion, and awoke to a consciousness of its heinous wickedness and abominations. Edited by a clergyman.* (London: Joseph Masters, 1857), pp. 37-42. [2495]

_____. (same, under title) *The "Fowler's snare," as craftily laid to catch unwary souls, now fully unmasked and exposed to view, by one who has broken the snare and escaped.* (London: Joseph Masters, 1858). [Identical to 1st ed.] [2496]

18. Emmons, S. B. *The spirit land by S. B. Emmons.* (Philadelphia: John E. Potter and Co., 1857; see chap. 8, "Mormon superstition: an account of the first vision and other delusions exposed by the Van Dusens"). [3163]

_____. (same) (Philadelphia: J.W. Bradley, 1859), pp. 101-102. [Van Dusen material deleted from this ed.]

19. Hyde, John. *Mormonism: its leaders and designs. By John Hyde,*

Jun. Formerly a Mormon elder, and resident of Salt Lake City. (New York: W.P. Fetridge & Co., 1857), pp. 40-41, 83-114. [4164]

_____. (same) 2d ed. (New York: W.P. Fetridge & Company, 1857). (4165)

20. Green, Nelson Winch. *Fifteen Years among the Mormons: being the narrative of Mrs. Mary Ettie V. Smith, late of Great Salt Lake City; a sister of one of the Mormon high priests, she having been personally acquainted with most of the Mormon leaders, and long in the confidence of the "Prophet" Brigham Young.* (New York: C. Scribner, 1858), pp. 41-53. [3703]

_____. (same) (New York: H. Dayton, 1858). [3704]

_____. (same) (New York: Dayton; Indianapolis, IN: Asher & Company, 1859). [Variant printing.] [3705]

_____. (same) (New York: H. Dayton, 1860). [c. 1857] [3706]

_____. (same, under title) *Fifteen years' residence with the Mormons. With startling disclosures of the mysteries of polygamy. By a sister of one of the high priests.* (Chicago: Phoenix Publishing Co., 1876). [3707]

_____. (same, under title) *Mormonism; its rise, progress and present condition. Embracing the narrative of Mrs. Ettie V. Smith, of her residence and experience of fifteen years with the Mormons; containing a full and authentic account of their social condition—their religious and political government . . . with other startling facts and statements, being a full disclosure of the rites, ceremonies and mysteries of polygamy. &c.* (Hartford, CT: Belknap and Bliss, 1870). [3708]

_____. (same) (Hartford, CT: Belknap & Bliss, 1872). [3709]

21. Remy, Jules. *A journey to Great Salt Lake City, by Jules Remy and Julius Brenchley, M.A.; with a sketch of the history, religion, and customs of the Mormons and an introduction on the religious movement in the United States.* (London: W. Jeffs, 1861); in 2 vols.; see vol. 2, pp, 65-77. [6867]

22. Waite, Catherine [Van Valkenburg]. *The Mormon prophet and his harem; or, an authentic history of Brigham Young, his numerous wives and children.* (Cambridge, MA: Riverside Press, 1866), pp. 244-60. [9505]

_____. (same) 3rd ed. (Cambridge, MA: Riverside Press, 1856). [9506]

_____. (same) 3rd ed. (Cambridge, MA; Riverside Press, 1867). [9507]

_____. (same) 4th ed., revised and enlarged. (Cambridge, MA: J.S. Goodman and Co., 1867). [9508]

_____. (same) 5th ed., revised and enlarged. (Chicago: J.S. Goodman and Co., 1867), [c 1866]. [9509]

_____. (same) 5th ed., revised and enlarged. (Philadelphia: Zeigler, McCurdy and Co.; Cincinnati: C.F. Vent and Co., 1867). [9510]

_____. (same) (Chicago: J.S. Goodman & Co., 1868). [c 1866]. [9511]

23. Beadle, John Hanson. *Life in Utah; or, the mysteries and crimes of Mormonism. Being an exposé of the secret rites and ceremonies of the Latter-day Saints, with a full and authentic history of polygamy and the Mormon sect from its origin to the present time.* (Philadelphia: National Publishing Co., 1878), pp. 486-502. [344]

_____. *The History of Mormonism; its rise, progress, present condition and mysteries: being an exposé of the secret rites and ceremonies of the Latter-day Saints; with a full and authentic account of polygamy and the Mormon sect from its origin to the present time.* (Toronto, Ont.: A.H. Hovey, 1873). [343]

_____. (same) [Under title, *Life in Utah.*] (Philadelphia: National Publishing Co., 1870). [345]

_____. (same) (Philadelphia: National Publishing Co., 1870). [346]

_____. (same) (Toronto: James Spencer, 1872). [347]

_____. (same, under title) *Life in Utah and on the plains; being an account of the settlement of the Great West, and embracing the history of the rise and progress of Mormonism, and the occupation of Utah by that people . . .* (Toronto: Dominion Publishing Co., 1876). [349]

_____. (same, under title) *Polygamy; or, The mysteries and crimes of Mormonism, being a full and authentic history of polygamy and the Mormon sect from its origin to the present time. With a complete analysis of Mormon society and theoc-*

racy, and an exposé of the secret rites and ceremonies of the Latter-day Saints. . . . (Philadelphia: The National Publishing Co., [c] 1882) [Copyright date mutilated on many copies, making it seem to be 1880.] [350]

_____. (same) (Boston: B. B. Russell, [c] 1882). [351]

_____. (same) (Auckland, N.Z.: A. F. Porter & Sons, [c] 1882). [352]

_____. (same) (Cincinnati: W. E. Dibble & Co., [c] 1882). [353]

_____. (same) (Philadelphia: National Publishing Co., [c] 1904). [354]

_____. (same) (Philadelphia: World Bible House, [c] 1904). [355]

_____. *Polygamy; or, the mysteries and crimes of Mormonism* (n.p., [c] 1904). [356]

_____. (same, in German) *Das Leben in Utah; oder, Die Mysterien und Verbrechen des Mormonenthums. Enthaltend eine Enthullung der Geheimenritualien und Ceremonien der Heiligen vom Jungsten Gericht . . . Aus dem englischen ubertragen von Carl Theodor Eben.* (Philadelphia: National Publications, 1870). [357]

_____. (same, in Russian) *Zhizn' Mormonov v Uta; ili Tainstva i prestupleniia Mormonizma; izlozhenie tainikh obriadov i tseremonii sviatikh posldnikh dnei.* (Sanktperterburg, Tip. M. Khana, 1872). [358]

24. Bundy, L. A. *Mormonism exposed; a faithful exposé of the secrets and evils of the Mormon country, by one who possessed the sixteenth part of a husband.* (New York: Ornum & Co., 1872 [?]), pp. 9-11, 55-56. [1006]

25. Stenhouse, Mrs. T. B. H. [Fanny]. *"Tell it all." The story of a life's experience in Mormonism. An autobiography by Mrs. T. B. H. Stenhouse of Salt Lake City, for more than twenty years the wife of a Mormon missionary and elder. With introductory preface by Mrs. Harriet Beecher Stowe.* (Hartford, CT: A.B. Worthington and Co., 1874). [8390]

_____. (same) *Full-page illustrations and steel-plate portrait of the author.* (Cincinnati: Queen City Publishing Co., 1874). [8391]

_____. (same) (Hartford, CT: A.D. Worthington and Co., 1875). [8392]

_____. (same) (Hartford, CT: A.D. Worthington and Co., Cincinnati: Queen City Publishing Co. [etc., etc.], 1875). [8393]

_____. (same) (Hartford, CT: A.D. Worthington and Co., 1876). [8394]

_____. (same) (Hartford, CT: A.D. Worthington and Co., 1876). [Publisher's sample.] [8395]

_____. (same) *Including a full account of the Mountain Meadows massacre and of the life, confession, and execution of Bishop John D. Lee.* (Hartford, CT: A.D. Worthington and Co., 1878). [8396]

_____. (same) (Hartford, CT: A.D. Worthington and Co., 1878). [8396a]

_____. (same) *Fully illustrated.* (Hartford, CT: A.D. Worthington and Co., 1890), pp. 352-69. [8397]

_____. (same, revised under title) *An Englishwoman in Utah: the story of a life's experience in Mormonism. An autobiography by Mrs. T. B. H. Stenhouse of Salt Lake City for more than twenty-five years the wife of a Mormon missionary and elder. With an introductory preface by Mrs. Harriet Beecher Stowe. Including a full account of the Mountain Meadows massacre and of the life, confession, and execution of Bishop John D. Lee. Fully illustrated.* (London: Sampson Low, Marston, Searle and Rivington, 1880), pp. 189-201, 320-21. [8398]

_____. (same) *New and cheaper ed.* (London: S. Low, Marston, Searle & Rivington, 1882). [8399]

_____. (same, under title) *The Tyranny of Mormonism, or An Englishwoman in Utah; an autobiography, by Fanny Stenhouse of Salt Lake City (25 years). With introductory preface by Mrs. Beecher Stowe. Fully illustrated.* (London: S. Low, Marston, Searle & Rivington, 1888), pp. 189-201, 320-21. [8400]

_____. (same, in Spanish) *Vida de una señora entre los Mormons; producto de la experiencia personal de una de las espousa de un sacerdote Mormon, durante un periode de mas de viente años.* (Mexico: Imprinta de Ignacia Escalante, 1873). [8401]

26. Young, Ann Eliza [Webb]. *Wife no. 19; or, the story of a life in*

bondage, being a complete exposé of Mormonism, and reveal-ing the sorrows, sacrifices and sufferings of women in polyg-amy, by Ann Eliza Young, Brigham Young's apostate wife. (Hartford, CT: Dustin, Gilman & Co., 1875). [10,046]

_____. (same) (Hartford, CT: Dustin, Gilman and Co., 1876 [c 1875]). [10,047]

_____. (same) (Hartford, CT: Dustin, Gilman and Co., 1876), pp. 349-72, 386-89. [Publisher's sample. Sold by subscription only.] [10,048]

_____. (same) (Hartford, CT: Dustin, Gilman and Co., 1877). [10,049]

_____. (same, under title) *Life in Mormon bondage; a complete exposé of its false prophets, murderous Danites, des-potic rulers and hypnotized deluded subjects, by Ann Eliza Young, 19th wife of Brigham Young. Limited ed.* (Philadel-phia/Boston: Aldine Press, Inc., [c] 1908), pp. 273-86. [10,050]

27. *The Gates of the Mormon hell opened, exhibiting the licentious abominations and revellings of the high priest of the Latter-day Saints Rev. Brigham Young and his 90 wives; and the vile scenes enacted by the elders and apostles with their many spiritual concubines in the secret chambers of the harem, or institution of cloistered Saints, privately attached to the temple. . . . with a most outrageous scene of disrobing and washing the new spiritual wife in a tub . . .* (London: Hewitt, Wych Street Strand, n.d.); [3531]
[A similarly titled pamphlet also was published in London by James Gilbert, n.d.]

28. "Mormon Masonry," in Mackenzie, Kenneth R. H., *The Royal Masonic Cyclopedia* (London: John Hogg, 1877), pp. 497-498.
_____. (same) (Wellingborough, Northamptonshire: Aquar-ian Press, 1987).
_____. (same) (Kila, MT: Kessinger Publishing, 1994).

29. Latham, Henry Jepson. *Among the Mormons. How an American and an Englishman went to Salt Lake City, and married seven wives apiece. Their lively experience. A peep into the mysteries of Mormonism. By Ring Jepson [pseud.].* (San Francisco: The San Francisco News Company, 1879). [4759]

30. *Salt Lake Tribune. The Mormon Endowment House! A graphic exposure of the treasonable institution, where polygamous marriages are solemnized. By an eye witness.* (Salt Lake City: Tribune Printing & Publishing Co., 1879. [Text dated 24 Sep. 1879, taken from the *Salt Lake Daily Tribune,* 28 Sep. 1879, p. 4, "Lifting the vail.– The endowment house mysteries fully exposed."). [7511]

_____. (same, under title) (Salt Lake City: 1879?). [Eight-page tract; signed: Mrs. G. S. R. Attributed to Mrs. Carrie Owen Mills by J. W. Buel, *Mysteries and Miseries of America's Great Cities.*] [7512]

_____. (same) (Salt Lake City: 1879?) [four pages] [7513]

31. Tenney, Edward Payson. *Colorado: and homes in the new West.* (Boston: Lee and Shepard; New York: C.T. Dillingham, 1880), p. 110. [8879]

32. Coyner, John McCutchen. *Hand-book on Mormonism.* (Salt Lake City: Handbook Publishing Co., 1882), pp. 23-30. [2567]

_____. (same) in *Tanner, Evolution of the Mormon Temple Ceremony: 1942-1990.* (Salt Lake City: Utah Lighthouse ministry, 1990), pp. 3-4.

33. Paddock, Cornelia, "Ms. A. G. Paddock." *The fate of Madam La Tour; a tale of Great Salt Lake, by Mrs. A. G. Paddock.* (New York: Fords, Howard, & Hulburt, 1881). (A typical Victorian novel, which mentions the Endowment House rituals and includes as an appendix, a form of the *Salt Lake Tribune* 1879 exposé.] [6042]

_____. (same) (New York: Fords, Howard & Hulburt, 1881). [6043]

_____. (same) (New York: Fords, Howard & Hulburt, 1882), pp. 333-36. [6044]

_____. (same) (New York: Fords, Howard & Hulburt, 1895). [6045]

_____. (same) (New York: Fords, Howard & Hulburt, 1900 [c] 1881). [6046]

_____. (same, in Danish) *Mrs. Paddock: blandt Mormoner en beretning om Madame la Tour og hendes born oversat efter: The fate of Madame la Tour or a tale of the Great Salt Lake af*

C. Menster. . . (Kobenhavn: Forlagt af Diakonissestiftelsens Depot, 1902). [6047]

34. Trumble, Alfred. *The mysteries of Mormonism. A full exposure of its secret practices and hidden crimes, by an apostle's wife.* (New York: Richard K. Fox, Proprietor, Police Gazette, [c] 1882), pp. 42-51. [9024]

35. McClintock, John. *Cyclopedia of biblical theological and ecclesiastical literature. Prepared by the Rev. John McClintock, D.D., and James Strong.* (New York: Harper and Brothers, 1883), vol. 6, p. 645. [5121]

36. Robinson, Phillip Stewart. *Sinners and saints. A tour across the states, and round them; with three months among the Mormons.* (Boston: Roberts Brothers, 1883), pp. 139-40. [7392]
_____. (same) (London: S. Low, Marston, Searle and Rivington, 1883). [7393]
_____. (same) New and cheaper ed. (London: Sampson Low, Marston & Company, 1892). [7394]

37. Sala, George Augustus Henry. *America revisited: from the bay of New York to the Gulf of Mexico, and from Lake Michigan to the Pacific.* (New York: I.K. Funk & Co., [c]1880). [7479]
_____. (same) 4th ed. (New York: I.K. Funk & Co., 1883), pp. 523-26.

38. Faithfull, Emily. *Three visits to America, by Emily Faithfull.* (Edinburgh: D. Douglas, 1884), pp. 150-78. [3296]

39. Jarman, W. *U.S.A., Uncle Sam's abscess; or, hell upon earth for U.S., Uncle Sam.* (Exeter, Eng.: Printed at H. Leduc's Steam Printing Works, 1884), pp. 57-92. [4364]
_____. (same) (Exeter, Eng.: H. Leduc's Steam Printing Works, 1884). [4365]

40. Nye, Edgar Wilson. *Baled hay. A drier book than Walt Whitman's "Leaves o' Grass."* (New York and Chicago: Belford, Clarke & Co., 1884), pp. 258-60. [5959]

41. Anderson, Scott. *Mormonism. By an ex-Mormon elder. Showing the true teachings of Mormonism and how converts are made. Mormon idolatry. Mormon slavery. Blood atonement as preached by Brigham Young. The character of the endowment*

house mysteries. Marriages and marriage laws, &c., &c. Also copy of a letter written to John Taylor, (the Mormon president), giving his reasons why he withdrew from the Mormon church. (Liverpool: T. Dobb & Co., 1885), pp. 24-26. [A1]

42. Wymetal, Wilhelm Ritter von. *Joseph Smith, the prophet, his family and his friends; a study based on facts and documents with fourteen illustrations.* (Salt Lake City: Tribune Printing and Publishing Co., 1886), pp. 267-72. ["volume first" of projected series called *Mormon Portraits.* No more issued.] [10,034]

43. *Few choice examples of Mormon practices and sermons.* (n.p., 1886[?].) [3341]

44. Clampitt, John Wesley. *Echoes from the Rocky Mountains.* (Chicago: Belford, Clarke & Co., [c] 1888). [Reprint of the 1879 *Salt Lake Tribune* exposé.] [2382]
_____. (same) (Chicago: Belford, Clarke & Co., 1888), pp. 325-36.

45. Kipling, Rudyard. *American Notes.* (New York: International Publishing Co., 1889). [Same account in "From sea to sea; letters of travel" (New York: Doubleday, Page & Co., 1907), pp. 112-13.] [4644]

46. Tullidge, Edward Wheelock. *Tullidge's histories (volume II) containing the history of all the northern, eastern, and western counties of Utah; also the counties of southern Idaho. With a biographical appendix of representative men and founders of the cities and counties; also a commercial supplement, historical.* (Salt Lake City: Juvenile Instructor, 1889), pp. 425-51. [Tullidge defends the temple ritual from the exposé-writers. He does not take issue with their accounts, but only with their interpretations and lack of sympathy.] [9045]

47. Bostwick, F. E. *As I found it; life and experience in Utah among the Mormons. Doctrines and practices of the Mormon church, polygamy, endoument [sic] secrets, destroying angels, Mountain Meadows massacre, present physical and political condition.* (St. Louis, 1893), pp. 8, 72-84. [756]

48. Feree, Barr. "Architecture," *Engineering Magazine* 6:1 (1893), p. 100. (Feree refers to the "largest bath-tub ever made," exhibited

at the World's Columbian Exposition of 1893 by the Standard Manufacturing Company, which had manufactured twelve of them on special order for the LDS church, for use in the Mormon temple in Salt Lake City.)

[Cited also by Laurel B. Andrew, *The early temples of the Mormons: The architecture of the millennial kingdom in the American west.* (Albany, NY: Suny, 1878), p. 25.]

49. *United States Circuit Court (8th District). The Reorganized Church of Jesus Christ of Latter Day Saints, complainant, vs. the Church of Christ at Independence, Missouri . . . Complainant's abstract of pleading and evidence.* (Lamoni, IA: Herald, 1893). [See esp. the testimonies of Wilford Woodruff at pp. 298-301, Mercy Rachel Thompson at 353-58, Bathsheba Smith at pp. 358-63, John Hawley at pp. 451-62, and Willard Griffith at pp. 462-66.]

50. Whitney, Orson Ferguson. *History of Utah, comprising preliminary chapters on the previous history of her founders, accounts of early Spanish and American explorations in the Rocky Mountain region, the advent of the Mormon pioneers, the establishment and dissolution of the provisional government of the state of Deseret, and the subsequent creation and development of the territory.* (Salt Lake City: George Q. Cannon & Sons, Co., 1893), vol. 2, p. 382. [Whitney refers to the *Salt Lake Tribune* exposés and complains that sacred LDS rituals were "revealed by apostates."] [9769]

51. Howard of Glossop, Winefred Mary (De Lisle) baroness. *Journal of a tour in the United States, Canada and Mexico by Winefred, Lady Howard of Glossop.* (London: Sampson Low, Marston, and Co., Ltd., 1897), pp. 48-49. [4102]

52. "Gentile" Bureau of Information. *Temple Mormonism.* (Salt Lake City, 190?.) [3542]

_____. (same) (Salt Lake City: 190?). [3543]

53. Folk, Edgar Estes. *The Mormon monster, or, the story of Mormonism, embracing the history of Mormonism, Mormonism as a religious system, Mormonism as a social system, Mormonism as a political system; with a full discussion of the subject of*

polygamy . . . (Chicago/New York/Toronto: Fleming H. Revell, 1900), pp. 102, 132, 156, 246, 318-41. [3387]

54. Linn, William Alexander. *The story of the Mormons, from the date of their origin to the Year 1901, by William Alexander Linn.* (New York: The Macmillan Co.; London: Macmillan & Co., Ltd., 1902). [4944]

_____. (same) (New York: The Macmillan Co; London: Macmillan & Co., Ltd., 1923), p. 355. [4945]

55. McMillin, Henry G. *The inside of Mormonism. A judicial examination of the endowment oaths administered in all the Mormon temples, by the United States District Court for the Third Judicial District of Utah, to determine whether membership in the Mormon church is consistent with citizenship in the United States.* (Salt Lake City: Utah Americans, 1903), pp. 9-53, passim. [5231]

[For LDS account of these hearings, see *Deseret News,* 14 Nov. 1889, "Base Falsehoods—Uttered in Court Regarding Mormon Church"; see also clippings from William Holland Samson Scrapbook, vol. 39 NR (local history).]

56. "The Mormon Endowment Ceremony," by a former Mormon, in *The World Today,* vol. 8 (Feb. 1905), pp. 165-70.

57. U. S. Congress. *Proceedings before the Committee on Privileges and Elections of the United States Senate in the matter of the protests against the right Hon. Reed Smoot, a Senator from the state of Utah, to hold his seat.* [16 Jan. 1904 - 13 Apr. 1906] (Washington, D.C.: Gov't. Printing Office, 1904-06). See testimony by J. R. Wallis, Sr. (v. 2:77-79, 148-49), August W. Lundstrom (v. 2:151-53, 160-62, 181-83), Annie Elliott (v. 2:189-90), Hugh M. Dougall (v. 2:759, 762-64), Alonzo Arthur Noon (v. 2:779), Walter M. Wolfe (v. 4:6-7), and William Jones Thomas (v. 4:495-97). [9173]

[Many newspapers carried stories of these testimonies; see, for example, the front pages of *The Washington Times* and *The New York Herald,* 14 Dec. 1904, for photographs of a man dressed in temple clothing modeling various oaths reportedly given in the endowment ceremony.]

58. *Salt Lake Tribune*. "Mysteries of the Endowment House," 12 Feb. 1906, pp. 2-4.

_____. *Mysteries of the endowment house and oath of vengeance of the Mormon church.* (Salt Lake City: *Salt Lake Tribune*, 1906). [16-p[age]. pamphlet reprint of the 12 Feb. 1906 *Tribune* exposé.] [7514]

59. Schroeder, Theodore Albert. *A reply to a defense of Mormons and an attack upon the Ministerial Association of Utah. By A. T. Schroeder.* (New York: *The Truth Seeker,* 1906), pp. 8-9. [Reprinted from *The Truth Seeker*. These thoughts are suggested by an article from Mr. V. S. Peet in *The Truth Seeker,* 25 Nov. 1905, p. 3.] [7582]

60. Tuttle, Daniel Sylvester. *Reminiscences of a missionary bishop, by the Right Rev. D. S. Tuttle.* (New York: Thomas Whittaker, [c] 1906), pp. 314-20. [9061]

61. Freece, Hans P. *The letters of an apostate Mormon to his son.* (New York: The Wolfer Press, [c] 1908), p. 58. [3438]
_____. (same) 2d ed. (Elmira, NY: [c] 1908). [3439]
_____. (same) 3rd ed. (New York: [c] 1908). [3440]
_____. (same) 5th ed. (New York: [c] 1908). [3441]
_____. (same) 6th ed. (New York: [c] 1908). [3442]
_____. (same) 7th ed. (New York: [c] 1908). [3443]

62. Marshall, Thomas Philip. *Mormonism exposed, by Thomas Philip Marshall, ex-elder of the Utah Mormon Church, with the secret workings, washings, anointings, and ceremonies performed in their temples. Together with the secret signs, grips, and their names by which they can make themselves known to one another, either in crowds, or walking along the streets of our cities. Also the horrible and barbarous punishments inflicted upon all who dare to divulge these secrets outside their temple walls.* (St. Louis: Ponath-Bruewer Printing Co., [c] 1908), pp. 43-66. [5285]

63. Major, Gertrude [Keene]. *The revelation in the mountain.* (New York: Cochrane Publishing Co., 1909), pp. 120-50. [5248]

64. Jones, Charles Sheridan. *The Mormons['] unmasked secrets of Salt Lake City.* (London: Jarrold and Sons, [c]1911). [4454]

_____. *The truth about the Mormons; secrets of Salt Lake City.* (London: William Rider & Son, 1920), pp. 91-92. [4455]

65. Jewett, J. M. "The hidden secrets of the Mormon church: An apostate describes the inner ceremonies of polygamous marriages and their treasonous oaths." *The Standard* (Chicago: vol. 58 [13 May 1911] no. 37, pp. 12-13.)

66. Stead, J. D. *Doctrines and dogmas of Brighamism exposed.* (Lamoni, IA: Board of Publication of the Reorganized Church of Jesus Christ of Latter Day Saints, 1911), pp. 107-32. Reprint of *Salt Lake Tribune* exposé.] [8369]

67. Kauffman, Ruth Hammitt. *The Latter-day Saints; a study of the Mormons in the light of economic conditions, by Ruth Kauffman and Reginald Wright Kauffman.* (London: Williams & Norgate, 1912), pp. 313-26. [Contains excerpts from Stenhouse's *Englishwoman in Utah* (1880, 1888), and McMillian's *The Inside of Mormonism* (1903).] [4526]

68. Kinney, Bruce. *Mormonism: The Islam of America.* (New York, Chicago, Toronto, London, Edinburgh: Fleming H. Revell, 1912), pp. 141-42. [4637]
_____. (same) (New York, Chicago, etc.: Fleming H. Revell Company, [c] 1912). [4638]
_____. (same) Rev. and enl. (New York, Chicago: Fleming H. Revell Company, [c]1916). [4639]
_____. (same, in Swedish) *Mormonismen. Amerikas Muhammedanism, av Bruce Kinney . . . med forord av Pastor E. Lundstrom Bemyndigad oversattning av. I.H—d.* (Stockholm: P. Palmquists Aktiebolag, 1914). [4640]

69. Nutting, J. D. *The secret oaths and ceremonies of Mormonism. The secret temple work which binds Mormons together under the power of their priestly leaders. Edited by Rev. J. D. Nutting.* (Cleveland, OH: Utah Gospel Mission, 1912), pp. 4-14. [Tract reprinting J. M. Jewett's 1911 exposé from *The Standard.*] [5934]
_____. (same) (Cleveland, OH: Utah Gospel Mission, 1821). [5935]

70. Baskin, R. N. *Reminiscences of early Utah.* (Salt Lake City: R. N. Baskin, 1914), pp. 86-103. [330]

71. Latimer, A. C. *Why I left the Mormon church.* (Pittsburgh: The National Reform Association, [c] 1916), pp. 6-11. [4762]

72. Danielsen, Vernon J. *Mormonism exposed: or the crimes and treasons of the Mormon kingdom. By Vernon J. Danielson. Ex-high priest and formerly secretary of European missions.* (Independence, MO: n.p., 1917), pp. 27-28, 30-50. [2660]
_____. *Mormonism exposed: or the crimes and treasons of the Mormon kingdom.* (Independence, MO: Herald, 1933), pp. 22-52.

73. Thomas, D. K. *Wild life in the Rocky Mountains, or the lost million dollar Gold mine by D. K. Thomas . . . A true story of actual experiences in the wild west . . . The secrets of Mormonism. A true story of the Mountain Meadows massacre . . .* (C. E. Thomas Publishing Co., 1917), pp. 110-17. [8899]

74. Martin, Stewart. *The Mystery of Mormonism.* (London: Odhams Press, Ltd., 1920), pp. 244-65. [5296]
_____. (same) (New York: E.P. Dutton, 1920).

75. Goodwin, Samuel Henry. *Mormonism and Masonry a Utah Point of View by S. H. Goodwin, P.G.M.* (Salt Lake City: n.p., 1921). [3631]
_____. (same) (Salt Lake City: Sugar House Press, 1921). [3632]
_____. (same) 3rd impression. (Salt Lake City: n.p., 1921). [3633]
_____. (same) 3rd impression. (Salt Lake City: n.p., 1922). [3634]
_____. (same) (Washington, D.C.: The Masonic Service Association of the United States, [c] 1924), pp. 50-59. [3635]
_____. (same) (Salt Lake City: Grand Lodge F. & A.M. of Utah, 1925). [3636]
_____. (same) (Salt Lake City: Grand Lodge F. & A.M. of Utah, 1927). [3637]
_____. (same) (Salt Lake City: Grand Lodge F. & A.M. of Utah, 1938), pp. 43-48.
_____. (same) Ninth Printing (Salt Lake City: Grand Lodge F. & A.M. of Utah, 1961), pp. 43-48.

_____. (same) Tenth Printing (Salt Lake City: Grand Lodge F. & A.M. of Utah, 1972), pp. 43-48.

76. Preuss, Arthur. *Dictionary of secret and other societies. Comprising Masonic rites, lodges, and clubs; concordant, clandestine, and spurious Masonic bodies . . . and many other organizations. Compiled by Arthur Preuss.* (St. Louis: B. Herder Book Co., 1924.) [6753]

77. Vellinga, M. C. *Mormon mysteries revealed . . .* (Los Angeles: West Coast Publishing Co., 1927.) [9460]

78. Paden, William M. *Temple Mormonism. Its evolution, ritual and meaning. By Dr. W. M. Paden.* (New York: A.J. Montgomery, 1931).
_____. (same) in Tanner, *Evolution of the Mormon Temple Ceremony: 1942-1990.* (Salt Lake City: Utah Lighthouse Ministry, 1990), pp. 3-4.

79. Brodie, Fawn M. *No Man Knows My History: The Life of Joseph Smith, the Mormon Prophet.* (New York: Knopf, 1946).
_____. (same, under title) 2d ed., revised and enlarged. (New York Knopf, 1971).
_____. (same) (New York Knopf, 1973), pp. 281-83.
_____. (same) (New York Knopf, 1982). pp. 281-83.

80. O'Dea, Thomas F. *The Mormons.* (Chicago: University of Chicago Press, 1957), pp. 57-60.

81. Ralston, Russell F. *Fundamental differences between the Reorganized church and the church in Utah.* (Independence, MO: Herald, 1960), pp. 215-31.

82. Harrison, G. T. *Mormonism now and then.* (n.p., 1961), pp. 232-34.

83. Tucker, William P. "Temples and ordinances and endowments." *Ensign*, Oct. 1964, Vol. IV, No. 8.

84. Jones, Wesley M. *Temple endowment ritual and ceremonies, "council of the gods," and a celestial drama of creation including man with sacred signs and tokens, secret oaths and penalties. By William Jarman, 1869, being an extract from his book, HELL UPON EARTH published in England, 1885, with notes by*

Wesley M. Jones. (Oakland, CA: n.p., 1965). [Typescript ms. in Bancroft Library, U.C. Berkeley.]

85. Whalen, William J. *The Latter-day Saints in the modern day world. An account of contemporary Mormonism.* (Rev. ed.) (Notre Dame, IN: University of Notre Dame Press, 1964), pp. 165-90.

86. Allen, Emily. "The Mormon Money Monster," in *Confidential* (Feb. 1969) xvii, no. 2, pp. 31-37, 70-73.

87. Smith, John L. *I Visited the temple. A book inspired by my visit to the Oakland Mormon temple before its dedication and containing other accounts and reports of the Mormon temples' [sic] and ceremonies.* (Clearfield, UT: The Utah Evangel Press, 1966), pp. 32-65.

88. Tanner, Jerald and Sandra. *The Mormon Kingdom, vol. 1.* (Salt Lake City: Modern Microfilm Co., 1969), pp. 123-72.

89. Ferguson, Charles W. *Fifty Million Brothers.* (New York: Farrar & Rheinhart Inc., 1970), pp. 27-29.

90. Holm, Francis W., Sr. *The Mormon churches: A comparison from within.* (Kansas City, MO: Midwest, 1970), pp. 130-42.

91. Packard, Clarence F. "The Mystery Religions of Paganism, Freemasonry, Mormonism." Photocopy. (Salt Lake City, 1965; Bountiful, UT, 1970).

92. Skousen, Max B. *The Temple Endowment. The Key to the Mysteries of Godliness.* (n.p., 1971.)

93. Tanner, Jerald and Sandra. *Mormonism: Shadow or Reality?* (Salt Lake City: Modern Microfilm Co., 1972), pp. 451-92.
    _____. (same) Enlarged, revised ed. (Salt Lake City: Modern Microfilm Co., 1982), pp. 451-92.

94. Muren, Joseph C. *The temple and its significance.* (Ogden, UT: Temple Publications, 1974). [Contains an outline of the endowment ceremony and covenants.]

95. Dolgin, Janet. "Latter-Day Sense and Substance." In I. I. Zaretsky and M. P. Leone, eds., *Religious movements in contemporary America.* (Princeton, NJ: Princeton University Press, 1974), 519-46; esp. fig. III.

96. Scott, Latayne Colvett. *The Mormon mirage: A former Mormon tells why she left the church.* (Grand Rapids, MI: Zondervan, 1979), pp. 196-204.

97. Smith, John L. *Has Mormonism changed ... Now?* (Utah Missions, Inc., 1979), pp. 67-75.

98. Young, Brigham. "Lecture before the Veil," St. George Temple, 7 Feb. 1877, in L. John Nuttall Journal, pp. 20-24, published by C. A. Vlachos in *Journal of Pastoral Practice*, III:2 (1979), 116-118. (Missions, Inc., 1979), pp. 67-75.

99. Ex-Mormons for Jesus. *What's going on here?* (Phoenix, AZ: n.p., [c] 1980).

100. Tanner, Jerald and Sandra. *The changing world of Mormonism.* (Chicago: Moody Press, 1980), pp. 524-47.

101. Witte, Bob, and Gordon H. Fraser. *What's Going on in Here? An exposing of the secret Mormon temple rituals.* (Gordon Fraser, Publisher, [c] 1980).

102. Christensen, Culley K. *The Adam-God Maze.* (Scottsdale, AZ: Independent Publishers, 1981), pp. 53, 83, 85-86, 116-17, 297.

103. Collier, Fred C. *Unpublished revelations of the prophets and presidents of the Church of Jesus Christ of Latter Day Saints, vol. 1.* (Salt Lake City: Collier's Publishing, 1979), 2d ed. 1981, pp. 113-18, 165-76. [The material on pp. 165-76 was not included in 1st ed.]

104. Sackett, Charles. *A Mormon temple worker asks some questions.* (n.p., n.d.; [c] 1981).

105. von Wellnitz, Marcus. "The Catholic Liturgy and the Mormon Temple," *Brigham Young University Studies* 21 (1981): 3-35.

106. Sackett, Chuck. *What's going on in there? The verbatim text of the Mormon temple rituals annotated and explained by a former temple worker.* (n.p., 1982).
_____. (same) 2d ed. (Thousand Oaks, CA: Ex-Mormons for Jesus, 1982).
_____. *The Mormon Priesthood Secrets Chart.* (Thousand Oaks, CA: Ex-Mormons for Jesus, 1982).

107. [Anon.] *Fact Sheet.* (Thousand Oaks, CA: Ex-Mormons for Jesus, n.d. [c] 1982]).

108. [Anon.] *Are Mormons Christian? Can a Christian be a Mormon?* (West Village, CA: Ministry to Mormons, n.d. [c] 1982).

109. Buerger, David J. "The Adam-God Doctrine." *Dialogue: A Journal of Mormon Thought* 15 (Spring 1982): 14-58.

110. Tanner, Jerald. *Pay lay ale; an examination of the charge that the Mormons call upon Lucifer in their temple.* (Salt Lake City: Modern Microfilm Co., 1982).

111. Decker, Edward, and Richard Baer. (Ex-Mormons for Jesus). *The God-makers: The Mormon Quest for Godhood (film).* (Ex-Mormons for Jesus, 1983). [Transcript of pertinent section made on 1 June 1983.]

112. Buerger, David J. "'The Fulness of the Priesthood': The Second Anointing in Latter-day Saint Theology and Practice." *Dialogue: A Journal of Mormon Thought* 16 (Spring 1983): 10-44.

113. Sackett, Chuck. *Mormon Temple Rituals—Preparation for Godhood?* (Thousand Oaks, CA: [Ex-Mormons for Jesus], 1983). [Includes excerpts from *What's Going on in There?*]

114. Greer, Thelma. *Mormonism, Mama & Me!* (Fort Washington, PA: Christian Literature Crusade, 1983), pp. 155-168. [Reprints the temple exposé from Beadle's *Life in Utah.*]

115. McKeever, Bill. *Behind Temple Doors.* (Tucson, AZ: Calvary Missionary Press, n.d. [c] 1983).

116. Tanner, Jerald and Sandra. *Mormonism, Magic and Masonry.* (Salt Lake City: Utah Lighthouse Ministry, 1983), pp. 62-71.

117. Brown, Lisle G. "Second anointings: A brief look at a little known ordinance." (n.p., n.d. ([c] 1980s). [Unpublished, but widely distributed.]

118. Azkin, Bojamah. *Elohim at the altar: The rituals and ceremonies of the Mormon priesthood.* Photocopy ([Utah?] n.p., 1986). [Unpublished, but widely distributed.]

119. Schnobelen, William J., and James R. Spencer. *Mormonism's temple of doom.* (Idaho Falls, ID: Triple J Publishers, 1987).

[Includes photographs of the tokens, signs, and penalties on pp. 37-41.]

120. Tanner, Jerald and Sandra. *The Lucifer-God Doctrine: A Critical Look at Some Recent Changes Relating to the Worship of Lucifer in the Mormon Temple.* (Salt Lake City: Utah Lighthouse Ministry, 1987).

_____. (same) Rev. and enl. (Salt Lake City: Utah Lighthouse Ministry, 1988).

121. Kimball, Stanley B., ed. *On the Potter's Wheel: The Diaries of Heber C. Kimball.* (Salt Lake City: Signature Books in association with Smith Research Associates, 1987), pp. 147-68. [Nauvoo temple diary extracts.]

122. Decker, Ed, and Bill Schnoebelen. *The Lucifer-God Doctrine: Shadow or Reality?* (Issaquah, WA: Saints Alive in Jesus, 1987).

123. Naifeh, Steven, and Gregory White Smith. *The Mormon Murders: A True Story of Greed, Forgery, Deceit and Death.* (New York: Weidenfeld & Nicholson, 1988), pp. 57-60.

124. Tanner, Jerald and Sandra. *Major Problems of Mormonism.* (Salt Lake City: Utah Lighthouse Ministry, 1989), pp. 232-41.

125. Tanner, Jerald and Sandra. *Evolution of the Mormon Temple Ceremony: 1842-1990.* (Salt Lake City: Utah Lighthouse Ministry, 1990). [Includes the initiatory ordinances (washing and anointings), complete texts of 1984 and 1990 endowment rituals, marriage/sealing, and ceremony for sealing children to parents.]

126. Hogan, Mervin B. *Free Masonry and Mormon Ritual.* (Salt Lake City: privately published, 1991).

127. Smith, George D., ed. *An Intimate Chronicle: The Journals of William Clayton.* (Salt Lake City: Signature Books in association with Smith Research Associates, 1991), pp. 199-258. [Nauvoo temple diary extracts.]

128. Laake, Deborah. *Secret Ceremonies: A Mormon Woman's Intimate Diary of Marriage and Beyond.* (New York: William Morrow, 1993).

INDEX

A

Aaronic priesthood, 37, 40, 61, 78, 116-18, 128-29, 137-38

Abraham, 12, 41, 43, 49, 61, 66, 88, 126

Adam/Michael, 12, 36, 42, 50, 58, 61, 80-81, 83-84, 105-106, 109-13, 128, 145, 178

angels, 13-15, 18, 20-23, 25-26, 28, 33, 38, 40, 42, 61-62, 67, 88-89, 98, 104, 107, 142, 144, 170

anointing, 1, 11-13, 15-21, 27-29, 31-34, 36-40, 56-57, 59, 61-63, 65-75, 77, 79, 81, 83-84, 87-94, 98-105, 109, 115-16, 118-26, 130-31, 142, 146-47, 155, 157, 160-61, 163-65, 171, 179

apostasy, 56, 62

apostles, 9, 13, 15-16, 18-19, 22, 28-31, 33-34, 36, 39-40, 57-58, 61-63, 66, 70-71, 73, 87, 91-93, 100-102, 105, 114-15, 118-19, 127-29, 133, 135- 36, 138-39, 147-50, 157, 160-63, 165

Arminianism, 3

B

Bennett, John C., 37, 50, 142

bishops, 13, 16-19, 22, 25, 74, 77, 85, 87, 99-100, 119-20, 122, 129, 168

Book of Mormon, 2-5, 16, 47-48, 104

C

calling and election, 2, 35, 123, 126

Calvinism, 3-5, 123

Campbell, Alexander, 3

Cannon, David H., 108, 117, 135, 139

Cannon, George Q., 63, 102, 114, 117-18, 126, 135

Carter, Jared, 5

Celestial kingdom, 12-14, 57-62,